North Park
A San Diego Urban Village

1896 – 1946

North Park
A San Diego Urban Village

1896 – 1946

By Donald P. Covington

North Park: A San Diego Urban Village, 1896-1946

Edited by Karon Covington and Katherine Hon
Book and cover design by Donald Covington
Back cover design by Katherine Hon
Printed in the United States of America

Published by: For the North Park Community Association History Committee (2007)
Hon Consulting, Inc.   For the North Park Historical Society (2010)
2226 Dwight Street
San Diego, CA 92104

ISBN-13: 978-0-9795005-0-3

For more information, visit the North Park Historical Society website at www.northparkhistory.org

Front and back inside cover maps Copyright © 2007 by Jerry Wallenborn, used by permission
Aerial photographs on inside cover maps courtesy of Google Earth Pro

Cover photo courtesy of the San Diego Historical Society (#Sensor 8-216)
        View of University Avenue looking west from 30th Street, early 1920s

Back cover photo courtesy of Karon Covington

In memory of Don Covington – an artist, author, teacher, and historian. Don was the inspirational leader of residents who love bungalows and the early history of our community. We finished his last book, which began as a committee project in 1988, in recognition of his contributions to the North Park community.

– North Park Community Association History Committee
2007

Table of Contents

Photos & Illustrations

Foreword

In many ways, the history of North Park is a case of "the more things change, the more they stay the same." Readers of this remarkable retrospective of one of San Diego's original and most influential neighborhoods will read of population explosions, housing shortages, drought, and infrastructure needs, but also of civic commitment, neighborhood pride, and a vision of the future. All of these are qualities of the present-day North Park. No one who has read this book will be surprised at the revitalization and renaissance that is taking place today; it is a North Park tradition.

Of course, some things have changed. We no longer can "grade, surface, and fence" a playground for $500, as they did when the North Park Recreation Center and Community Park was first created in 1908. It is also very unlikely that an annual community picnic would feature "a scramble after 30 chickens, each of which will belong to the catcher," as it did in 1930.

And some North Park mainstays have endured – Stern's Gym, where Arnold Schwarzenegger and Toni have both worked out (although never at the same time); the venerable Rudford's diner, which will soon serve the residents of the new La Boheme and Renaissance projects; and the beautiful and historic North Park Theatre, where once again audiences are being delighted and entertained.

It is one of the great pleasures of representing the Third City Council District that we get to work hand-in-hand with the residents of North Park, who are such a vital component of the preservation and revitalization of this historic neighborhood. We commend this book to all of them, as well as to those in any other community who want to know more about how an urban village successfully grows from infancy to maturity.

Don Covington's loving tribute to North Park is an exceptional portrait of old and new San Diego and an invaluable addition to our history.

– Senator Christine Kehoe
and
Toni Atkins, Councilmember,
Third District, City of San Diego

Preface
Our Neighborhood, Our Legacy, Our Treasures

Neighborhoods are like rings inside a tree trunk. The oldest ones are near the center. Also, the neighborhood rings that radiate outward from San Diego's earliest days give a look at our architectural history.

Old Town and New Town began near the water. Early settlers needed access to our great natural harbor.

We can find early Spanish and Early California architecture in Old Town to this date. Take a neighborhood ring inland a bit and we have a wonderful cache of Victorian and Edwardian homes in Bankers Hill. For a quick tour of that era, just find your way to Second Avenue and go north from Quince.

As the neighborhood tree grew, we come to the neighborhoods ringing Balboa Park. South Park, North Park, Hillcrest, Burlingame, Marston Hills, University Heights, Sherman Heights and Golden Hill arrived on the scene during the Arts & Crafts era (1895 to 1920). Seventh Avenue north of Upas gives us a majestic glance of high end Craftsman homes, and 28th Street in North Park shows off our town's slice of everyman's Bungalow Heaven.

A bit further out we find a Spanish Revival ring beyond North Park in Normal Heights, Kensington and parts of Talmadge.

And, being American, we also find all architectural styles interspersed throughout the neighborhoods.

Since this wonderful book is about North Park, you'll soon launch into reading how our neighborhood came to be. But North Park or any neighborhood didn't come to be in a vacuum. External commercial forces played a big role.

Many of us know the 1915 and 1916 International Fairs brought a lot of new residents to the area. They needed to live someplace. The area around the park was being developed as water and transportation routes reached out like those rings on a tree. Homes were built to house the boom in population between 1910 and the first world war. But, Balboa Park's expositions weren't the only reason for early growth.

Geographically, San Diego is the nearest natural harbor to that brand new (1912) eighth wonder of the world called the Panama Canal. At the beginning of the 20th century, our City Fathers and Mothers were embarrassed that when the U.S. Navy's Great White Fleet came to call on us – our harbor was too shallow. The Fleet was on a world tour and the fact that they had to anchor off of Point Loma rankled city officials like U.S. Congressman William Kettner, for one. It wasn't long before our harbor became a dredged port.

Soon, San Diego became a hotbed for building those new-fangled flying machines. And, of course, the Navy was trying to land those biplanes on the decks of ships they had converted to floating landing strips.

The aircraft carrier and the aircraft industry (commercial and defense-wise) took root in San Diego during the teen years. And, all those folks needed homes to live. The demand was so great for housing during the first two decades of the 20th century that master builders like North Park's David Owen Dryden could crank out a home in six weeks (weather permitting).

Don and Karon Covington's home took longer because of Mr. Hatfield's Flood.

But that's another story and another ring in the tree. Enjoy this wonderful work by Don and Karon Covington. Their work defines who we are as North Parkers. This book makes the point that we don't live in old houses, we live in architecturally splendid Craftsman bungalows, whether they be Spanish Revival or Arts & Crafts in style. As a colleague, John Brinkmann, Editor and Founder of *American Bungalow*, pointed out, "North Parkers live in the single largest collection of bungalows in the country. There are more variety of bungalow styles here than anywhere else."

– Thomas Shess
Founder, *North Park News*

Acknowledgements

This book was prepared by the History Committee of the North Park Community Association (NPCA). The Committee was formed in 1988 by those members of NPCA who were interested in the old homes and commercial buildings. It became clear to us that North Park had been blessed from the beginning with community leaders who had vision, adventurous spirits, and a willingness to invest themselves and their money in what one of the early leaders referred to as "A City of Our Own." The curiosity of the present-day North Park residents prompted this book, the purpose of which is to acquaint the reader with the origin and history of a very livable community.

The author of this book is Donald Covington. It was based on research conducted by History Committee members, and was edited by Karon Covington and Katherine Hon. Jerry Wallenborn donated his graphics skills to create the tract and landmarks maps, Carl Moczydlowsky helped with final formatting, and Thomas Shess provided timely editorial comments. We are grateful to the Hartley Family and Klicka Family for sharing their photographs and stories. We also appreciate the photographs of the Lafayette Hotel from Tina Colmenero. The book was printed through the generous contributions of the following Book Sponsors: Karon Covington, Ruth Dahl, George Franck, Steve Hon, Katherine Hon, and NPCA. Members of the History Committee past and present are listed below. We apologize if we missed anyone. The late Architectural Historian Kathleen Flanagan, though not an attending member, also contributed important research.

Ernestine Bonn	George Franck	Jack Illes	Joey Perry*
Dennis Campbell	Vicki Granowitz	Anita Johnson	Rob Powell
Joan Campbell*	Lorraine Halac	Lloyd Kirkpatrick	Art Seamans
Jay Coles*	Marcella Hamlin	Bertha Klann	Beth Swersie
Don Covington*	Brett Harris	Chris Milnes	Michael Thornhill
Karon Covington	Katherine Hon	Ricardo Moran	Kristine Wade
Ruth Dahl*	Steve Hon*	Dan Perkins	Paul Wade
			Betty Whitaker

*History Committee members who have served as Chair

An Urban Village

In its 2001 General Plan Update, the *Strategic Framework City of Villages* project, the city of San Diego defined its concept of an urban village as a: "community-oriented center where residential, commercial, employment and civic/education uses are integrated. Villages are intended to be unique to the community, pedestrian-friendly, and have elements to promote neighborhood or civic gatherings."

By this definition, North Park has been an urban village since its inception. It is one of San Diego's two oldest such communities, both of them emerging on the northern border of Balboa Park in the first decade of the twentieth century. In the era before the mass popularity of the automobile, North Park and its sister, Hillcrest, were just remote enough from San Diego's civic center to require for its residents the full development of services and institutions. This book traces that development in its first half-century.

WELCOME TO NORTH PARK
AN HISTORIC CRAFTSMAN
NEIGHBORHOOD

Introduction
Where Is North Park?

"The City Council has as yet been unable to determine the exact boundaries of the North Park Addition."

– *San Diego Daily Transcript*, February 11, 1909

Introduction
Where is North Park?

The problem of determining the official boundaries of North Park has continued to trouble each generation since the early years of the 20th century. At the end of the 19th century, all of that territory within the city limits east of Sixth Avenue and north of Balboa Park was officially designated *University Heights* with no mention of any other community or tract.

On a map drawn for the College Hill Land Company in 1906, University Heights had been restricted to that section east of Tenth Avenue, west of Boundary Street and north of University Avenue, with no label for that land south of the Avenue. Five years later, North Park had emerged as two small tracts subdivided by Stevens & Hartley and McFadden & Buxton. In that year, 1911, Jack Hartley was at work establishing at 30th and University the commercial core of the new North Park community. In spite of that, as late as 1922, land developer Oscar Cotton could identify the area as "The Great West End District;" West End being the tract that lay immediately west of Hartley's North Park Addition.

In 1909, although the City Council had been using the descriptive nomenclature *North Park* for several years, the members could not decide just what were its geographical boundaries.

Today, the confusion continues. In recent years, in an effort to clarify individual suburbs within the historic Mid-City, the Planning Department of the City of San Diego published a series of maps entitled <u>Potential Historic Sites and Areas</u>, one of which was <u>Greater North Park</u>. That map established Interstate 805 as the eastern boundary, Park Boulevard as the western boundary, and the southern slopes of Mission Valley as the northern boundary. Upas and 28th Streets formed the southwestern border, and Juniper Street marked the southern boundary.

During the period that the History Committee of the North Park Community Association was laying the research foundation for this book, many long-term residents with memories of early years in North Park were interviewed. One question that each interviewer always asked concerned the boundaries of historic North Park.

Although there were many opinions offered, no one recognized the City's designated "Greater North Park" as the historic district. Almost without exception, the junction of 30th

Street and University Avenue was given as the "heart" of the community. Boundary Street, the old city limits, was often given as the eastern border and Switzer Canyon the southern line. Florida Street and Georgia Street Bridge seemed to most people to represent the western edge of North Park, and El Cajon Boulevard the northern boundary.

North Park landmarks most often mentioned by those residents interviewed were the Georgia Street Bridge, the University Heights Water Tower (the "tank"), the North Park Theatre, and the former Imig Manor Hotel (now the Lafayette), which, with its Mississippi Ballroom was a glamorous focus of North Park entertainment in the immediate post-World War Two era.

For purposes of this book, the map of North Park is drawn in response to those oral histories with a few exceptions made in deference to sites within the city's Greater North Park which had significant relationships to the development of Historic North Park. Those sites include the Valle Vista Tract north of Adams Avenue along Panorama Drive, where many of the early structures were built by North Park's premier builder of Craftsman style houses, David Owen Dryden; the historic streetcar route along Adams Avenue, sister to that of the line along University Avenue, both of which opened the Greater North Park district to settlement in 1907; and the Burlingame tract, Kalmia Place and Eastern Addition, closely related to North Park by way of the McFadden & Buxton partnership.

All of these considerations resulted in defining Historic North Park with El Cajon Boulevard as the northern border; Boundary Street as its eastern edge; Juniper Street as the southern line; and Upas and 28th Streets as the southwestern wedge. Due to the recent emergence of an historic University Heights district with its center along Park Boulevard and Adams Avenue, this book establishes the western boundary of Historic North Park at Texas Street from El Cajon to University, with a jog west to Georgia Street and its Bridge, then south to Upas Street. The area, therefore, includes that portion of the original University Heights district between University Avenue and El Cajon Boulevard east of Texas Street.

The Map of Historic North Park

The historic district with which this book is concerned is bordered in red on the official San Diego city map of Greater North Park (opposite).

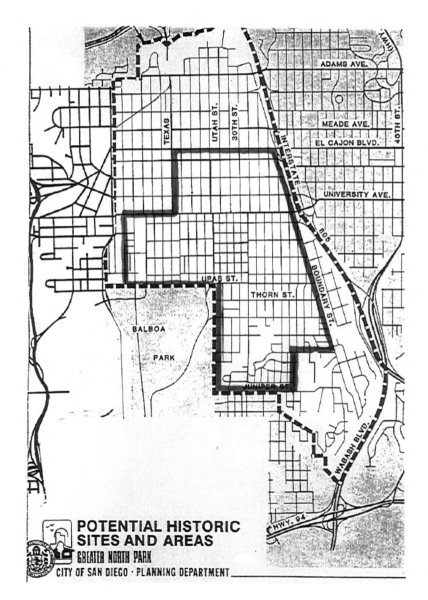

POTENTIAL HISTORIC SITES AND AREAS
GREATER NORTH PARK
CITY OF SAN DIEGO · PLANNING DEPARTMENT

Part One
In the Beginning ~ 1896-1906

"In the Fall of 1896, we moved to the lemon ranch, into a six room house facing what is now University Avenue, at 31st."

– Maud Hartley MacDougall, 1950

Chapter 1
The Hartleys

On an early morning in mid-January 1882, hours off its schedule, the little side-wheeler steamship, Orizaba, rounded the horn of Point Loma into San Diego Bay and made land at La Playa. Among its many passengers, wearied by rough seas of the previous night's storm, James Monroe Hartley led his wife and five children down the gangplank and onto the rocky shore of the final destination for each of them. As individuals and as a family, they would become the chief generating force for the emergence of one of San Diego's earliest suburban communities: North Park.

The family had spent a fortnight traveling from their farm home in Oswego, Kansas. By train, stage and ship they made their way across the southwestern territories and into Southern California. Boarding the Orizaba at San Pedro, the family embarked upon the final leg of the long journey. Years later, Maud, the youngest Hartley daughter, wrote about the experience and of her father's first response to the view of San Diego from the deck of the Orizaba:

> "There was no harbor in San Pedro then and the steamer was anchored some distance out from shore. Some of the passengers had to be taken out on a flat boat . . . transferred to the steamer, clamoring over the side on rope ladders. However, they were all taken safely aboard, down to the babe in arms, and after an all night voyage, reached their destination."

> "As the boat steamed around Pt. Loma, into the clear blue waters of San Diego bay (sic), with the rolling hills as a perfect background, there seemed to unfold in my father's heart, a contentment that lasted throughout his life, and he always thought that there was no place like San Diego. He believed, even then, that one day, it would be a big city, and while he lived, worked to that end."

> – Maud Hartley MacDougall
> *Memories of Mary Jane Tibbetts Hartley*
> *1852-1940*

James Monroe Hartley and his wife, Mary Jane (nee Tibbetts), spent their childhoods in Iowa, but met and married in Oswego, Kansas on the border of the Cherokee Nation, Indian Territory. Hartley, a Union veteran of the Civil War, was traveling through southern Kansas as a fire insurance salesman when he met Mary Jane Tibbetts. The two were married during the morning service of the Oswego Methodist Church, August 6, 1871. The same day, they returned by rail to Hartley's home in Cedar Rapids, Iowa.

After nine years in Iowa and the birth of four children, the Hartley family returned to Oswego where in the summer of 1880 they bought a farm from Mary Jane's father, Henry Tibbetts, who had moved to San Diego County.

James Hartley also had a brother in San Diego; and the news from each of the new San Diegans painted an irresistible picture of life in the dusty little town on the Mexican border. The Iowa farm was sold and a few days before Christmas 1881, the Hartley family began its journey.

The first home for the Hartley family was in the Tijuana River valley where they began a small fig orchard next to Henry Tibbetts' farm near Nestor. After an unsuccessful year, James joined his brother "Mark" (Marquis DeLafayette Hartley) in a tannery business on Fourteenth and L Streets in downtown San Diego. The *San Diego Sun* ran the following notice in its edition of September 13, 1882:

> ". . . Hartley Brothers, for the purpose of
> manufacturing boots, shoes and harness, or
> any other business they may see fit to
> engage in."

James Hartley soon returned to his prior employment as a traveling salesman of fire insurance policies. His route took him throughout the back country of San Diego County.

During one of his travels he discovered a small, picturesque valley near Dehesa and urged Mary Jane to file homestead claims with him on land there. They and Mark were awarded Federal homesteads on neighboring acreages in the winter of 1883-84.

While James traveled, Mary Jane and the older children managed the ranch in Dehesa. Then, during the land boom of 1887, James decided that he could make more money by moving back to town and entering the real estate business. Although many people acquired quick fortunes, just as many lost all they had invested and more. James Hartley was among the latter group, and lost his health as well. After he recovered, the family once again returned to the ranch in Dehesa.

James Monroe Hartley
1846-1904

Advertisement courtesy of the Hartley Family

By 1891, James Hartley was doing so well with the insurance business that he was appointed Special Agent for the Continental Insurance Company. The family moved from the ranch to Los Angeles where the company's regional offices were situated.

The two older daughters, Mary Catherine and Delia Anna, entered the Los Angeles Normal School for preparation as teachers. Their graduation in June, 1893, was a very important occasion for the Hartleys and there was much talk among family members in the final year of their studies concerning some special event to celebrate the occurrence. The event settled upon was a summer visit to the popular Columbian Exposition in Chicago for the two daughters and their parents. Money was put aside for the trip and many plans were made by the two young women and their mother.

However, in January, 1893, James Hartley used the excursion money, four thousand dollars, for the purchase of forty acres of land in the Park Villas Addition of Pueblo Lot 1127 on the northeast edge of the city. This tract was bordered on the north by University Avenue, on the south by Dwight Street, on the east by 32nd Street, and on the west by Ray Street. The land was immediately planted with lemon trees. The orchard was named by James, "Hartley's North Park," a name that appeared on all city maps at the turn of the century. The family lived in Logan Heights while James Hartley traveled for work.

In 1894, there was trouble with the Dehesa ranch tenants, and the family moved there. Sadly, the night after the household goods were brought from town, a fire destroyed the ranch house, leaving them only the few odds and ends they were to take the next day. But the family was resilient. Maud continued the story:

"A makeshift house was soon built, and it was the home for two years. . .

In the Fall of 1896, we moved to the lemon ranch, into a six room house facing what is now University Avenue, at 31st. The barn was where the first Smith Clinic stands. When we first went there to live, the boys had to haul water in barrels, from El Cajon Ave., a country road then, where the main pipe line was laid into San Diego. Water was eventually piped into the place, and although we never had water in the house, the tap was on the porch.

For awhile both places were worked. Sometimes I would be at Dehesa with one of the boys and mother with the other at the lemon ranch but after awhile, the Dehesa ranch was given up, because it took all the time for the lemon orchard.

The boys worked very hard, driving the mules, Beck and Laurie, to the ploughs and cultivators, digging irrigating ditches, filling them with water, and when dry, cultivating, only to do the same thing over again in another month."

– Maud Hartley MacDougall
Remembered Incidents in the Lives of the
James Monroe Hartley Family
1882-1940

Jack and Paul Hartley (and Don the dog)
at the Lemon Ranch - now North Park, circa 1900
Photo courtesy of the Hartley Family

In 1901, James Hartley gave up the insurance business and took a position with a building and loan association in Washington State. James and Mary and the two youngest children, Maud and Paul, moved to Tacoma, head office of the association. The two oldest daughters remained in Dehesa where they taught school. John, the eldest son, married Ella Dodge and left San Diego for a job in North Dakota selling fire insurance.

In the absence of his parents and siblings, George Hartley took over the management of the lemon grove. George married Jane Denby in February 1901, and a son was born to them two years later. In May 1903, Jane died leaving George with a four-month-old infant. This death precipitated a return of the family from Tacoma so that Mary Jane could assume the care of her grandson, and James could help with the lemon grove. John also returned to San Diego in order to relieve George of the responsibility for the management of the family business of the production and distribution of citrus.

The long hours and hard labor in the family packing house began to affect James Hartley's fragile health. In the summer of 1904, he collapsed and was taken by ambulance to the Agnew Sanitarium where he died on the 23rd of July. Reverend Crabtree officiated at the military service, and James Hartley was buried in Mount Hope Cemetery.

In the months that followed, the bereaved family made the decision to give up the orchard business. Maud wrote in her *Remembered Incidents*:

"John went into the real estate business, after they decided to give up the orchard, gradually the equipment for the place was sold off, the house was sold, and moved down on El Cajon Ave., near Texas

12

and made into a store building. The other buildings were torn down and the trees all dug up, and the 40 acres was just flat land again but ready to be sold."

The production of citrus on the dry mesa northeast of the city had always been an arduous affair. However, the severe drought of 1903-04 intensified the problems of irrigation and, no doubt, played a large part in the demise of the family's lemon orchard.

The severity of the 1903-04 drought and its effect upon the citrus industry in San Diego is dramatically recorded in letters of G. Harold Powell, a U.S. Department of Agriculture pomologist sent to Southern California to help citrus growers solve the problems of shipping produce to the East. His letters home in the early months of 1904, published in Letters from the Orange Empire by the Historical Society of Southern California in 1990, clearly delineate the problems brought on by that period of drought.

"Hollenbeck Hotel (Los Angeles, California)
January 28, 1904 7:30 p.m.
My dearest Gertrude: . . . My but the country is dry. There have not been 2 inches of rain since last spring. Every mountain and hill and valley not supplied with water is as dry as a road.

Thousands of cattle and sheep are dying in some of the counties from lack of food and water . . . Today the air is very hazy and smoky. It is dust from the desert. The winds have been blowing at a high rate for several days, filling the southern part of the state with a fine dust that sifts over the mountains . . .
Affectionately, Harold"

"Hotel Del Coronado
1st March (1904)"
My Dearest Gertrude: I have had a busy day driving through a desolate country where the lemon business has been badly injured by the short water supply. . .
Affectionately, Harold"

Following the decision to give up the lemon orchard business, John Charles ('Jack'), the eldest Hartley son, and his brother-in-law, William Jay Stevens, who had married Delia Anna Hartley in 1901, established a partnership in Real Estate. The Stevens & Hartley firm opened an office at 844 Sixth Street in downtown San Diego in 1905. The first edition of their weekly bulletin advertising properties for sale and rent was published on October 18, 1905. Although the lemon orchard was fallow, the family kept the land that would become the heart of North Park's commercial district.

The Amos and Lizzie Richardson House, circa 1900
(Still standing with a stucco façade at 3425 31st Street)
Photo courtesy of the San Diego Historical Society (#89:17482)

Chapter 2
Neighbors

In the autumn of 1896, when the Hartley family moved from the farm in Dehesa to their Park Villas lemon ranch on the northeast corner of then City Park (Balboa Park), they were not the only occupants of that arid mesa. They were preceded in 1895 by two orchardists, Henry and Hiram Stiles and their families. The Stiles family homes were situated near the intersection of the old La Mesa Road and Nash Avenue (the present-day corner of University Avenue and 32nd Street) on the northeastern edge of the Hartley lemon grove. Two granddaughters of Mary and Hiram Stiles were close in age to Paul Hartley, the youngest child of James and Mary Jane Hartley. If the newspaper is to be trusted, there may have been a financial connection between the Hartleys and Stiles families as well. On February 9, 1893, the *San Diego Union* noted under the heading "Local Intelligence – In General" that, "A forty-acre tract in pueblo lot 27, in the vicinity of the city park has been purchased by H. Stiles and J. M. Hartley and will be set to lemon trees."

Supplemental water for farming on the mesa was pumped up from the San Diego River in Mission Valley and ran down El Cajon Boulevard in an open wooden trough on its way into the urban neighborhoods. Farmers collected in barrels their portions of water from the trough. The meager introduction of water to the northeastern section of the city spurred the first developments there of a small and tenuous citrus industry in the years before the turn of the century. Between 1895 and 1900, six other families and their hired hands joined the Stiles as nearby neighbors of the Hartleys.

The Federal Census in 1900 recorded seven landowners and 55 residents between the City limits at Boundary Street on the east and Florida Canyon on the west, Adams Avenue on the north and Switzer Canyon on the south. In the year that the Hartleys moved to the Park Villas section of the City, four other families established residences there.

Siegfried Michel, an immigrant from Switzerland, and his English-born wife, Marie, purchased a home site on Alabama Street near University Avenue. The Michel family in 1896 included three young children, contemporaries of Paul Hartley. Siegfried and Marie married in 1890 and were reported to be the founders of the first Jersey dairy in San Diego County.

August and Stephanie Storme, two naturalized citizens who emigrated from Belgium, also moved onto the mesa top in 1896. Their two teen-aged children, Achilles and Ida, worked with them in their citrus orchard near present-day 30th and Polk Streets.

Another naturalized citizen, Jacob Lenz, a German photographer, moved to the northeast corner of 30th and Myrtle Street in 1896. Mr. Lenz and his artist wife Ella operated the Temple of Music and Art, and Photographic Arts on Fifth Avenue in downtown San Diego.

The fourth family to join the Hartleys in the Park Villas section in 1896 was that of Amos and Lizzie Richardson, who along with their two adult daughters had come to San Diego from New England. Amos Richardson had previously owned a ranch in Mission Valley. His efforts at establishing a citrus ranch in the Park Villas must not have been successful as by 1900 he had retired. The eldest daughter, Ida, was a teacher in the Encinitas school.

The Richardson home, with a superficially altered exterior, remains at 3425 31st Street on the southern boundary of the original Hartley lemon grove. The house is one of the oldest early structures remaining in North Park, having been built in the mid-1890s. In the photograph, it is shown with its original columned porch, crested false gable and carpenter gothic widows-walk.

In 1899, two other families moved to the nascent North Park community and planted citrus orchards. Thomas Works, son of United States Senator John Works, established his ranch and home near Adams Avenue and Idaho Streets. His household included a wife and three small children, his wife's parents, and a teen-age servant and farm laborer.

The last member of that pioneer group of ranchers on the periphery of the Hartley's lemon grove at the turn of the century was John M. Highett, who came to California from Australia with a wife, four children and Ling, a Chinese cook. John Highett purchased 20 acres in the vicinity of Landis and 32nd Street on the eastern border of the Hartley property. The drought of 1903-04 was as discouraging to him as it was to the descendents of James Hartley, and in 1905 the Highetts moved to England. Mr. Highett returned in the autumn of 1922 in order to sell his farm which lay fallow while the community of North Park grew up around it. At that time, the *San Diego Union* ran an article about him in which he told of his experiences in the early days of the community.

"In those days . . . I always kept a span of horses and we drove to town down the Big Grade (Pershing Drive) which was pretty steep and awful narrow, but afforded the quickest route to town for the five or six families that lived out near what is now the Thirtieth and University section. The property I have just sold to Welsh and Campbell had been subdivided in the Big Boom (1886-87) which collapsed before any lots were sold, I guess, because I just naturally took the streets and all and nobody ever complained about it. I planted lemons, oranges, wheat and barley and did some garden trucking but the water problem was a serious one and I had to catch all I could in a hole for future use when the city pumped any into my line. One year, I had to haul it from town and finally . . . I left for England . . . "

– *San Diego Union*, November 26, 1922

Paul Hartley, who was born in October 1894, attended elementary school in a building at El Cajon and Park Boulevards between 1900 and 1905. On December 9, 1949, he was interviewed by a reporter from the *San Diego Union* and reflected upon those early school years at the turn of the century:

> "Pershing Dr., which follows the same route today that it did then from the country to town, was unpaved and only one lane wide. And there was not a single house between Ray and University and Sixteenth and C Sts."

> "There were only two or three houses between our home and the old school building as late as 1903. All the area was devoted to lemon groves."

> – Paul Hartley, 1949

By the time the Hartley family moved from the North Park lemon ranch to Logan Heights in 1905, many of those groves were gone. Some of the Hartleys' neighbors followed their lead and that of the Highett family by moving on or adapting to the arid conditions of the high mesa.

Jacob and Ella Lenz left San Diego and the Temple of Music and Art in 1904. The following year, Siegfried Michel moved his dairy from the vicinity of University Avenue and Mississippi Street to the flood plain of Mission Valley. August Storme held out until 1906 before giving up his ranch near Polk Avenue and Ohio Street.

Those who remained on the mesa found other means of livelihood. The Stiles family converted their orchards to a poultry ranch in 1905. Mary's son Herbert became the proprietor of San Diego Poultry Supply Company in downtown San Diego and established the Park Villa Poultry Yard on the family's North Park property in 1908. Thomas Works continued to operate his ranch near Adams and Utah until 1911 when he became a street grading contractor. Mrs. Richardson began teaching in the public schools in 1904, while Amos turned to selling real estate by 1907. Following Amos Richardson's death, his widow and daughters continued to live in the house on 31st Street for a few more years. The oldest daughter, Minnie, was the last family member to live in the old home. By 1920, she had remodeled the house into four rental apartments and was living there with three other families. As shown in the photograph, the house is still standing, albeit with stucco façade, at 3425 31st Street.

The rapid decline of citrus ranching on the mesa northeast of City Park in the years between 1905 and 1910 coincided with the emergence of several building blocks of urban development. Those building blocks were all in place by the time Will Stevens and Jack Hartley cleared the former family citrus grove in preparation for the development of the North Park suburban tract in 1910.

Part Two
Building Blocks ~ 1907-1919

"University Avenue Electric road is now under construction. The beautifully located territory at the intersection of that Avenue and 30th Street is sure to be the most valuable of that section. NOW is the time to purchase."

– *San Diego Union*, August 11, 1907

Chapter 3
Transportation, Water & Sewer

During the period between the national Panics of 1907 and 1913, the return of confidence in the financial markets and funding sources stimulated population growth and expansion of San Diego into its northeast territories. The elements upon which an urban community is built began to transform the previously arid citrus groves and cattle pastures of the high mesa northeast of Balboa Park into an urban village. The crucial building blocks included:
- Efficient streets and transportation systems
- Water
- Good available housing
- A commercial market core
- Public services

The demand for new housing, neighborhoods, and community centers lasted until the summer of 1913. Key to growth in this time was the extension of electric car lines for public transportation. It was the electric rail system of the city, prior to the popularity of the motor car, that brought the potential of urban development to a region.

Electric Rails to Suburbanization

The pattern of growth in early San Diego was profoundly affected by Balboa Park. In the late 19th century, the 1,400 acres of reserved parkland (then called City Park) on the northeast edge of Horton's New Town had caused the city to grow directly north along the western boundary of the park and east along its southern boundary. Once expansion had reached Golden Hill, on the eastern side of the park, it turned north into Brooklyn Heights. On the western side of the park, the city expansion was swift to make the highlands of present day Hillcrest, where it once again turned eastward into University Heights several blocks north of the park.

In these two neighborhoods, expansion was stymied by similar geographical features. To the north of Brooklyn Heights lay the depths of Switzer Canyon. To the east of Hillcrest was the formidable ridge of Georgia Street. That spine of earth rose gradually from the flatlands east of Hillcrest and then fell suddenly into the ravine of Florida Canyon. These extreme contrasts in the contours of terrain interrupted the steady progress of the iron rails. For Greater North Park, development hinged on the completion of three electric car lines: the Adams Avenue line that terminated at Mission Cliff Park and Ostrich Farm (part of Route #1 in 1910), the University Avenue Shuttle (which became part of a new Route #7 in 1917), and the 30th Street line that originally terminated at Upas Street (part of Route #2 in 1910).

The Adams Avenue Line

The first electric car line to penetrate the territory that today is Greater North Park was the Adams Avenue Line. That extension to the San Diego Electric Railway system was announced on the first of January 1906. The stated purpose of the line was "to open up a new residence district to be known as Normal Heights."

Colonel David C. Collier Jr., George M. Hawley and the Southern Construction Company were granted the franchise for the extension of the line that was to run from the Mission Cliff Pavilion to the eastern boundary of the Normal Heights Addition. On the way, it would run along the northern rim of the future North Park community.

Work began on the Adams Avenue Line on Monday morning, May 27, 1907, when a large force of men began putting up poles for the trolley wire. In June, the first rails and ties were laid out past the Bentley Ostrich Farm, Valle Vista Terrace, around the curve of Adams Avenue and over old Sandrock road. By the middle of July, the track had reached the City limits.

Construction of the line was completed late in August and service on the line was begun at 6:35 a.m., Sunday, August 25, 1907 when the first car left the end of the line for Mission Cliff Pavilion.

A formal celebration of the opening of the line was held that afternoon by the Ralston Realty Company. A large tent near the end of the line was erected on Adams Avenue in Normal Heights. More than 400 guests, including stockholders of the College Hill Land Association, officials of the city and county, and real estate men, were invited to lunch and entertainment by the City Guard Band under the direction of Maestro Iannuggiello. Four special cars brought some of the guests from downtown San Diego to the tent in Normal Heights.

Following the luncheon and band concert, guests were given free round trip rides on the new electric line.

Special excursions by autos and carriages were offered around Mission Drive.

"D.C. Reed, former mayor of San Diego, and who has been in this city since the days of '88, made the only speech of the afternoon. It was short and to the point. It was left to Mr. Reed to announce the tally-ho rides, and in addition he stated that the occasion reminded many of the old-timers present of the days of yore, when trips were made into what was then the country for the purpose of booming new residence tracts and selling real estate. He ended by saying that the opening of the Adams avenue line was but the beginning of a lasting prosperity for University and Normal Heights.

A rush for the tally-ho's was then made, and for more than an hour the unparalleled view of Mission valley, the mountains and the ocean was enjoyed while the conveyances rolled over the smoothest and best scenic automobile ride in the west."

– *San Diego Union*, August 26, 1907

Upon the completion of the Adams Avenue line, a spur was added. That 1,000-foot extension north of Adams Avenue on the easterly edge of Normal Heights was made for the purpose of giving access to the Southern Construction Company's quarry. Decomposed granite from this quarry was used for the grading of most streets in the new additions north of Balboa Park. The San Diego Electric Railway Company also used the material from this quarry to ballast tracks of its street railways.

Opening of the Adams Avenue Line Celebration, August 6, 1907
Photo courtesy of the San Diego Historical Society (#7774)

Opening of the Adams Avenue Line Celebration, August 6, 1907
Photo courtesy of the San Diego Historical Society (#7774-A)

The University Avenue Line

In order to extend San Diego Electric Rail line along University Avenue from Hillcrest to the eastern city limits, it was necessary to cut through the high ridge of Georgia Street and to bridge Florida Canyon with a level bed for the rails.

Early in 1907, a 32-foot deep cut through the high ridge of Georgia Street at University Avenue made the extension possible. With earthen sides, the gap was wide enough for a narrow roadway and a single line of rails. Over the gap, the two separated sections of Georgia Street were joined by a redwood truss bridge. When this bridge was completed in the summer of 1907, grading began along University Avenue, the old La Mesa Road.

In July 1907, the project for extension of the car line to City Heights was approved and rails began to be laid on August first. On the morning of Monday, November 18, 1907, the first electric car made its way under the new Georgia Street Bridge and out along the single track laid upon the mud of University Avenue. Its final destination was the intersection of Fairmount and University Avenues in the heart of what would become City Heights.

"University Avenue Electric road is now under construction. The beautifully located territory at the intersection of that Avenue and 30th Street is sure to be the most valuable of that section. **NOW** is the time to purchase. 30 or 60 days hence, when the cars are running, values will be decidedly advanced. Thirtieth Street will soon be completed in grading.

With two lines of transportation, (the area) is to become a highly favored section."
– *San Diego Union:* August 11, 1907

"Ties and rails are being laid on the University avenue extension of the San Diego Electric Railway company. The trolley poles have all been erected and the wire is being strung. Work on the track was started at University boulevard and the line will be extended eastward along University avenue to Fairmount avenue. The line runs along the southern boundary of University Heights and when completed will, with the Adams avenue line, afford good car service to the residents of University Heights."
– *San Diego Union,* August 17, 1907

"If work on the construction of the University avenue car line extension to and through City Heights continues to progress as rapidly as it has for the past few weeks, it will only be a short time before the track is ready for service. The trolley wires have already been strung to the end of the city limits from the beginning, a distance of about three-quarters of a mile and the ground has been plowed to within a distance of a block and a half of the city limits.

The car track is laid complete to Texas avenue, the grading is complete to Idaho and the street plowed clear to Missouri [32nd Street]."
– *San Diego Union,* August 29, 1907

View of University Avenue (Old La Mesa Road) Single Rail to the East from the Georgia Street Bridge, 1907
Photo courtesy of the San Diego Historical Society (#1597)

View to the East on University Avenue of the Newly Completed Georgia Street Bridge (Redwood Truss Construction), 1907
At the crest of the hill lies Texas Street. In between are a few remaining citrus or small cattle ranches with limited human habitation
(*San Diego Union,* August 29, 1907)
Photo courtesy of the San Diego Historical Society (#1597A)

The opening of the University Avenue line, three months following that of the Adams Avenue line, was heralded by the Columbian Realty Company in a manner similar to that given by the Ralston Realty Company in Normal Heights. The Columbian Realty Company, which had the franchise for the City Heights Addition, contracted with the city for the grading of University Avenue, and with the San Diego Electric Railway Company, for the construction of the University Avenue Line.

By 1913, the single track of the University Avenue car line had become inadequate to serve the increased population of the mesas to the east of Park Boulevard. Double tracking that line required a wider gap in the ridge at Georgia Street and a new bridge was ordered to replace the one built in 1907.

The city engineer, J.R. Comly, designed the new bridge to be constructed of reinforced concrete, which he declared to be more nearly permanent than steel. He also stated that concrete "lends itself more readily to artistic treatment than any other material." The aesthetics of the replacement bridge echoed contemporary ideals of the *City Beautiful* movement in civic design of monumental character.

Whereas the earlier cut in the ridge at Georgia Street had been narrow with sloping earthen sides, the new cut was widened and buttressed with perpendicular concrete walls. These buttressed walls were paneled to reflect the pattern of the columns and spandrel arches that supported the roadway of Georgia Street. Those columns rested upon the grand arch of reinforced concrete that had a clear span of 66 feet.

Georgia Street Bridge Wall under Construction, circa 1913
Photo courtesy of the San Diego Historical Society
(#83:14659)

More than any other man-made feature, the Georgia Street Bridge stands as a landmark and symbol of the event that opened the northeast mesa to urban development. Mr. Comly's masterwork still stands today as the western gateway to the Greater North Park community.

Georgia Street Bridge by J. R. Comly, circa 1929
Reinforced concrete construction, completed 1914
Photo courtesy of the San Diego Historical Society (#6852)

The 30th Street Line

At the same time work on the Georgia Street Bridge was begun, the City initiated an additional project meant to open up the section of land lying northeast of the Park. That project was the bridging of Switzer Canyon in order to extend 30th Street north to El Cajon Boulevard.

In the late Spring of 1907, crews were grading 30th Street north from Brooklyn Heights. In June, it was announced that upon completion of the grading, construction of the bridge over the canyon would begin. It was estimated that construction could start within a few days at North Park. However, problems in obtaining bridge materials caused a serious delay and construction did not begin until winter.

The 30th Street Bridge was finally completed in June 1908. The total cost of the project, including the entire infrastructure, was estimated to be $40,000. Structure of the bridge was an imposing combination of steel and reinforced concrete with a wood deck. The Cotton Brothers Construction Company of Oakland, California built the bridge.

Spanning more than 700 feet between the north and south abutments, the bridge rose 80 feet above the canyon floor at its deepest point. The structure had five "Queen truss rod" trestles, each one 20 feet long. The main section was made up of five trussed-rod spans of 102 feet each.

On the January 1, 1909, a group of property owners living on the north side of the new 30th Street Bridge petitioned the Vice President of the San Diego Electric Railway Company for an extension of the South Park line up 30th Street to Upas. The single track line for the 30th Street trolley line and the bridge combined to open the 30th Street corridor between North Park and Downtown. The immediate result for the old Pueblo Lot #1128 north of the bridge was a garden of budding new residential tracts. Two years after the opening of the line on 30th Street, it was double-tracked in response to heavy demand from the rapidly expanding area. In autumn of 1911, the line was extended from Upas northward along 30th Street to University Avenue, connecting to the line that had made its way eastward.

As predicted, the opening of the three new electric lines through the heretofore-undeveloped regions north of Balboa Park spurred an immediate burst of interest in land development for new residential tracts. The first of these, simultaneous with the development of the new electric car lines, was the Valle Vista tract of George Hawley's Southern Construction Company. But before residential development could flourish, another key building block was needed: a reliable source of water.

Streetcar Crossing New 30th Street Bridge over Switzer Canyon, circa 1920
Photo courtesy of the San Diego Historical Society (#10251)

PIERS UNDER
30TH ST. BRIDGE.

30th Street Bridge over Switzer Canyon, circa 1920
Photo courtesy of the San Diego Historical Society (#15144)

An Improved Water Supply System

Opening the arid mesa north of Balboa Park to public transportation in 1907 stimulated a new interest in real estate. The major land development companies such as Ralston, Columbian, and Pacific Building Company, as well as realty companies such as Stevens & Hartley were quick to seize the opportunity to sell property in the vast and empty acres of University Heights north of University Avenue and Park Villas south of it. However, it was not until an improved source of water for homes and gardens became available that potential community development could become a reality.

That altered status in water supply began to take place in the spring of 1908. The old system of collecting water pumped up from wells in Mission Valley to a small reservoir on El Cajon Avenue was improved upon during 1907-1908. The Southern California Mountain Water Company initiated improvements in the water supply system by way of the construction of Barrett Dam (completed January 1909), and filter plant and reservoir at Chollas Heights.

The Chollas Heights facility was connected to a new aeration plant and reservoir at Howard and Idaho Streets. In April 1908, $151,933 in bond money was turned over to the City Treasurer for the purpose of enlarging the University Heights reservoir. The result was a boarded-over, concrete structure with a capacity of 19 million gallons. The structure covered the entire block now the site of the North Park Community Park at Howard and Idaho Streets. The reservoir work was noted as starting soon in the *San Diego Union* on May 3, 1908. On July 3, 1909, the *San Diego Union* heralded, "Immense Municipal Reservoir on University Heights Nearly Finished." On July 27, 1909, the *San Diego Daily Transcript* reported that "No decision has as yet been reached by the City Council as to the kind of waterproof coating to be used in the University Heights reservoir to prevent possible leaks." The uncompleted reservoir was the unusual venue for an organizational event, when "Permission has been given the Woodmen of the World to hold their initiation on August 14th in the unfinished City reservoir on University Heights" (*San Diego Daily Transcript*, July 28, 1909). Finally, the new reservoir was finished December 28, 1909, with the *San Diego Daily Transcript* noting, "Late this afternoon, water was turned into the new reservoir on University Heights, just completed at a cost of over $100,000." Water was delivered from the reservoir into a new iron main on El Cajon Avenue. In early 1909, with the new reservoir underway, the community pressured for a new water pipeline.

"Want Water Main Past Their Lots – University Heights residents along University Avenue petition to have the wooden water main running along that Avenue replaced with a larger, metal one to connect with the new reservoir under construction."

– *San Diego Union*, February 24, 1909

A new 24-inch iron main was extended down University Avenue to its intersection with Fifth Avenue in Hillcrest. This water main supplied the new suburbanites in Hillcrest, University Heights, and the future Greater North Park.

With the improvements imminent in February 1908, Emery Smith, a San Francisco chemist and engineer of the Chollas Heights and University Heights reservoirs, declared that San Diego would now receive "as fine a supply of water as any city in the state and that there should be no uneasiness of a shortage."

However, in May of 1908, city officials declared that even with the large capacity of the new University Heights reservoir, its elevation would not be high enough to carry the water to some of the higher territory north of El Cajon Avenue. The pessimistic predictions of pressure too low to supply water adequately to customers proved to be accurate. New households in Pacific Building Company's Tract #3 in the immediate vicinity of the new reservoir began to complain about the low water pressure and to demand a solution.

That solution came in the spring of 1910 with a water tank raised above the reservoir. Water was pumped into the tank from the reservoir and then released through a pipe into the water mains. Enough pressure was supplied by gravity to satisfy the needs of the local houses until the real estate boom of the early 1920s. The population explosion in San Diego that began in 1921 created a severe housing shortage and rapid build-up of North Park and University Heights. Water supply to the area again became inadequate for all of the new houses. The solution was a larger water tank and reservoir.

In the autumn of 1923, a municipal bond issue was authorized by a local election for the construction of a new tank with a capacity of 1.2 million gallons. Bids were received from a number of contractors. The one accepted was made by the Pittsburgh-Des Moines Steel Company.

Partially Completed Water Tank, 1924
Photo courtesy of the San Diego Historical Society (#2621)

Construction of the Water Tank at Howard and Idaho Streets in University Heights, 1924

The tank as constructed was supported 50 feet above ground by 12 steel columns. The columns taper from footings to the balcony. The diameter of the structure is 54 feet. The height of the tank is 52 feet. Overall, the structure from foundation to the overflow cap is 127½ feet in height. When fully loaded, the tank held approximately 5,000 tons of water. The steel structural plates and members add about 400 tons to the load. The water storage system was purported to be the largest elevated tank in the world (see 1924 photo on page 34).

The 1920s tank and enlarged reservoir served the Mid-city well until the late 1940s. The water treatment plant and its block-long reservoir were removed in the 1950s, when the Alvarado Water Treatment Plant went into service. In the 1990s, new seismic safety standards required the City of San Diego Water Department to retire the tank, which now stands empty, but is a registered historic landmark.

Modern Sewers

In January 1909, Mayor John Forward, Jr. identified an additional problem of urban development that concerned the territories north of Balboa Park: a lack of sewers. Mayor Forward recommended to the city council that steps be taken for the extension of the city's sewer system.

"I respectfully submit for your consideration a communication from the city engineer, requesting permission to take up the matter of surveys and plans for sewer extensions, covering sections of the city now rapidly building up but without sewer service. Some of the most sightly and desirable sections of the city, which are building up in fine improvements and actual homes, must, in the nature of things, soon acquire sewers. Take University Heights east of Georgia street . . . etc."

"Those localities are making wonderful progress and deserve the hearty encouragement of the municipality and I therefore suggest that . . . the city engineer be directed. . . to make . . . surveys and plans for sewers . . . covering the localities mentioned."

– Mayor Forward, January 6, 1909

In 1911, bonds for $26,000 funded the construction of the Switzer Canyon Trunk Sewer, an 8-inch pipeline that ran south from the east side of Balboa Park in Golden Hill to Oregon (now Pershing Avenue) and B Streets, where it entered the downtown system. This was only the second trunk sewer for the city, placing North Park at the leading edge of the modern sewage system in San Diego.

36

Chapter 4
Early Housing Tracts

A First Tract: Valle Vista Terrace

In the spring of 1907, the College Hill Land Association was making improvements to all of the streets and avenues in the immediate vicinity of the cliffs overlooking Mission Valley. The Ralston Realty Company acted as the general agent for sales promotion in this northern section of the University Heights Addition. The College Hill Land Association formed in the late 1880s during an exciting boom time in San Diego. The founding members envisioned a community with a great university as its centerpiece. Arrangements were made with the Methodist University of Southern California in Los Angeles to establish a branch in what is now University Heights. The University was to be called the San Diego College of Arts of the University of Southern California, and it was to be located where the present day Board of Education is on Normal Street. The *Golden Era Magazine* in November 1888 said, "Where could a more desirable location be found? Here nature has eclipsed art, and here art will do its utmost to eclipse nature." When the "Boom Went Bust" in the 1890s, construction of the college ceased, and in 1896 the USC directors reconveyed the site and unfinished foundation to the company, provided land would be donated to the state for a normal school. Part of the State Normal School building that was built as a result and dedicated on May 1, 1899 still graces Washington Street and Park Boulevard near El Cajon Boulevard, and the legacy of the

land development company lives on in street names, including University Avenue in North Park.

Prime development by the College Hill Land Association in the Valle Vista area began with the grading of streets on Valle Vista Terrace, Saturday, May 4, 1907. By mid-June, the grading of Cliff Street and Panorama Drive had been completed and workmen began laying the cement sidewalks and curbing. Four cobblestone pillars marked the eastern and western entrances into the tract. Ornamental electric lights topped these pillars.

George Hawley, whose father founded the store that later became San Diego Hardware, became a partner with Col. D. C. Collier in the land development business in 1899 with the incorporation of the South-Western Investment Company. They started the early building and improvements within the Valle Vista tract. The first house built there on a villa lot of Panorama Drive was Hawley's own residence, designed by architects William S. Hebbard and Irving Gill. Gill was the project architect on the job.

The Hawley house, a modified half-timbered, Arts & Crafts design was completed about the August 1, 1907. The canyon side of the house looked out across Mission Valley to the northwest with a glimpse of the Pacific Ocean. Two giant palms, taken from Hawley's former home on Third Street, were placed in the front lawn of the house. Other palms were planted on both sides of the U-shaped Panorama Drive throughout the tract.

Following the completion of George Hawley's home, other houses began to fill in the spaces around the horseshoe curve of Panorama Drive. An early neighbor of the Hawley Family was Mrs. Hattie F. Carey, for whom the architect Edward Quayle designed a home in the late summer of 1907.

Two other early residents of the neighborhood, A. E. Roberts and Claude Woolman, built houses side by side on Cliff Street in the Fall of 1909. A. E. Roberts, a real estate agent, had his home built by the contractor, F. M. Powell. The house later was the home of author Carobeth Tucker Harrington Laird. Carobeth's father, James Harvey Tucker, who moved his family from Texas to San Diego in 1915, purchased the house at 2204 Cliff Street when Carobeth was 19 years old. Her first book, *Encounter With An Angry God*, was published in 1975 when she was 80 years of age.

Next door to the Roberts house, F. M. Powell built a house for city councilman, Claude Woolman (1909-1911). Woolman was an advocate for the issuance of municipal bonds to fund the purchase of the entire water system of John D. Spreckels' Southern California Mountain Water Co.

It was under Woolman's jurisdiction as municipal water superintendent that the 20-million-gallon reservoir on University Heights was completed in 1909. Councilman Woolman also was responsible for the placement of iron water mains down University Avenue. This addition of a major water system for that section made possible the first important housing development in the future North Park addition, Pacific Building Company's Tract #3.

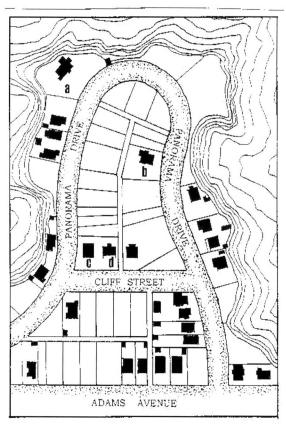

Map of Valle Vista Terrace

a. George Hawley House, Hebbard & Gill, 1907, 4744 Panorama Dr
b. C .O. Reinbold House, M. P. Kellogg, 1910, 4769 Panorama Drive
c. A. E. Roberts House, F. M. Powell, 1909, 2204 Cliff Street
d. Claude Woolman House, F. M. Powell, 1909, 2216 Cliff Street

Another of Hawley's nearby neighbors and a business associate was C. O. Reinbold whose home was built at 4769 Panorama Drive in 1910. Mr. Reinbold was secretary-treasurer for Col. Collier's real estate company. His house was built by M. P. Kellogg.

In 1914, master craftsman David Owen Dryden built another six houses in Valle Vista Terrace, including possibly his first two-story house at 4780 East Panorama Drive. This luxurious home was purchased by Helen Crenshaw, a Vice President of the San Diego Title Guaranty Company, one of Dryden's early lenders. By 1920, there were 27 homes in the tract that was being touted as one of San Diego's new "high-class" residential districts.

Tracts Developed 1909-1914

Large scale development of the high mesa northeast of Balboa Park had to wait upon the acquisition of two of the key building blocks of urbanization: public transportation and a reliable source of water. By 1909, these two pieces of the jigsaw puzzle were in place.

On the morning in 1907 when the first trolley made its way down University Avenue, the *San Diego Union* reported that 41 homes scattered throughout City Heights were being served by the electric railway. Only four of those had existed prior to the start of construction on the line in the summer of that year.

The Columbian Realty Company had been so certain that a new trolley line would open the entire high mesa beyond the city limits that it purchased 2,000 acres in City Heights; land that was covered by nothing more than sagebrush and cactus. At Fairmount Avenue, the terminus of the University Avenue trolley line, the Company built a modern sales office and waiting lounge, and proceeded to sell improved lots as building sites for homes and commercial establishments.

"San Diego Electric Company
Will Open University Extension Line"

"At the present terminal of the line, just opposite the home of R. Quartermass, the Columbian Realty company, which controls the larger part of the property reached by the new line, has erected a most attractive office and station, the surrounding grounds of which have been converted into a bower of beauty by means of palms, rose bushes, grass and other plants. In the interior of the structure, which with its wide veranda and large windows has a most pleasant exterior appearance, are numerous easy chairs, lounges, reading and writing tables for the accommodation of the general public and free to all."

"At a distance of some fifty feet in the rear of the office, a long stable 54 by 15 feet, has been constructed. This stable is likewise open for the use of anyone. It being the idea that ranchers from the outlying districts may drive as far as the station, hitch their horses in a place protected from the weather and take a car downtown, happy in the thought that their horses will be thoroughly rested for the drive home, when they return."

– *San Diego Union*, November 17, 1907

Pacific Building Company Tract #3

The real estate boom spread west from Fairmount Avenue all along the University Avenue line. In May of 1909, Oscar Cotton's Pacific Building Company announced plans to construct the third of its residential tracts in "the best part of University Heights."

Pacific Building Company Tract #3 at Idaho and Lincoln, 1907
Photo courtesy of the San Diego Historical Society (#618)

That tract was centered upon the immediate blocks north of University Avenue, south of Polk, east of Idaho and west of Kansas, an area that later would be identified as North Park. In February 1909, the San Diego City Council admitted that it was finding it difficult to identify the western and southern boundaries of the new North Park addition.

" . . . A little city by itself"
San Diego Union, May 2, 1908

Pacific Building Company's Tract #3 got under way in June 1909 with the construction of five cottages on the east side of Idaho Street in the block south of the University Heights water reservoir. All were constructed in variations upon the California Arts & Crafts bungalow style with wood frame and sheathing. In August, the company issued a promotional statement declaring that Tract #3 would "be the only thoroughly developed property in University Heights and the most modern section in San Diego" and that it would lead to "a little city by itself" *(San Diego Union,* August 6, 1909, page 7).

The company's design and construction policy required that no lot be sold without a custom built house of less than $1,200 at cost. In order to prevent unsightly gaps in the neighborhood of new homes, the lots were sold in order beginning at the north end. No lot was sold until the lot to its north had been sold and a house contracted for. The method ensured that once all lots on a block were sold, there would be a solid row of houses facing the street.

Single lots were 25 feet wide by 140 feet deep and were sold in pairs for $1,200 each. Houses cost a minimum of $1,200. For $2,400, a North Park resident could obtain a minimal two bedroom, one bath home. Good mountain water was supplied with strong pressure guaranteed by the new water tower nearby. Frequent trolley service to downtown was available less than two blocks away. Term purchases could be made for $25 a month.

By the time the 1910 Federal Census was recorded, there were 28 working-class households in Pacific Building Company's Tract #3. In the entire district centered on 30th and University, there were more than 75 households. The suburbanization of North Park was underway.

West End Tract

The West End tract was bordered by 28th Street and Ray Street on the west and east, and University Avenue and Upas Street on the north and south. The tract encompassed the east side of 28th Street, while the west side of the street was part of the neighboring Park Villas Tract. Although West End as a subdivided tract had been laid out on paper as early as 1872, it did not receive its first residential improvements until 1907, contemporary with the construction of the electric car line on University Avenue. The first "paper" tract map #590, dated May 17, 1873, followed the precedent of Horton's Addition of that same year. The 80-foot wide streets, blocks 200 feet by 300 feet, and lots 50 feet by 100 feet gave it a different configuration from the typical 60-foot wide streets and 50-foot by 125-foot lots in the surrounding tracts of Park Villas and University Heights, hence the multiple dog-leg intersections at the tract boundaries.

Concerning the sudden interest in property in the West End that occurred in the Fall of 1910, the *San Diego Union* reported: "Principally owing to lack of transportation, it has been for many years without a single house or other improvement, but has now suddenly come into notice" *(San Diego Union,* December 11, 1910, page 7). Among those taking notice were some of North Park's most active realty men, including Joseph McFadden, who would later play a key role in development of the Burlingame tract.

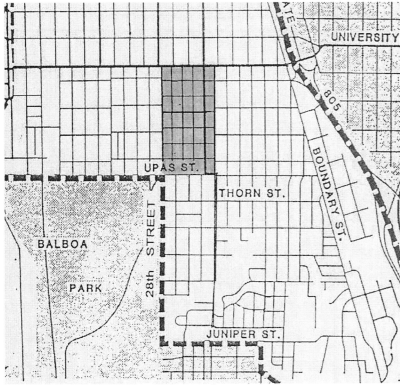

West End Tract

NOTE: All tract maps in this section are based on a mapping by the Planning Department of the City of San Diego of "Potential Historic Sites and Areas in Greater North Park" (date unknown).

Following a brief career as proprietor of a downtown restaurant, Joseph McFadden re-entered the real estate market in November 1910 as a partner of Maurice Essery. This was at about the same time that Charles O'Neall (a future mayor of San Diego) began to deal in properties in West End. McFadden announced in December 1910 that he also would be specializing in sales in the West End tract (*San Diego Union*, December 11, 1910, page 5).

Also in December, the *San Diego Union* reported that:

"Building operations are becoming more active in that section of the city every day. New houses have been erected by the score during the past few months and others are being started every few days. Fine homes are being built in all sections of that district."

– *San Diego Union*, December 16, 1910, page 18

With all of the attention given to the sales of property in West End by both O'Neall and McFadden, 20 homes had been completed by the end of 1910 and ten more were under contract for construction early in 1911.

McFadden established the West End Building Company, and the first house was permitted in February 1911. Job 1 of the company was recorded in the *Daily Transcript* on February 11, 1911 as Building Permit #220 for a bungalow and shed on 30th Street between Capps and Dwight streets (Block 22, Lot 4). In June 1911, the *Daily Transcript* recorded five building permits by Joseph McFadden or the West End Building Company in the tract. These were each for $2,000 cottages on Kansas (now 29th) Street. The homes were at the southwest corner of Capps and Kansas streets (Block 28, Lot 1); between Capps and Myrtle streets (Block 28, Lots 3 and 5); and between Dwight and Capps streets (Block 22, Lot 9 and Block 23, Lot 5). The latter, now 3560 29th Street, was Joseph McFadden's residence for two years.

In August and September 1911, the *Daily Transcript* recorded three additional building permits for

Joseph McFadden or his company: on Kansas between Capps and Dwight streets (Block 22, Lot 8), later 3563 29th Street; on 30th Street between Upas and Myrtle streets (Block 31, Lot 10); and on 30th Street near Capps Street (Block 22, Lot 5).

By October 1911, Joseph McFadden had taken on a new partner, George Buxton, and the partnership moved from real estate sales to tract development with their first success in the West End tract. By December, McFadden's West End Building Company had completed 72 houses. In a published statement, McFadden claimed that the "West End Addition is the choice location – where the cream is fast rising and waiting to be skimmed." He further predicted, rightly so, that:

> "Fortunes are being made by many foresighted people in San Diego realty. The city is forging to the destined position among cities of the United States. The progress for the next two or three years will be marvelous in our eyes."
>
> – *San Diego Union,* December 11, 1910, page 31

McFadden's statement verified that the critical building blocks of infrastructure were in place: "Two electric routes available. Main water pipe, gas, electric light, sewers provided for in the last bond issue."

In the autumn months of 1911, the #2 electric car line, which had terminated at Upas and 30th streets, was extended north along 30th to an intersection with the electric car line on University Avenue. Adjacent property became more valuable and sales of lots increased on 30th Street as well as on 29th Street to the west and Ray Street to the east. A new land boom was on, and by 1920 more than 200 additional homes had been built within the West End addition. In those years, McFadden & Buxton, one of North Park's most dynamic land development firms, was launched.

The West End tract attracted prominent builder/craftsmen, including David Owen Dryden. His first house on 28th Street is renowned for being his most extroverted attempt at an oriental mode. The house was built on property owned by George H. and Anna Carr at 3553 on the corner of Capps Street. George Carr was Secretary of the Independent Sash and Door Company, a manufacturer and supplier of fine doors, sashes, mill work, and art glass. The house was completed on June 22, 1915. Other West End homes built by Dryden include 3505 and 3571 28th Street.

Edward F. Bryans, who would build extensively on Oregon Street (later Pershing Avenue) in the Park Villas tract, built two stucco homes on Granada Avenue at Upas Street, obtaining the building permit for 3401 Granada Avenue on April 29, 1926, and the permit for 3411 Granada Avenue on March 31, 1927.

Alexander Schreiber, who earned a reputation for the electrical installations in the homes he built, received the building permits for a set of five homes along Utah Street on March 5, 1919. These wood frame homes near Capps Street are at 3519, 3552, 3562, 3569, and 3577 Utah Street.

Lynhurst and St. Louis Heights Tracts

In January 1910, the San Diego Construction Company announced that it had bought a ten-acre tract of land in the former Wallace partition of Pueblo Lot 1128. In January 1898, an interlocutory decree had subdivided Pueblo Lot 1350 and 1128. The two major land holders of Pueblo Lot 1128 following the subdivision were James Wallace and Robert J. Blair. San Diego Construction Company's ten-acre plot, the Lynhurst Tract, was bordered by 29th and 30th Streets on the west and east, and Upas and Thorn streets on the north and south. It was a highly marketable plot of real estate at the end of the new #2 trolley line.

The company promised a development of the two city blocks into a tract that would be "improved at once and fitted up as a high class residence district." The subdivision map for the tract was filed on May 25, 1910 (Map #1262). The first house (Lot 12 in Block 2) was completed in the following July.

By the end of 1912, more than a dozen structures had been completed in the tract, including *The Lynhurst,* a commercial building of mixed use with seven shops on the ground floor and five apartments on the second floor. The structure, designed by the architect Eugene Weathers, was sold in August 1913 for $26,000. The building permit was obtained December 27, 1912, and the building was constructed by the San Diego Construction Company.

The 1909 terminus of trolley line #2 at Upas and 30th Streets and the completion of the Lynhurst Building stimulated the growth of a small commercial nucleus at the intersection of these two streets. In the 1920s, in order to distinguish the nucleus from the North Park center at 30th and University, the merchant group named it "Pershing Heights" and held their meetings in the Lynhurst Building. The chairman of the Pershing Heights Business Club was D. M Parker, a local realtor. He said in an interview that the mission of the organization was "to boost San Diego and the 'Buy-in-San Diego' movement." The first meeting and social

gathering of the club occurred on March 25, 1924 in the new one-story row of shops at 2965 Upas Street, an extension of the Lynhurst Building constructed in 1923 by C. M. Williams.

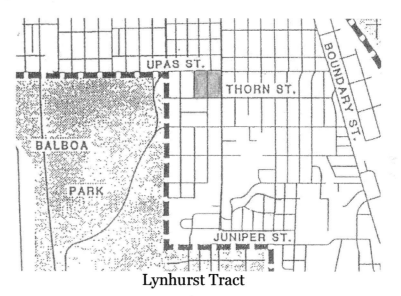

Lynhurst Tract

The name Pershing Heights was obviously taken in reference to the newly widened, paved and re-named old one-lane wagon trail that wound its way through the eastern canyons of Balboa Park up the steep grade from downtown San Diego to the heights above the northeast corner of the Park. Named for General John J. Pershing, the hero of World War One, the new highway was a memorial to the San Diego military men and women who had given their lives in service to their country during that conflict. The highway, the most expedient and fastest automobile and truck route between the commercial centers of downtown San Diego and North Park, did for the new bustling business community at the junction of 30th and University what the street car lines on those two avenues had done for it in the previous decade.

Immediately west of the Lynhurst tract, St. Louis Heights encompassed the ten acres between 28th and 29th streets on the west and east, and Upas and Thorn streets on the north and south. Subdivision Map #907 filed May 24, 1904 indicated lots measuring 25 feet by 120 and 127 feet. Edward F. Bryans built in the St. Louis Heights tract at the southwest corner of Granada Avenue and Upas Street, as well as in the Lynhurst tract on the west side of Dale Street.

The 1909 extension of trolley line #2 over the Switzer Canyon Bridge along 30th Street to Upas Street stimulated the development of several new residential tracts east and west of the line. As early as 1905 in the newly subdivided Pueblo Lot 1128, several small but important tracts began to be created: Frary Heights, Gurwell Heights, Blair's Highlands, Wallace Heights, and O'Neall's Terrace.

Lynhurst Building, circa 1921
Photo courtesy of the Historical Collection, Union Title Insurance Company (San Diego Historical Society #1657)

46

Frary Heights Tract

On March 9, 1905, Map #940 for Frary Heights was filed in the County Office of the Recorder. This tract was bordered by 30th and 32nd streets on the west and east, and Upas and Redwood streets on the north and south. The subdivider of the tract was Frank P. Frary (1857-1911), Mayor of San Diego from 1902 to 1906. Frary was a founder and partner in the Pioneer Truck Company (1889) who came to San Diego from Ohio in 1877. The first house built in the tract was one for Mayor Frary and his wife, Maude, at 3227 Grim Avenue. As the Frarys continued to maintain their permanent residence on Ivy Street, the Grim Avenue house was most likely a weekend retreat on the semi-rural outskirts of the city.

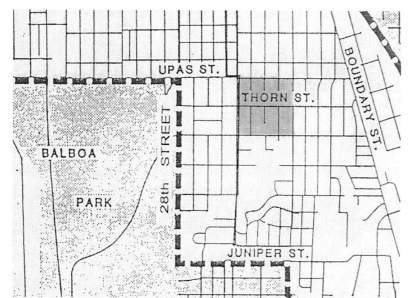

Frary Heights Tract

Gurwell Heights Tract

South of Frary Heights, Gurwell Heights extended from 30th to 32nd streets on the west and east, and from Redwood to Nutmeg streets on the north and south. Subdivision Map #992 was filed for this tract on June 4, 1906. One of the early listings in the *San Diego Daily Transcript* was a September 25, 1911 building permit for Mrs. E. D. Orendorff, for a cottage near 30th on Quince. David Owen Dryden built two homes on Palm Street (3039 and 3049) for Casper Kundert in March and April of 1912. In 1924, Dryden obtained multiple building permits for cottages and garages along Olive Street and 30th Street in Gurwell Heights.

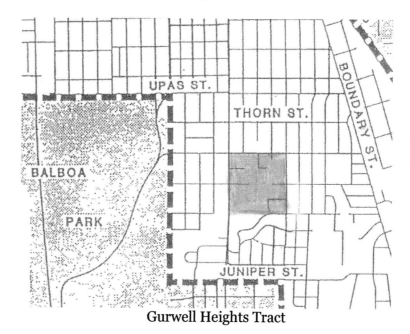

Gurwell Heights Tract

Blair's Highlands, Wallace Heights, and O'Neall's Terrace Tracts

An interlocutory decree of January 28, 1898 authorized the partition of Pueblo Lots #1128 and #1350. The decree was recorded September 17, 1903. Among those who owned large portions of the undivided lots were James Wallace and Robert J. Blair. New subdivided tracts within Pueblo Lot 1128 were named for both of those investors. Blair's Highlands included seven blocks extending from 28th to 30th streets on the west and east, and Redwood to Nutmeg streets on the north and south. On January 24, 1906, Subdivision Map #971 for Blair's Highlands was drawn and filed by Blair. The remaining southeastern block bordered by Dale and 30th streets on the west and east, and Palm and Nutmeg streets on the north and south was called Aurora Heights. Subdivision Map #1489 was filed November 6, 1912 for this tract with irregular lots.

Wallace Heights, directly to the north and split lengthwise, was bordered by Granada Avenue and Dale Street on the west and east, and Thorn and Redwood streets on the north and south. Subdivision Map #902 was filed January 20, 1904 for this tract. The one-block tract directly east of Wallace Heights was called M. Gurwells' Subdivision, with Map #1715 filed February 24, 1921. The one-block tract directly west of Wallace Heights was named for a third investor, Charles F. O'Neall, the realtor who, prior to his becoming mayor of San Diego in 1913, handled property in all of the new subdivisions of the city north of Balboa Park. O'Neall's Terrace was bordered by 28th Street and Granada Avenue on the west and east, and Thorn and Redwood streets on

the north and south. Subdivision Map #999 for this tract was filed July 16, 1906.

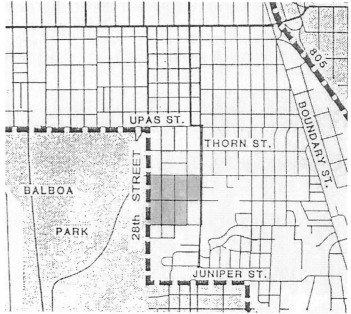

Blair's Highlands Tract

R. J. Blair (1871-1939) was a co-founder and Vice President of Union Title Insurance and Trust Company in San Diego. Blair was "a nationally recognized authority on land titles" (James D. Forward, *San Diego Union*, September 27, 1939). He was born in Cincinnati, Ohio and entered the title business in San Diego as a young man of seventeen.

In January 1909, Robert Blair, Sr. and Robert Blair, Jr. were prominent members of the small group of property owners north of the new 30th Street Bridge who petitioned the San Diego Electric Rail Company for an extension of car line #2. It was their contention that "until the project was carried through, the development of these ideal residential territories would be retarded" (*San Diego Union*, January 31, 1909, page 16). The following year, the extended line was completed and in January 1911, Charles F. O'Neall announced the new subdivided tract south of Lynhurst. In advertising the Blair Highlands tract, O'Neall proclaimed it "the ideal home spot on the hills; overlooks the Bay and Park and has a fine mountain view" (*San Diego Union*, January 2, 1911, Section 9, page 7).

Blair and his wife Ethel acquired Lots 25 through 28 in block 5 of Blair's Highlands on April 3, 1908 from his father. In the summer of 1911, the Blairs had a small house moved onto the back of Lots 25 and 26 in Block 5 (Notice of Completion #MR 38-268, September 18, 1911). In that month, he contracted with the Andrew Brothers, building contractors, for a house to be built on the same property. The two story dwelling, north of Nutmeg Street on the west side of Granada Avenue, was completed on February 1, 1912 (MR #38-439).

The Andrew Brothers, Daniel and William, were born in Scotland and immigrated to the United States in the 1880s. A carpenter, Daniel Andrew (1862-1946) arrived in San Diego in 1886 during the city's first land boom. His initial construction work was on the Hotel Del Coronado project in the late 1880s. Although he was the contractor for several public buildings, his main work was in home construction. Several of his early houses were built in the North Park neighborhoods. At his death in August 1946, it was estimated that he had built several hundred San Diego homes in a career that spanned more than 45 years.

Also in the tract, a home for Reverend W. E. Crabtree was built on the southeast corner of 28th and Palm streets by T. T. Harding in October 1912. Edward F. Bryans built a cottage on Dale Street south of Redwood in Blair's Highlands.

Park Villas Tract

This large tract spanned two areas north of Upas Street and south of University Avenue. Separated by the West End tract and James Hartley's 40 acres of the North Park Addition, the eastern Park Villas tract was bordered by Boundary Street on the east, and by 32nd Street (northern portion) and Ray Street (southern portion) on the west. The western Park Villas tract was bordered by Arizona and 28th streets on the west and east. This large area had been surveyed for Joseph Nash in May 1870, and Subdivision Map #438 was filed October 14, 1887.

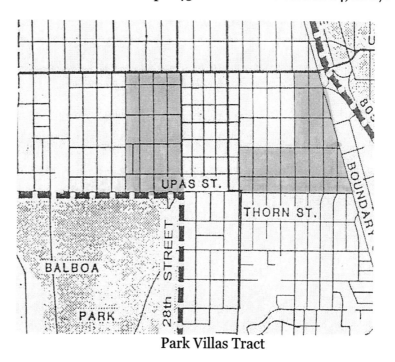

Park Villas Tract

Joseph Nash was an early San Diego entrepreneur who opened his general merchandise store on the New Town waterfront in 1868. It was Nash's business that a young clerk in the store, George Marston, and his friend Charles Hamilton, bought for $10,000 in 1873. The Marston Company ultimately became San Diego's leading department store. Nash was a contemporary of Alonzo Horton, founder of San Diego's New Town. A 1914 news article about Nash noted, "He purchased a lot in the business district for $25 and erected a building to house his stock. He purchased other business property at the same price." Nash is quoted as saying, "I purchased whole blocks for $200 per block. We divided up some of the blocks into lots and tried to sell the lots for $5 each. I remember one man who claimed he had been cheated and demanded his $5 back. He threatened us with lawsuits and made such dire intimations against our characters that we gave him back his money."

The Ralston Realty Company advertised 34 western Park Villas tract lots for sale in the Sunday morning *San Diego Union* on November 17, 1907, noting the lots were "one short block south of University Heights and the new car line on University avenue which will be in operation Monday . . . These lots are level, on high ground, desirable for immediate building and the best buy at the price fixed, in all San Diego." Barnson for Bargains enthusiastically advertised lots in the blocks between Villa Terrace and 28th Street on the west and east, and Landis and Dwight streets on the north and south, extolling the:

> "Panoramic view of all creation to the horizon at every point of the compass. Unobstructable view of the mountains to Mexico, Point Loma, Coronado Islands and

down over the big park to the EXPOSITION grounds. Considering the magnificent view, unequalled car facilities, proximity to what is very soon to be most unique play grounds and wonderful International Botanical Gardens in the world, and its nearness – 20 minutes by car, or 10 minutes through park to the business district. This section is sure to become the favorite residence district of the city and will undergo a most wonderful change in the next twelve months."

One of the early building permits for Park Villas listed in the *San Diego Daily Transcript* was for a cottage and store on Arnold near Landis, issued to W. A. Winnege on October 25, 1909. A building permit was issued for Park Villas School on Idaho (now 28th Street) between Wightman and Landis in Park Villas block 63 on December 8, 1910. Charles Cheesewright was issued a building permit for a cottage on Arnold between Dwight and Landis on January 3, 1911. W. B. Ricketts received a building permit for a barn and shed at the northwest corner of Herman and Myrtle streets on February 14, 1911, and a permit for a cottage at the same location on March 18, 1911.

Many notable builders constructed homes in the Park Villas tract. In 1912, T. F. ("Jack") Carter, who also built the three-story commercial building for Stevens & Hartley at 30th Street and University Avenue, built homes on Ray and on Grim between Dwight and Myrtle streets, and apartments and a store at Idaho (28th) Street and University Avenue. Maurice Essery was issued permits for three houses and garages on Landis between Oregon (Pershing) and Idaho (28th) streets on January 21, 1913. James Blaine Draper built three residences in a row along

28th Street. He built the home at 3630 28th Street in November 1915 (which was altered in January 1919), 3638 28th Street in February 1916 (which was altered by Dryden in October 1917), and 3644 28th Street in May 1916. He also built 3574 28th Street in August 1915. Alexander Schreiber built the home at 3432 Oregon in October 1919. William E. Gibb, who built numerous buildings in North Park's commercial core for the Hartleys, built a large Craftsman home in April 1915 at 2738 Upas Street, at the corner of 28th and Upas streets.

Francesca Croxall-Bale built homes in the Park Villas tract at 2527 Landis Street (November 1922), 3571 Bancroft Street (October 1924), and 3439 Villa Terrace (March 1926).

Edward F. Bryans built more than a dozen homes along Oregon Street (now Pershing Avenue) and the west side of 28th Street in the Park Villas tract. He received a building permit for 3420 Oregon Street on January 20, 1913, and for 3544 Oregon Street on May 15, 1913. The latter was his own residence. Other homes built by Bryans in the tract include 3510-12, 3530, and 3536 Oregon Street and 3570 28th Street (1916); 3612-14 and 3652 Oregon Street (1917); 3607 Oregon Street (1919); 3521, 3552, and 3635 Oregon Street, 3520 28th Street, and 2728 Upas Street (1921); and 3593 Oregon Street (1923).

David Owen Dryden built about 20 homes in the Park Villas tract, most on the east side of Oregon and the west side of 28th Street during 1915 to 1918. He built a bungalow for his own family at 3536 28th Street, and the home next door at 3546, which were completed in December of 1915.

San Diego Union, November 17, 1907

In 1916, Dryden had seven major houses under construction in Park Villas. The first of these, begun on the 7th of January, was a two-story house at 3446 28th Street in the classic redwood board and shingle tradition of the Craftsman style. Delayed by the continuous rains and high winds of Hatfield's flood, the house took two months to build instead of the usual six weeks. When the house was finally completed in early March 1916, it was quickly purchased by a retired Chicago manufacturer and proprietor of a paint and varnish company, John Carman Thurston, who ironically had recently moved to San Diego for its more benign climate. Other homes built by Dryden along 28th Street include 3516, 3554, 3614, 3676, and 3712 (1916); and 3412 and 3706 (1917). Dryden homes along Oregon Street include 3503, 3543, 3559, and 3575 (1917); and 3511, 3527, and 3728 (1918).

Pauly's Addition Tract

Adjacent to Nash's western Park Villas tract, Pauly's Addition was bordered by Alabama and Arizona streets on the west and east, and University Avenue and Upas Street on the north and south. Subdivision Map #65 was filed April 1, 1873. Aaron Pauly was an original "forty-niner" and San Diego pioneer who came to the young town in 1869. He set up a large and successful general merchandise store at the foot of Fifth Street, renting the wharf and store from Alonzo Horton. Aaron Pauly, who was the first president of the San Diego Chamber of Commerce, ran the store with his sons Frederick and Charles W. George Marston was an assistant bookkeeper in this store for a year before clerking at Joseph Nash's business, and he took his meals at the Pauly home. Both Aaron and Charles entered the real estate business in 1875. Upon Charles's death in 1925, George Marston recalled, "It was my happy privilege to be a junior bookkeeper in the wonderful Pauly store when Fred, Charlie and George were adventurers together in the golden west." He said of his friend, "Mr. [Charles] Pauly has an honorable record in the history of our city: first as a merchant, then as a realtor, and in later years as a bank director. Pauly's addition is a tract of land northeast of Balboa park, a section of the city that was developed by Mr. Pauly. Other parts of the city have felt the touch of his guiding hand." Charles W. Pauly was the receiver for the Mission Cliffs gardens when it went into bankruptcy.

Some of the early building permits in this tract were issued to W. Chadwick for four cottages on Arizona Street between Dwight and Landis (*San Diego Daily Transcript*, June 19, 1909). W. Chadwick received another building permit September 30, 1909 for a cottage on Arizona and Dwight streets. F. L. Edwards received a building permit for a bungalow on Texas at the northeast corner of Landis on February 2, 1910, and D. L. White received a permit for a bungalow on Texas Street in the same block, between Landis and Wightman streets, the same day. On April 12, 1910, the Hillcrest Company received building permits for three cottages on Texas Street, two between Dwight and Myrtle streets, and one between Wightman and Landis streets. The Hillcrest Company obtained a building permit on June 4, 1910 for a bungalow on Arizona Street between Landis and Dwight streets. A. A. Findley and T. W. Coates obtained a building permit on August 12, 1910 for a cottage on Louisiana Street between Wightman and Landis streets.

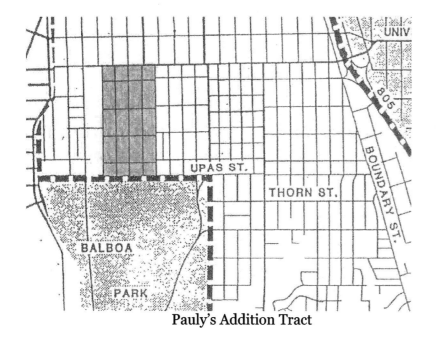
Pauly's Addition Tract

As with other tracts, skilled Craftsman builders worked in Pauly's Addition. Edward F. Bryans obtained a building permit for a frame cottage at 3694 Texas Street on March 14, 1912, and a permit for a house at 3567 Mississippi Street on May 25, 1925. This home was built for Fred Bartlett, manager of Peerless Laundry, one of the earliest North Park businesses. Alexander Schreiber received a permit for a frame cottage and garage at 3545 Mississippi Street on March 31, 1922. Francesca Croxall-Bale obtained the building permit for 3535 Mississippi Street on November 19, 1928. The architectural designer team of Ralph Hurlburt and Charles Tifal obtained a building permit for a home on the northwest corner of Mississippi and Upas streets on December 3, 1924 for George M. Hawley Company, owner.

John Pearson obtained a building permit for a Spanish Colonial Revival house at 3435 Texas on October 19, 1925, and permits for four similar houses on Mississippi Street, at 3530 (December 1, 1926), 3536 (March 21, 1927), 3544 (June 28, 1926), and 3575 (January 23, 1928).

Hartley's North Park Tract

Sometime in 1910, Jack Hartley and Will Stevens made the decision to subdivide the family's former lemon grove for development as commercial and residential plots. It was determined that in order to pay for the street grading and other improvements, one half of the 40 acres would have to be sold. The 20 acres that they kept, bordering University Avenue between Ray and 32nd (formerly Missouri) Streets, became a large part of the future commercial center of North Park. The caption on the following photo from the Hartley album reads,

> "1910 – Breaking ground for residential development on Hartley's North Park – Ray street to 32 and south 1 quarter mile. This was the old Hartley lemon ranch – planted in 1892 by James Monroe Hartley, who was living at the time in Dehesa with Mary Jane and five children. Penny Company bought this corner in 1941 for $14,500. Old time San Diegans thought they paid too much."

The opening sale of property in the Hartley's North Park tract took place on September 29, 1912. The Addition was advertised as follows:

> "TWO CAR LINES (No. 1 and No. 2, same distance each way) will take you to "Hartley's North Park," the most up-to-date

restricted residence district in San Diego. Streets graded and surfaced with decomposed granite; sidewalks and curbs, ornamental corner posts, etc. Building restrictions $2000, except property facing on University avenue, which will be sold in 25-foot lots for business purposes. Watch the growth of buildings and values."

Subdivision Map #1428 was filed April 8, 1912 for Hartley's North Park. Among the prominent designer builders active in the tract were Hurlburt and Tifal, who obtained a building permit within the tract for a frame cottage and garage at 3751 Herman Street on June 13, 1923. William Gibb built a frame cottage and garage at 3115 University Avenue for Mary Jane Hartley, owner, obtaining the building permit on December 14, 1924.

Breaking Ground for Residential Development on Hartley's North Park, 1910
Photo courtesy of the Hartley Family
(San Diego Historical Society #5590)

Hartley's North Park, 1907
Photo courtesy of the San Diego Historical Society (#UT 8248-444)

Hartley's North Park, View from 30th and Upas Streets, circa 1910
Note Streetcar on 30th Street
Photo courtesy of the San Diego Historical Society (#64)

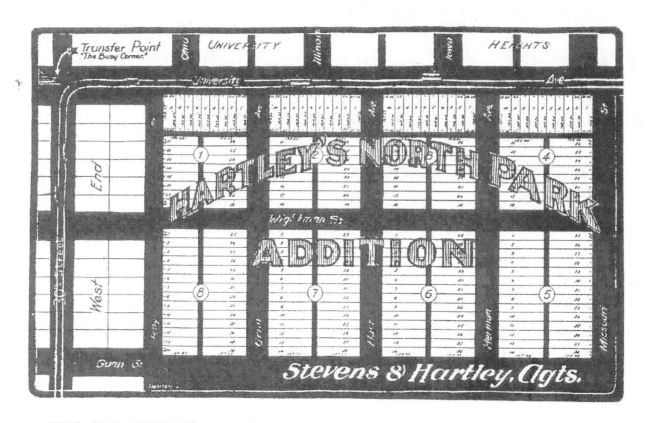

TWO CAR LINES (No. 1 and No. 2, same distance each way) will take you to "Hartley's North Park," the most up-to-date restricted residence district in San Diego. Streets graded and surfaced with decomposed granite; sidewalks and curbs, ornamental corner posts, etc.

Building restrictions $2000, except property facing on University avenue, which will be sold in 25-foot lots for business purposes. Watch the growth of buildings and values.

Hartley's North Park Tract Advertisement

McFadden & Buxton's Tracts

The part of Hartley's original 40 acres that was sold lay south of Gunn and north of Dwight streets, between Ray and 32nd streets. The purchaser of that other half was a syndicate headed by the firm of McFadden & Buxton, which paid $38,000 for 22 acres of the Hartley property. The joint development project was McFadden & Buxton's responsibility.

Joseph McFadden and George Buxton formed their real estate development partnership in October 1911. It was a partnership destined for notoriety. The two men were each at that critical stage in life wherein plans of heroic proportion seem, at last, to be achievable.

Both were in their mid-thirties. Each had a record of maintaining successful business enterprises. And, each had recently made a professional break from a secure and predictable life-style.

Furthermore, the times favored entrepreneurial ventures in land development. The national economy was surging ahead again after the Panic of 1907. San Diego was in the throes of a population explosion and a housing shortage. Additionally, the city had begun construction of the buildings in Balboa Park that would house the 1915 Panama-California Exposition.

Together, McFadden and Buxton met the new era of opportunity with creative ideas and innovative concepts. The incredible burst of professional energy that immediately followed the formation of their partnership resulted in several significant land development schemes.

Joseph McFadden was born in Canada in 1878 and settled in San Diego soon after the turn of the century. Following several years of work as a real estate agent, in March of 1909, he became joint proprietor of the Palace Café. Overlooking the Plaza in San Diego's town center, it was one of the most fashionable local restaurants. Across Broadway from the Plaza, the U.S. Grant Hotel was nearing completion when McFadden became a proprietor of the Café. In 1910, with the opening of the hotel, McFadden's investment in the restaurant business was greatly enhanced.

In November 1910, McFadden sold his interest in the café and, with his profits, re-entered the real estate business. McFadden's expressed interest at that time was in promoting real estate in the recently re-opened West End Addition near the budding commercial center at 30th Street and University Avenue.

A native of California, George Buxton was born in 1875. He spent his early years in Arizona where as a young man he entered the retail business of his father, a Phoenix merchant. Soon after the turn of the century, he moved to Bisbee, the mining community on the Mexican border. In Bisbee, his coal and wood firm, Buxton-Smith, was incorporated in June 1902, and thereafter prospered through investments in mining and milling. In 1904, Buxton became President of the Bisbee Board of Trade.

On November 12, 1910, George Buxton took temporary residence at the newly opened Grant Hotel in San Diego, at the same time that McFadden was terminating his ownership of the Palace Café across Broadway from the hotel. While retaining his interest in the Bisbee partnership, Buxton decided to permanently transfer his residence to San Diego. His intention was to enter the real estate business in association with Ed Fletcher. In October of the following year, McFadden and Buxton became associates in a new partnership. Two of their major tract development projects on the northeast border of Balboa Park soon followed: Hartley's North Park and Burlingame.

The Systems Firm

Late in 1911, Joseph McFadden and George Buxton created a complex land investment and development syndicate that they called The Systems Firm. That firm was as modern as the new century. It was organized as a network of thirty specialists who coordinated their individual areas of expertise for the singular purpose of developing, promoting, and selling suburban tracts.

Burlingame was the first major tract development undertaken by the firm. It was there that all of the elements of the network came into play. The result was a coordinated effort on the part of the builders, developers, architects, salesmen, insurers, and public relations personnel. McFadden & Buxton held that "this is the age of specializing, the jack-of-all-trades is obsolete." The firm lasted two brief years before dissolution in October 1913. McFadden & Buxton's major accomplishment was the integrated tract of Burlingame. The unique attributes of The Systems Firm were the network of specialists, the marketing schemes, and the promotional advertising. Those marketing schemes were masterpieces of showmanship that rivaled Hollywood hi-jinks and often resulted in corporate cinematography. Newspaper advertisements were classic forerunners of current commercial "hype."

McFadden & Buxton "The Record Breaker" Advertisement
San Diego Union, January 15, 1913

McFadden & Buxton Advertisement, circa 1911-1912
Photo courtesy the San Diego Historical Society (#91:18564-1611)

Burlingame Tract

On Saturday, January 13, 1912, the Burlingame tract (Subdivision Map #1402) was opened for public inspection. On that first weekend, 34 lots were sold. Throughout the following weeks, scores of mule teams labored to grade the streets with crushed granite and generally to improve property in the tract. Late in January 1912, the distinctive red curbs, crosswalks and sidewalks were laid, thereby paving the way for the beginning of residential construction.

McFadden & Buxton promised a community of refinement, and used rose colored sidewalks as part of an effort to set Burlingame off as a unique and cultured setting. Additional features such as streets contoured to the shape of Switzer Canyon's rim, cast-iron street lamps, and a fully-equipped children's canyon playground drew families looking for a suitable neighborhood in which to build the architectural fantasy of their dreams.

On August 12, 1912, a group of visiting young ladies, daughters of wealthy railroad men from Arizona, agreed to help the developers promote plots in this exclusive Tract of Character. The 21 girls, their escorts, and of course a chaperone, motored out to a plot in Burlingame where they all posed under a billboard. The billboard promised, "The first young lady from Arizona becoming the bride of a San Diego man shall receive this lot. McFadden & Buxton." A mock wedding was held under the sign. Miss June Salliday, first row, second from the right, was persuaded to play the bride. Fred T. Peyton, who became one of the original residents of Burlingame, jumped at the chance to be the groom. Peyton is located in the top tow, first person on the left.

In the years following the opening of the tract, which was generally bounded by 30th and 32nd streets on the west and east, and Burlingame and Kalmia streets on the north and south, Burlingame became a showcase of diverse architectural concepts. Between 1912 and 1930, the Burlingame microcosm unfolded in a rare collection of architectural fantasies.

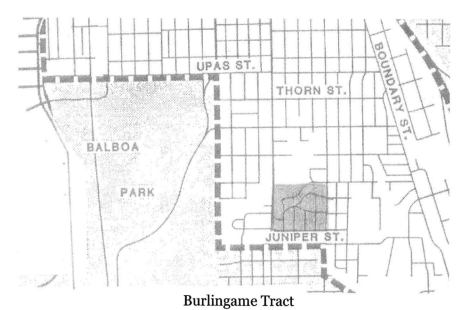

Burlingame Tract

ARIZONA · SAN DIEGO

THE FIRST
YOUNG LADY

OF THE ARIZONA
GAZETTE PARTY

BECOMING THE BRIDE OF A SAN DIEGO MAN
SHALL RECEIVE THIS LOT
McFADDEN & BUXTON

McFadden & Buxton Burlingame Advertisement, 1912
Photo courtesy of the San Diego Historical Society (#91:18564-2203)

The developers poetically extolled the views available.

"From the level acres of Burlingame, the eye sweeps over a wonderful panorama. In the foreground lies [Balboa] park, its mesas and canyons soon to be covered with exposition buildings. Beyond, the silver sheen of the bay meets the white strip of sand that separates it from the blue Pacific. Far out at sea, the Coronado Islands rise out of the blue depths . . . of the heaving sea . . . To the east, the frowning Cuyamacas, their peaks covered with snow in the winter, supply a fitting frame for the picture . . . At night, the lights of the city gleam below in silent splendor, and the shipping leaves luminous streaks on the bay's inky water."

By March 1912, Erwin Norris had constructed Burlingame's first home, a handsome two-story Craftsman with a full front verandah at 3170 Maple Street. Soon after, Archibald McCorkle completed a unique Spanish Revival-Craftsman-Mediterranean style house at 3048 Laurel Street. Then William Henry Wheeler finished the Moorish-style Rinehart house at 3128 Laurel Street, complete with a tower designed to take advantage of the spectacular 360-degree view. By early April 1912, the first nine of the houses were under construction and each of them was unique in style. At the end of the first year of building in the tract, 34 homes had been completed. Examples of Mission Revival, Spanish Colonial Revival, Craftsman, Swiss Chalet, Prairie School and several hybrid styles could be found along the streets of the tract.

Many of San Diego's leading architects, craftsmen, and designers worked out their earliest inspirations within Burlingame's residential blocks. Architects and architectural designers such as Carleton Monroe Winslow, Earl Josef Brenk, Walter Keller, Charles Salyers, and Ralph Hurlburt, as well as master craftsmen such as Alexander Schreiber, Pear Pearson, Archibald McCorkle, and David Dryden played significant roles in the aesthetic development of Burlingame. Most important of all, however, was William Wheeler, who served The Systems Firm as chief architect and designed most of the earliest homes in the tract. Born in Australia, Wheeler became a citizen of the United States in 1900. Travels in Mexico affected his aesthetic awareness of Spanish colonial architecture, about which he later remarked: ". . . to my trained sense of observance for proportion, form of detail, color and harmonious treatment . . . the treasures to be found in this land of romance were a revelation."

Within a year of the tract opening, the Burlingame Club was organized with six charter members. The women held meetings every two weeks. Besides socializing, the women's mission included philanthropic activities and "Preventing the neighborhood from becoming slovenly." They made it their business to foil entrepreneurs who attempted to set up boarding houses, or even worse, houses of prostitution, in the neighborhood. Later, when members got wind of plans for the 805 freeway to plow right through the middle of Burlingame, they got the route changed. Philanthropic works included assisting injured soldiers during World War I and II, and donating money to battered women's services and the Marston House Museum.

This 1912 Burlingame home at 2525 San Marcos Avenue is a Smith & Hawkins house in a *Churrigueresque* style. Churrigueresque, a sub-style of Spanish Colonial Revival, was a hallmark of the 1915 Panama-California Exposition held in Balboa Park. The style became popular in the western United States following World War One. Its appearance here in 1912 made this house one of the most avant-garde structures in North Park. Photo courtesy of the San Diego Historical Society (#91:18564-64)

The address in the photo may say 3955, but this home at 3055 Kalmia Street in Burlingame is one of architect William Wheeler's earliest houses in San Diego. The house was built over the winter months of 1912-13 by contractor Henry Sparks. The design of the house is distinctly English in style with many overtones of the small Elizabethan manor revived during the late 19th century as the *Tudor Revival* style, one of the roots of the English Arts & Crafts. Photo courtesy of the San Diego Historical Society (#91:18564-41)

This Burlingame home at 3048 Laurel Street was the second house under construction in the tract. Built by Archibald McCorkle in the spring of 1912, the style of the house is a builder's hybrid of *Mission Revival* and *Craftsman* style. It was one of McCorkle's last houses before an early death. At its completion, the house was sold to Nathan and Edith Cottee, two employees of George Marston's department store in downtown San Diego. The photograph shows a group of flappers gracing the entrance pergola of the house. Photo courtesy of the San Diego Historical Society (#91:18564-46)

Arizona Street Tract

In the five years prior to the 1915 Panama-Pacific Exposition in Balboa Park, an explosion of population brought a new boom to San Diego along with houses that were fabricated and partially assembled in factories, shipped to the purchaser and joined by carpenters on the site. Several companies such as the Southern California Home Builders were active in both Los Angeles and San Diego. The old Park Villas addition north of Balboa Park was the site of much of the local activity of this company during the years preceding World War One.

One of the company's unique experiments was the Arizona Street Tract, a one block development just north of the Park bordered by Arnold, Arizona, Myrtle and Dwight Streets. Unique in its development was the internal, one-block narrow little street, Park Villa Drive, to which the bungalows on the inner ring faced. Typical 120-foot lots in the Park Villas Addition were in this case divided into two back-to-back lots, each 60 feet deep by 50 feet wide. Subdivision Map #1495 filed November 14, 1912 established the "Park Villas Block 80" tract with irregular lots.

The first eleven houses were under construction during the early spring of 1913. By March of that year, most of those unfinished, ready-cut frame structures had been sold. Harry A. Malcolm, Superintendent of Construction for the company, became one of the first residents of the tract when he moved into 3593 (now 3589) Park Villa Drive. The Southern California Home Builders Company reported that another ten houses would be commenced immediately in an effort to satisfy the "urgent demand" for the "pretty little homes." Selling prices for the houses in the tract were set at $2,400 to $2,900 to appeal to buyers of modest incomes. The first bungalows constructed within the tract were completed by the late autumn of 1913.

The map of the tract included in the Sanford Fire Insurance survey of 1921 delineates the first 17 houses. The remainder of the tract was not completed until the end of the 1920s. Unique in its development, the private inner drive or "court" was designed by the company's landscape engineer to include palms, acacias and other tropical plants and trees. Today, most of the original plantings are gone and some alterations to the historic dwellings have occurred, but the unique, private environment of the diminutive bungalow neighborhood still reflects the intimate charm of the once "affordable" tract.

Chapter 5
The Commercial Core

Emergence of a Business Center, 1909-1912

While the former Hartley's North Park lemon grove was fallow, the realty firm of Will Stevens and his brother-in-law, Jack Hartley turned its attention to rural properties. Operating from offices on Fifth Street in downtown San Diego, the firm of Stevens & Hartley made its early reputation by specializing in property in the El Cajon Valley and the east county. Then, in 1907 with the University Avenue car line running through their North Park property, they began to turn the firm's attention toward suburban lots there. In 1909, Pacific Building Company predicted that its bungalow Tract #3 would "start a nucleus which will attract other buildings in the surrounding property." The new University Heights water reservoir, and the approaching car line #2 up 30th Street made it apparent to the partners that 30th and University would soon become the center of a new suburban community. That junction was centered upon their undeveloped property.

In December 1909, construction of a small wooden building was begun on the northwest corner of 30th and University. When it was completed, it became the North Park branch office for the Stevens & Hartley firm. By the spring of 1910, the development of the commercial center at the junction of the two avenues was underway. Stevens and Hartley began clearing the old family lemon grove and constructed an additional small frame shack on the southeast corner of the junction for the first grocery store in the community.

Meanwhile in November 1910, on the northeast corner of University at Texas Street, Joseph W. Sefton, Jr. commissioned a building from Irving Gill. When it was completed, Arthur and Anna Valentien opened a pottery workroom there. The Valentiens had moved to San Diego from Cincinnati where the notable Rookwood Pottery had employed them as artists. Arthur, a painter, was the first pot decorator hired by Rookwood, and was chief decorator for 24 years. Anna, who was also a talented sculptor, was with Rookwood for 21 years. They moved to San Diego in 1908, and in April purchased the first house north of the new Georgia Street Bridge on the east side, at 3903 Georgia Street. They continued to operate the pottery workroom on Texas Street until late 1913 when residents of the newly developed neighborhood around them complained of the pollution from the kiln. The pottery factory was closed by the end of 1913, and the Valentiens went on to other art work. Anna taught at San Diego State Normal School from 1914 to 1916, and then at San Diego Evening High School, where one of her pupils in sculpture was Donal Hord. Albert worked on a commission from Ellen Browning Scripps to paint the wildflowers of California, which became a compilation of 1,500 specimens by the time of his death in 1925. Anna died in 1947 in the bungalow on Georgia Street that had been her home for 40 years.

The Stevens & Hartley Real Estate Office in North Park, 1912
Photo courtesy of the San Diego Historical Society (#12180)

30th & University Center, 1912-1917

The first significant development of a commercial center in North Park began in the years 1912-1913 with the cluster of emerging buildings and the businesses that filled them at 30th and University. The most impressive of the buildings was the three-story multi-use structure erected on the northwest corner of the junction by the Stevens & Hartley firm at a cost of $14,000. Construction of the building got under way in August 1912 by the Carter Construction Company. Early in 1913 when it was completed, Stevens and Hartley moved the main office of their real estate firm from downtown San Diego to North Park. Their headquarters for the next few years in the new facility became one of the busiest storefronts on University Avenue.

The drug store that opened in the Stevens & Hartley building in 1913 was the first in a continuous line-up of pharmacies there for more than 80 years. The first proprietor was Mr. J. L. Haggard who for several years had been in the manufacture of syrups and flavoring extracts in San Diego. His new store featured an up-to-date soda fountain with all mahogany cases. Haggard was soon succeeded by Joseph L. Hallowell, an experienced San Diego druggist. From that time until the late 1920s, a special counter in the drug store was the U.S. Post Office #8 for the North Park community. That facility combined with the major soda fountain made the drug store a popular public center.

The third commercial space of the building at 3829 30th Street was North Park's first barbershop attended by John Roberts who lived in the community at 3134 Granada Avenue. The apartments on the second and third floors of the Stevens & Hartley building contained twenty rooms divided into four two-room and four three-room apartments. These rooms were leased to Edward G. Straub who furnished and managed them. The apartments were said to be "modern in every respect, having wall beds and all other built-in features . . . with hot and cold water." One of Mr. Straub's first tenants was Addie Griffith who had recently moved to San Diego from Redlands. Mrs. Griffith opened a millinery shop in the building on May 1, 1913. Other tenants who followed included doctors, dentists and nurses.

The Stevens & Hartley building was joined on the southwest corner by a one-story building of four stores built for William Younkin with construction also beginning in August 1912. These four stores became a support center for the new homebuilders and homemakers with two plumbing shops (Curtis and Joseph Mann; A. F. Thompson), a hardware store (Henry Berger) and furniture store (John Andrew). Across 30th Street from Younkin's stores, a cluster of four small cottages was built on a single lot in 1913. These cottages served as housing for some of the proprietors of local businesses including the grocer, Clayton Hill (at 3829). Next door to this bungalow cluster at 3835 29th Street was an additional small cottage that became the office of the community's first doctor, Frank Drake, M.D.

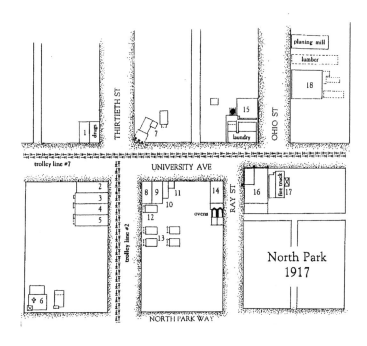

Thirtieth & University Center 1912-1917

1. Stevens & Hartley Building 1913
2. Bank
3. Furniture store 1913
4. Mann brothers plumbing 1913
5. Berger hardware / plumbing 1913
6. Immanuel Evangelical Church
7. Winter/Hill Oil Station 1918
8. Clayton Hill grocery 1912
9. Hardy's North Park Market
10. Stevens & Hartley
11. Stevens & Hartley
12. Dr. Frank Drake 1912
13. North Park Cottages 1912
14. Merritt Bakery 1917
15. Peerless Laundry 1914
16. North Park Garage 1914
17. S.D. Fire Station #14
18. North Park /Dixie Lumber Co.

The Stevens & Hartley Building , circa 1919. Will Stevens and Jack Hartley are seen standing in front of their real estate office on the left. Standing next to them on the right is probably the proprietor of the North Park Drug Store, Joseph Hallowell. Stevens & Hartley moved their real estate office back to North Park immediately following the Armistice of World War One. Photo courtesy of Historical Collection, Title Insurance & Trust Company (San Diego Historical Society #6941)

On the southeast corner of 30th and University, next to Clayton Hill's grocery store at 3001, Stevens & Hartley built a shop to house Charles S. Hardy's North Park Meat Market. Hardy was the proprietor of a string of San Diego's most notable butcher shops. Meat cutter for the North Park Market was Peter Cappel who opened his own market at 3830 30th Street in 1919. Hill's grocery and Hardy's meat market began the development of what by 1920 would become a shopping strip known as "Hartley's Row," named for its developer and owner, Jack Hartley.

At the other end of that block, the next most important building in the strip was constructed by L. C. White for Stevens and Hartley in the summer of 1916. The one-story frame and plaster building with two brick ovens was leased in 1917 to the Merritt Bakery. Merritt was followed by Ideal Bakery in the early 1920s, and throughout that decade there was always a bakery within the building. Directly east of the bakery, on the south side of University, Block 1-4 of the Hartley's North Park tract offered ten 25-foot by 90-foot wide business lots for each block. These lots were placed on the market by Stevens and Hartley early in 1913. Each 25-foot lot was offered at $1,750.

Across University Avenue, at 3038, a laundry and dry cleaning plant was established in 1914. The first manager of the firm was William F. Crane. Crane was one of the North Park businessmen who chose to live in the Pacific Builders Tract #3 (at 3960 Utah). Others were Henry Berger (3945 Idaho) and A. F. Thompson (4021 Idaho). The Peerless Laundry more than doubled its plant in a 1918 expansion and remained at 3038-48 University until 1927 when, under the management of

Fred Bartlett, it moved one block north to 3972 Ohio Street for another expansion.

Sharing the northwest corner of Ohio and University at 3048 University Avenue was another Stevens and Hartley enterprise, the Barnes and Wolfe Garage, which was leased to Joseph J. Wolfe, "an experienced auto machinist" in 1914. The Wolfe Garage moved in 1918 down the street to 3049 University Avenue in order to make way for the Peerless Laundry expansion. The gasoline engine automobile, first introduced to San Diego in the early years of the century, rapidly became a standard item on graded roadways around town. What was estimated as a handful of those machines in 1907 and a few hundred in 1910, became several thousand at the close of the Panama-California Exposition. By the time North Park got its first commercial garage in 1914, innovative businesses to service and maintain the new conveyances were sprouting in all the recently developed suburbs.

North of the laundry and garage on the east side of Ohio Street, a large lumber yard was begun in 1913. This was the North Park Lumber Company, renamed in 1915 the Dixie Lumber & Supply Company. The firm was organized by J. H. Bjornstad, who ran the business alone for the first two years. By the early 1920s, however, it had become a major business in the North Park community employing more than 50 people with an annual payroll in excess of $100,000. East of the Dixie Lumber Company, very few business establishments existed prior to the mid-1920s.

The Stevens & Hartley Garage, managed by J. J. Wolfe, was followed in 1919 by the Winter & Hill Oil Station at 3000 University Avenue. The proprietor, Albert Winter, lived in a cottage next to the station on the northeast corner of 30th Street. Howard H. Johnson, a banker and investment broker, purchased this property in February 1912 for $10,000. The same property had been purchased in 1906 for $2,050. The phenomenal inflation in value reflects the rapid growth of interest in the newly forming community at 30th and University. By the fall of 1912, the streetcar junction had been dubbed "The Busy Corner" for the heightened activity that had occurred within one short year.

The real estate boom and commercial development of the years prior to the Panama-California Exposition continued in North Park well beyond that of the city in general. However, with the entrance of the United States into World War One in 1917, real estate investment and suburban development came to a temporary halt. With little local activity in the district, Stevens and Hartley temporarily moved their firm out of North Park and back to a downtown office.

The Winter/Hill Oil Station on the Northeast Corner of 30th Street and University Avenue, circa 1924
Photo courtesy of the San Diego Historical Society (#20252-33, detail)

The W. B. Younkin Store Building on the Southwest Corner of 30th Street and University Avenue, circa 1926
Photo courtesy of the San Diego Historical Society (#Sensor 8-192)

Fire Station #14

Mary Jane Hartley, widow of North Park founder, James Monroe Hartley, was commonly known by community residents as the "Mother of North Park" for her many philanthropic contributions to the welfare of the community. An example of her philanthropy was Fire Station #14.

Following the early emergence of commercial and residential buildings at the junction of 30th and University in 1910 and 1911, property owners petitioned the city for fire protection. The response was installation of a fire alarm box mounted on a pole at the corner of those two streets. A signal from that box would bring a fire truck and crew lumbering up from downtown by way of the narrow and rutted canyon trail that ran through the park from 16th street to Upas. With luck, the truck would make it before the building burned to the ground.

In order to persuade the city to improve these conditions, Mary Jane Hartley donated to the city a prime plot of ground facing University Avenue near Ray Street in the Hartley's North Park tract. The plot was given and accepted with the condition that the city would establish an official fire department station. The building constructed for that purpose gave North Park not only increased security from fire but an important civic structure as well. The campanile tower used for drying hoses, visible for miles around, became a landmark for the community center.

In the winter of 1941-42, the Hartley's North Park Garage next door to the fire station was sold to the J. C. Penney's Stores. The garage was demolished and a deep pit was dug for the building's foundation and basement. Unfortunately, a freak rainstorm filled the excavated pit with water, undermining the foundation of the fire station next door. The inevitable collapse of the west wall of the fire station and partial destruction of the truck shed signaled the end of the fire station on University Avenue.

San Diego Fire Station #14, circa 1925
Photo courtesy of the San Diego Historical Society (#3030)

Early Development of El Cajon Boulevard

Before University Avenue was cut through the Georgia Street ridge in 1907, El Cajon Avenue had been the main wagon road connecting Horton's New Town San Diego with the rural settlements of east San Diego County. In the years before World War One, that single lane dirt road was the site of many auto races between the few men who could afford the early recreation machines.

El Cajon Boulevard Auto Race, Looking West to Park Boulevard and the Normal School, 1913
Photo courtesy of the San Diego Historical Society (#15069)

By 1911, with the growing popularity of the automobile as a primary mode of transportation, a national movement formed to link up roads to create intercontinental highways. One of those was the southernmost highway across Arizona through Phoenix to the California border at Yuma.

In 1912, Los Angeles made a bid to be the western terminus of the interstate highway by obtaining the link from Yuma. Four of San Diego's leading citizens took that bid as a challenge and set out to prove that a San Diego to Yuma link was more practical and shorter. Those four, Col. Ed Fletcher, Rufus Choate, John Forward Jr., and Fred Jackson, were appointed as the official representatives of the San Diego-Arizona Highway Association. They managed to raise $60,000 by public subscription, to cut a road through the mountains and across a wooden plank highway in the sand hills east of El Centro. To prove that the road was not only passable but also faster than one to Los Angeles, in October 1912 they sponsored a race of automobiles leaving San Diego at the same time as those leaving Los Angeles. One of the San Diego cars won the race, arriving in Phoenix approximately 16 hours after the start. San Diego became the official terminus of Interstate Highway 80, which intercepted the eastern end of El Cajon Avenue at the San Diego city limits (*San Diego Union*, Oct 10, 1937, section 2, page 2). McFadden & Buxton advertised they were "in to win" with their entry.

McFadden & Buxton In to Win, 1912
Joe Fernando is the driver in the racing car in front of the McFadden & Buxton Burlingame Headquarters, October 1912
Joseph McFadden is in the right foreground, George Buxton is in the left foreground
Photo courtesy of the San Diego Historical Society (#91:18564-19)

Jefferson Elementary School, circa 1913
T.C. Kistner, Architect
Photo courtesy of the San Diego Historical Society (#2701)

Chapter 6
Pioneer Schools & Churches

A First Schoolhouse

The new development of homes in Pacific Building Company's Tract #3 brought with it a community of young children remote from any of the City's schools. Therefore, in December 1910, the school district began the construction of a small wooden bungalow schoolroom at a cost of $500. The building was put up two blocks south of Tract #3 in the middle of Park Villas Addition Block 63 facing Idaho Street (28th Street). It was named the Park Villas Elementary School.

Eighteen months later, in June 1912, the Board of Education announced that an entire block in West End had been purchased for $12,000 for the purpose of building a new elementary school "to relieve the congested condition now existing in the northeast district." The site was directly across Idaho Street from the little bungalow schoolhouse. The new school was to be named Jefferson Elementary.

Plans for the new building were drawn by the architect T. C. Kistner. The specifications called for a sixteen-room building of "fireproof" hollow tile and stucco construction in the decorative Spanish Revival style of the Exposition currently under construction in Balboa Park. The preliminary phase of the expandable building included four classrooms of the "open air" type with entire walls of French doors that could open the schoolrooms directly to the play yard. The first phase of the plan, a single story, four-room building was opened for classes in the spring term of 1913.

North Park Community Church

The North Park Community Church started as a tent in 1910. In that year, a young couple, Isaac and Ann Hardy, came to San Diego from the Northwest. They had been advised to come for Isaac Hardy's health. They bought a lot in the newly developing community of North Park and pitched a tent on it. Isaac was able to spend much of the day outside in the sun and fresh air, and regained his health. Both Hardys were devout Advent Christians, and Ann walked around the tiny North Park settlement calling on others of that faith. Eight people gathered in their tent and began to plant the seeds that would grow into a church building.

On October 19, 1911, the group met to consider the possibility of building a church. The Reverend and Mrs. MacFadyen, and Reverend W. C. Tingle of Los Angeles attended as representatives of the Advent Christian Conference of Southern California, to give its aid and blessing. In less than a month after the organizational meeting, a lot committee was appointed to find suitable property on which a church might be built. Two adjoining lots on the corner of 29th Street (then Kansas) and Landis Street were recommended.

Meanwhile, the Reverend Tingle had returned to Los Angeles and had visited D. A. Davis of Pasadena, telling him enthusiastically about what the ardent little group in San Diego was trying to get started. Davis bought both lots for the young church.

In June 1912, a tent was pitched on the property, and services were held regularly all summer. During the winter, services had to be held downtown at 7th and B Streets. This exposure in downtown attracted passersby, and the congregation grew. In 1913, a structure with wooden walls and a canvas roof was completed on one of the lots the congregation owned. The little group had been having temporary visiting pastors, but in June 1913, Reverend Samuel Forsey was assigned as the first permanent pastor. Reverend Forsey and his family were new citizens of the U.S., having recently emigrated from England.

By 1914, it was decided to begin constructing a permanent church building. D. A. Davis, whose strong interest in the fledging congregation had continued, came down from Pasadena with a group of workmen. The first church building was erected under his personal supervision. He and his wife also paid all the construction expenses, so that the church was free of all debt.

Park Villas Congregational Church

The "Golden Anniversary 1912-1962" of the Plymouth Congregational Church reports their beginnings as follows:
"Four Sunday School Scholars met at the home of Mrs. Robert Dick in the year 1908 for the study of the lesson. This number increased until the place of meeting was too small to accommodate the children. Then came the Rev. H. P. Case who assisted in organizing a permanent school, aiding with supplies and advocating the need of a suitable building. Lots were donated by Mr. Robert Dick and money was solicited for the building. A house 30 x 40 feet was planned and at great sacrifice, was built."

That little building was on 28th Street across the street from what is now Jefferson School, and served as the home of the first North Park church until 1923 when a new, larger building was constructed at 2717 University Avenue in 1924. The church has been known as the Park Villas Congregational Church (1912), Plymouth Church; The Community Church (1922), Plymouth Center of the First Congregational Church (1923), and Plymouth Congregational Church (1927).

28th Street Congregational Church Building (Plymouth Congregational) as a Meeting Hall, 1926
Photo courtesy of the San Diego Historical Society (#UT3249)

Immanuel Evangelical Church

At the corner of 29th and Wightman (now North Park Way), was the Immanuel Evangelical Church, which was headed by Reverend Philip Sachs, a German immigrant. The church first appeared in the City Directory in 1913. Reverend Philip Sachs was the pastor until 1922. He lived with his wife Catherine at 3431 Oregon Street (now Pershing Avenue). Also at this address in 1919 was his son, Alvin B. Sachs, a cashier for Union Oil Company, and another son, Karl P. Sachs, a clerk at the Western Metal Supply Co. Karl Sachs was the builder of 3424 Oregon Street in 1920, and 3425 Oregon Street in 1922, both with Philip Sachs as the first owner. Reverend O. D. Wonder became pastor in 1922. Reverend U. S. Schauer became pastor in 1927, when the street address of the church was given in the City Directory as 3803 29th Street. From 1928 to 1950, the City Directory lists the church name as the Emmanuel Evangelical (sometimes Lutheran or United Brethren) Church. Reverend E. C. Schneider presided in the later years, when the address is given as 3801 29th Street. The church is long gone; there is now a multi-story parking garage at this location.

The University Heights Public Playground

Before being named the North Park Recreation Center and Community Park, the two-block area between Lincoln and Howard avenues and Oregon and Idaho streets was officially dubbed the University Heights Public Playground. As such, it was a small part of an historic movement that, at the turn of the century, emerged from progressive concepts of socialist doctrine.

One of those concepts held that an urban community was responsible for the physical health and moral development of its youth. In response to that concept, the Public Playgrounds Movement, empowered by the patronage of such figures as President Theodore Roosevelt (Honorary President of the Playground Association of America), swept the nation in the first decade of the century and San Diego was said to be "likely to be among the leaders in the movement."

That optimistic declaration was made by Jessie Tanner, Director of the Physical Education Department of the San Diego Normal School (later San Diego State University) during a lecture which she gave to the Golden Hill Improvement Club in March 1908. In that presentation, she offered the opinion that modern educators "believe that right play develops right habits of thought and action." She stated that:

> "San Diego's greatest need at present is several small playgrounds. These, in connection with the large park ground already planned, would provide well for the boys and girls. To organize a local playground association would mean the formulating of a plan, not only providing for the present, but one looking toward the future, when increased population will mean increased demands upon the recreation grounds."
>
> – *San Diego Union*, March 22, 1908, page 19

Local interest came to fruition in July 1913, when the playground commission recommended to the city council that a city playground and recreation center be located in the "half block on the west side of Idaho street between Polk and Lincoln avenues, just below the University Heights reservoir." The *San Diego Union* reported that:

> "Several weeks ago a large number of residents of University Heights petitioned the commission to make a playground for the children of that district, declaring that it would not only keep the children off the street and tend to conserve the morals of young people of both sexes, but that it would also serve as a much needed place for neighborhood gatherings. The petition was signed by the University Heights Improvement Club, the University Heights Mothers' Club, the Vista Villas Congregational Church Ladies Aid Society and the teachers of Garfield school.
>
> According to Superintendent Frank Marsh of the playground commission it will cost about $500 to grade, surface and fence the ground. If the Council will give the land the commission will bear the cost of preparing the grounds and furnishing the necessary equipment.
>
> Members of the Mothers' Club, it is said, have promised to raise sufficient money to build a field house. A number of fathers have offered to build the house and it is proposed to have these men do the work on some Saturday, setting aside the day as one of dedication."
>
> – *San Diego Union*, July 11, 1913

The completed playground and "field house" were inaugurated early in 1914, making it the first major suburban recreation center in the San Diego Playground Movement.

In 1924, the University Heights Playground obtained its own tennis courts, which the *North Park News* reported "will be used also for dancing as the weather gets warmer." The North Park Business Club held many popular community dances on those courts in the following years, and some of San Diego's finest tennis players learned to play there. In 1969 the playground was named the North Park Recreation Center, which had grown to include meeting rooms, classrooms, baseball fields and a basketball court in addition to play areas.

Part Three
The Boom Years ~ 1920s

"Will J. Stevens and J. C. Hartley, local realty men, made a prophecy in 1905 that the corner of Thirtieth street and University avenue would some day be one of the busy corners in this city. This prophecy, made 16 years ago, when they started a realty firm here, has seen its fulfillment, and today it can be said with safety that there is no part of this city which is building faster."

– San Diego Union, October 2, 1922

Chapter 7
The Hartleys and the Klickas

The business and mercantile center at 30th and University was quick to respond to the improvement in the general economic climate of the region. In the early years of the 1920s, a period of expansion occurred that was unmatched until the second boom years of the early 1950s. That expansion, although contributed to by many new entrepreneurs and civic boosters, was chiefly the result of a convergence of two families and their individual and joint projects of mercantile, business and community development: the Hartleys and the Klickas.

The Hartley Family

The Hartleys, the founding family of North Park in 1896 and owners of 40 critical acres of the undeveloped land, had dispersed and left the area following the death of the senior member of the family, James Monroe Hartley, in 1904. Beginning in 1905, the Stevens & Hartley firm had been instrumental in establishing a nascent business and residential community centered on the junction of University Avenue and 30th Street. The period of initial growth of that center had lasted until the involvement of the nation in the European war during 1917-18. In those years, the Stevens & Hartley firm had closed its branch office on University Avenue and worked entirely from its main office in downtown San Diego.

"Will J. Stevens and J. C. Hartley, local realty men, made a prophecy in 1905 that the corner of Thirtieth street and University avenue would some day be one of the busy corners in this city. This prophecy, made 16 years ago, when they started a realty firm here, has seen its fulfillment, and today it can be said with safety that there is no part of this city which is building faster.

"Stevens & Hartley. . . not only made the prophecy but backed up their judgment with plenty of cash and built the first large business block in that neighborhood."
– M. C. Robertson, *San Diego Union*,
October 2, 1922

Following the return of the Stevens & Hartley Real Estate firm to North Park in 1919, family members resumed the development of the little community on the outskirts of the city and began to re-establish their residences there. Mary Jane Hartley, widow of James, moved into a new house at 3827 31st Street, and was joined there by her youngest son, Paul Hartley, following his discharge from the U.S. Army in August 1919. Paul became an eager participant in the family real estate business. For several years, he built and sold houses in the Hartley North Park tract for the firm before assuming ownership in 1927 of the North Park Garage and Service Station on the corner of Ray Street and University Avenue. Mrs. Hartley's oldest son John C. "Jack" Hartley, made his permanent home at 3827 Herman Street in 1919 and his brother-in-law and real estate partner, William Jay Stevens, moved into 3819 31st Street in the same year.

Maud Hartley tells this part of the story:

"Meanwhile John and Will had gone into the real estate business together as the Firm of Stevens and Hartley, and in 1912 put up a small building on 30th and University for an office and began selling vacant lots. Mother sold 20 acres of the 40 commenced to develop the 20 she kept, facing University ave. and so began the first development of North Park. Father had named his lemon orchard 'Hartley's North Park' but eventually, the whole district became just North Park. However, it is shown on the City Map as the original name. John told me once that father's plan was to divide the 40 acres into plots and give us each 5 acres. How little he could foresee how the whole thing would be.

In 1917, Paul was graduated from U.C. and got a job on a ranch near Sacramento, and mother lived for a time in a cottage on Herman St. and when she had to give him up to the War the next year it was very hard on her. She had had the flu and it had left her hard of hearing and she was so lonesome with Paul so far away, in France, so that I came down for awhile, with my two babies. It helped a little.

After the War North Park grew up in earnest, and John and Will were doing well. Houses sprang up by leaps and bounds and 30th and University became a busy corner.

Where we used to count ten houses looking in all directions, soon it was a city of homes. Mother finally established in one of them at 31st and University . . . John, who was running her affairs saw to it that she had everything she wanted and so he made her very happy. He used to take her around among his business associates, and to the gatherings they had, so she knew them all and they called her the mother of North Park, and Grandma Hartley."

– Maud Hartley MacDougall,
Remembered Incidents in the Lives of the James Monroe Hartley Family 1882-1940

The Stevens & Hartley firm continued to dominate the real estate development market in the North Park district. However, by 1922, several other important realty offices moved to the 30th and University area from around the city. W. A. Allen, a successful San Francisco real estate broker with offices on Adams Avenue, opened a branch office in the new Ramona Theatre building in the summer of 1922. Fred Peyton, one of the city's most prominent realtors formerly associated with McFadden & Buxton, and his partner, builder John N. D. Griffith, moved their office from the Spreckels Building downtown to 3810 30th Street. Peyton stated that the firm had been "exceptionally busy since the first day it moved into its new offices."

"This section has certainly developed into one of the most beautiful parts of this city. I recall the difficulty that I had in trying to locate stakes where Granada, Oregon and Twenty-eighth streets are now. At that time there was nothing but sagebrush there. In fact, it was so all about this section. We were compelled to leave the electric car or auto at Upas street and then start out through the brush. One can hardly realize the changes."

– Fred Peyton, *San Diego Union*,
June 18, 1922

Throughout 1920 and 1921, there was a steady growth of real estate and building activity along the commercial streets of North Park. By the fall of 1921, 40 businesses were operating in the district. Among them were a pharmacy, dry goods store, bakery, several grocery stores, three butcher shops, many produce markets, an automobile garage and several oil stations, a shoe store, a major laundry, a hay and feed store, cleaners and dyers, several restaurants, doctors and dentists offices, ice cream parlor, a barber shop, a bank, and a blacksmith shop.

"It is most gratifying to know that this part of the city is being built up so fast."

– Will Stevens, *San Diego Union*,
October 2, 1921

The Klicka Brothers

Emil and George Klicka moved to San Diego from Chicago in 1921 and became a major force in the opening phase of North Park's dynamic post-war development. Creative entrepreneurs and successful businessmen approaching middle age, the two were drawn to San Diego as a potential site for adventurous new beginnings. The family firm they left behind in Chicago, the Joseph Klicka Company, was a producer of wood veneers, picture frame and room moldings. Emil, who served his father's firm as president, had joined the company in 1896 at the age of 17. In February 1922, the Klicka brothers opened a large lumber yard in the 3900 block of 30th Street and began to sell lumber, paint, cement, hardware and other materials.

Business acquaintances and some family members criticized the two brothers for their choice of North Park as a site for an investment of personal time and fortune. In 1922, the community was still considered by many to be "out in the sticks." But to the Klicka brothers, it offered welcome challenges and a break from the stable and routine lives they led as Chicago manufacturers. They could also see the great potential the area had for becoming another satellite town in the city's urban complex.

San Diego was not unknown to Emil and George Klicka. In the early years of the century, Emil, then a young Chicago banker, spent a few years as a novice cowboy in the backcountry of San Diego County. His chronic bad health in the severe Chicago winters had resulted in a doctor's advice to seek a milder climate and employment in the fresh, open air. That prescription led Emil to San Diego where he purchased a horse and headed for the remote county ranches in the Laguna Mountains. Emil's employer in San Diego County was rancher Tommy Gray of Buckman Springs. Emil's admiration for his employer was matched by his affectionate feelings for his employer's wife Jessie, a member of the Weegar family. To Emil, Jessie Weegar Gray was the epitome of womanhood. To others, Jessie, who excelled in marksmanship and horsemanship, was the Annie Oakley of backcountry San Diego.

John C. "Jack" Hartley
1876-1937

Paul James Hartley
1894-1969

Photos courtesy of the Hartley Family

With restored good health, Emil returned to Chicago where he assumed the new role of President of the family business in wood products. Emil, a bachelor, remarked to members of his family that he would gladly marry if he could find a woman like Jessie Gray. Several years later, Emil heard from former acquaintances that Tommy Gray had drowned in the Colorado River. A return to San Diego gave him the opportunity to pursue his friendship with the widow Gray and in 1907, they were married. Following the wedding, the two returned to Chicago and his involvement in the family business. Fourteen years later, they returned to San Diego and began a new mature phase in their lives.

The youngest Klicka brother, George, having heard all the tales about the romantic far west from Emil, made his own trek to California with a friend by motor car in 1915, a rugged adventure reported later in the January 1916 issue of *The Headlight* magazine of the Lawndale Automobile Club of Chicago. George was a salesman for the family firm in Chicago and often traveled about the country on the job. However, the trip to California in the days before major paved highways were common proved to be an unforeseen adventure with mud the major hazard. Thirteen days and nine tire changes after leaving Chicago, he drove into San Francisco for a week of rest before continuing down the coast to San Diego. George began his saga noting, "Having made all necessary arrangements we left Chicago during a heavy rain on July 7th, at 11:15 a.m. Our destination was California, no matter what trouble or experiences we might encounter." Excerpts of his story follow.

"A turtle-back road for an eight-mile stretch [outside of DeKalb, Illinois] put us down in a deep ditch four times in that distance. At this point we were informed that several tourists in the past week had abandoned the idea of driving to the coast and had either shipped their machines or turned back. Very readily we understood that.

We encountered our first trouble at Grand Island, [Nebraska] where we struck a deep mud hole which compelled us to $5.00 worth of horses. It took a half hour for the four horses before we finally were out.

There are some very dangerous passes and divides around Reno and Carson City, and steep mountain grades that forces all makes of cars to stop every 15 minutes to fill up the radiators with water.

After traversing through many beautiful Redwood forests we pulled into Sacramento where we saw our first palm trees and flowers lined along both sides of the roads and streets. This was California! And how good the roads looked after passing through what we had.

Having checked everything up we found we had made the trip from Chicago to Frisco in 13 days actual driving. Speedometer showed 3216 miles. 264 gallons of gas were used, costing $62.95. Nine tire changes were made.

After four days in Los Angeles saw us driving over the 'prettiest coast scenery road in America,' headed to San Diego, where we arrived at 4 p.m., in time for the San Diego newspapers to take pictures of us and also for details of our experiences of the trip."

– George Klicka, *The Headlight*
Issued by the
Lawndale Automobile Club of Chicago,
Vol. 1, No. 8, January 1916

One of the Chicago firm's San Diego customers was Frank Orr, whose gallery in Old Town San Diego stocked Klicka moldings for picture frames. Although San Francisco was the primary destination for George, the contact with Orr and the Exposition in Balboa Park drew him south along the coast before his return trip to the Midwest. On his return to Chicago, he declared the San Diego exposition to be superior to San Francisco's. He also thought that San Diego had the best climate of any town on the Pacific coast.

In April 1921, George and Wilhelmina Klicka were the first of the family to settle in North Park. They purchased from Stevens & Hartley a home at 3543 Oregon Street. The shingled, California Craftsman style house had been built by David Owen Dryden in 1917. In this home, their son Robert Emil Klicka was born. They lived here until 1925, when the family moved to 1419 Granada Avenue for two years. In 1926, George Klicka had a new house built by Southern California Home Building Company in the Valle Vista Terrace tract, and the family moved to 4869 East Panorama Drive in 1927.

In May 1921, Emil and Jessie Klicka commissioned a home from Lance Consaul and Theo Lohmann, a large Midwestern style Craftsman house at 3506 28th Street. This was their home until 1944, when they moved to 3404 Pershing Avenue.

The Klicka Brothers Company (name changed to Klicka Lumber Company in November 1923) was incorporated in December 1921. Its intended purposes were stated "....to make & execute contracts for all kinds of construction work.." and ".....to build, construct, alter, repair, move, decorate, furnish and improve houses, office buildings and other structures..." Other branch ventures of the new firm followed immediately: the Klicka Mortgage Company and the Klicka Development Corporation.

In December 1921, Emil and George established the Plymouth Company, which held offices at 313-319 Fifth Street. The Articles of Incorporation for the firm state the purpose of the company was to manufacture paper, pasteboard, cardboard, etc., such as cartons, boxes, books, and magazines, and to operate a business of stationers, printers, publishers, lithographers, engravers, bookbinders, etc. Directors of the company were Emil and George Klicka, and Gordon Gray, attorney-at-law. Among the publications of the Plymouth Company were the *North Park News, Homecraft, Motorist's Guide Handbook, and Southwest Magazine*.

The *Southwest Magazine* began publication with the September 1923 issue and seems not to have been in publication after 1925. The editor was Eva B. Stiles-Adams. One of the purposes of the magazine was encouraging literary pursuits of new authors. Among the professional contributors were architect William H. Wheeler and Charles Lummis.

A second *North Park News*, named in honor of the Klicka publication, was founded by Thomas Shess in 1993. The first issue of the reincarnation, dated May 1993, was called Vol. 2, No. 1 to recognize North Park's early heritage.

Klicka Lumberyard, circa 1926
Photo courtesy of the San Diego Historical Society (#81:10386)

Emil and Jesse Klicka at 3404 Pershing Avenue, circa 1944

George Klicka, circa 1940

Photos courtesy of the Klicka Family

Chapter 8
The Boom Begins ~ 1920-1924

Post-war, 1919-1921

By December 1918, as the victorious American troops began their return from the battlefields of France, Jack Hartley could see signs of a renewed residential real estate market and moved the Stevens & Hartley office back to its former site at 30th and University. By the early Spring of 1919, the firm had 20 new houses under construction in the neighborhoods of North Park. After two years of limited home construction combined with an unprecedented expansion of the local populace, a shortage of dwelling units had developed throughout the San Diego suburbs. Other shortages such as that of automobile fuel and domestic servants helped to re-define the day-to-day experience for San Diegans as well as for all Americans. These shortages and rising inflation in the cost of domestic goods and services were reflected in the post-war popularity of small, compact houses that incorporated efficient, easy-to-care-for interiors within exterior shells of Mediterranean fantasies.

"The shortage of houses in this city is declared serious, as it is almost impossible to find houses for rent. There is great building activity, but not enough houses are being built to accommodate the expected influx of home seekers. The high cost of living and high taxes, which will take a jump upwards in the next tax levy, are reported deterring many owners of property from building."
— *San Diego Daily Transcript,*
August 31, 1920, page 2

"It is certain a system of rationing gasoline will have to be devised if everybody is to get a share. The constant increase in the number of pleasure cars, trucks and tractors, will make it imperative at no distant day to have recourse to some other kind of fuel than straight gasoline."
— *San Diego Daily Transcript,*
August 14, 1920, page 2

"The difficulty experienced by local housewives in solving the servant problem which is apparently hopeless is not, as some San Diego ladies seem to think, confined to this section of the country."
— *San Diego Daily Transcript,*
August 28, 1920, page 2

Children of the 'progressive' pre-war generation, who too early had met the challenges and hardships of war and pestilence, eagerly cast aside the constraints of their parents' Arts & Crafts philosophy in exchange for a brand of modernism that combined mass-consumption, industrial technology and cinematic style romance. No rambling, handcrafted, rustic bungalow appealed to them. The exposition buildings in Balboa Park set the pattern in Mediterranean style. The ideal became the sanitized, all-electric, stucco hacienda, a romantic amalgamation of Edison, Bell, Ford and Zorro with telephone jacks and radio aerial intact. The patio succeeded the verandah; the tiled breakfast room challenged the paneled dining room; the screened sleeping porch gave way to the two-tray laundry porch; and the motor car became the new house pet with its own attached garage. Floor plans grew tighter and area square-footage shrank, as more women became their own domestics and construction costs doubled.

> "There is no question that the exposition buildings and the planting about them constitute one of our very greatest assets. Those buildings set a precedent which has exerted a profound influence on all architectural design in southern California during the past five years . . ."
> – San Diego Architectural Association,
> March 5, 1922

Better roadways, comfortable town cars, and an efficient system of municipal street railways opened up more remote suburbs. Downtown San Diego got the first challenge to its status as the main shopping and business center in the early 1920s. The largest and most successful of those challenges began to emerge in 1921 around 1912's "Busy Corner," the junction of 30th Street and University Avenue in North Park.

The first major expansion of the business center and the residential neighborhoods began in the spring of 1921. Following the inauguration of President Warren G. Harding, early reports from the Government predicted an improvement in the economic conditions of the nation and a return to controlled and balanced growth of commerce and industry. A major increase of population, stimulating an expansion of business and home building in North Park, seemed to support the Government's predictions. Local businessmen and contractors sensed a boom forming.

> "Strauss & Company, New York: Reports indicate particular activity in residential operations. Unless unforeseen events transpire, the ensuing season will bring considerable relief to the housing situation throughout the country."
> – San Diego Daily Transcript,
> March 18, 1921, page 2

> "The building boom that has struck this City has gathered such momentum that another deputy building inspector has been added to the regular staff."
> – San Diego Daily Transcript,
> September 14, 1921

The numbers validated the boom. The total number of building permits in 1921, valued at $8,228,952, more than doubled that of the previous year.

> "The year of the exposition in this city is the only year which in the history of San Diego showed greater activity in building than the year just closed."
> – San Diego Union-Tribune,
> January 2, 1922

Pershing Memorial Drive

North Park's post-war development boom was enhanced by the improvement of Pershing Drive. Prior to World War One, the road was a nameless, hazardous and often impassable, wagon trail that led up from downtown through the canyons of Balboa Park's east mesa to the rural lands beyond the eastern boundary of the city's pueblo lots. In 1908, stimulated by real estate interests in the undeveloped northeast section of town, a municipal bond issue had allowed funds for turning the trail into an improved road (*San Diego Union*, April 8, 1909, pages 5-6). Ten years later, those early improvements had become inadequate to serve the transportation needs of the rapidly expanding residential neighborhoods of the new community of North Park.

The efficient network of street railways that had encouraged the development of outlying suburbs offered convenient links to the city's center. However, in the post-war era, the lure of transport by personal conveyance created a new demand for better roads and streets. The "big grade" was North Park's best potential connection to downtown San Diego. It was, however, too steep, too narrow, and unpaved. An opportunity to change that with city help arose in the immediate days following the Armistice in November of 1918.

Riding the high surge of local patriotism following the victory in Europe, a group of San Diego businessmen with residences in North Park conceived an adventurous plan to turn the "big grade" into a 25-foot wide, paved boulevard as a memorial to the San Diego men who died in the war. Three days after the Armistice, R. A. Chapman presented to the Board of Park Commissioners his plan for a drive through Balboa Park to connect 18th Street downtown with the northeast corner of the park at 28th Street. The road, paid for in part by public subscription, would be named Pershing Memorial Drive in honor of the popular military leader of the American forces, General John Joseph "Black Jack" Pershing. The proposal received unanimous support of the board. The City Council soon followed with its approval and pledged to match funds raised through public subscription.

"This would be a lasting tribute to the work of the American army in France... While San Diego is erecting a monument make it one that will be a substantial improvement, in keeping with the government's idea of stopping waste. This road is one of the main traveled roads leading from the heart of the city to the back country, and it is believed that after the monuments are placed and the road paved that it will be lined with beautiful ornamental trees that will make it one of the finest drives of the city."

– R. A. Chapman, *San Diego Union*
November 15, 1918

In the days following Chapman's proposal to the Board of Park Commissioners, a War Memorial Committee was established to begin the task of acquiring public subscription. The first meeting of the group was scheduled to be held at the U.S. Grant Hotel on Friday, December 7, 1918. However, the meeting was postponed due to the city's enforced quarantine of public meetings as a result of the Spanish Influenza epidemic. Subscriptions began to be collected, nevertheless. By April of 1919, $2,000 was on deposit in the Committee's account.

Eventual supporters included many of San Diego's prominent citizens including Mrs. Schumann Heink, who gave a concert in the Spreckels organ pavilion, raising an additional $1,600. However, the early lists of those who made contributions of time and money in support of the project were largely made up of North Park residents and businessmen such as Jack Hartley, Will Stevens, John Griffith, Fred Peyton, Dr. A. C. Ekern, and Charles A. Small.

It was estimated that approximately $26,000 would be needed to complete the project. Although early enthusiasm resulted in statements from the Memorial Committee that such a fund could be raised in a week, three years later, the goal had not been realized. In January 1922, a meeting of supporters of the project was called to encourage a re-commitment to raising the funds and completing the work of road building.

"A meeting of subscribers to the Pershing Drive paving fund, and others, has been called for Monday night (January 23) to ascertain if efforts to complete the fund should be continued or money collected returned to subscribers."

– *San Diego Daily Transcript*,
January 20, 1922, page 2

The new Memorial Committee, including G. A. Davidson, president, and George Marston, vice-president, was chaired by Charles A. Small, a North Park resident and manager of the Bishop Cracker & Candy Company on Market Street in downtown San Diego. In the months that followed, a renewed effort brought in enough donations that the Committee was able to turn over $8,000 to the City Council which in turn provided a matching contribution. In June 1922, the Council awarded a paving contract in the amount of $14,476 to the California Construction Company.

"The new Pershing Drive fund, through C. A. Small, has presented the city with $8,000 contributed by public spirited citizens. The Council will now apportion a similar amount to start the work of paving part of the drive."

– *San Diego Daily Transcript*,
May 30, 1922, page 2

"The City Council has awarded the contract for the paving of Pershing Drive in Balboa Park to the California Construction Company for $14,476."

– *San Diego Daily Transcript*,
June 20, 1922, page 2

On Friday, July 28, 1922, Charles Small held a public meeting of the subscribers and other supporters of the Pershing Drive project. The meeting was held in the newly expanded Jefferson Elementary School for the purpose of celebrating the beginning of the first phase of work on the road. Mr. Small remarked on the work completed and outlined what needed yet to be accomplished. Others who spoke included attorney E. E. Hendee of Burlingame.

By October 1922, the citizens committee had successfully raised additional funding.

"The Citizens Committee to raise funds to pave Pershing Drive has secured a total of $16,135.80, and the City Council will appropriate a like sum for the work beside doing the grading."

– *San Diego Daily Transcript*,
October 19, 1922, page 2

In January 1923 paving was completed and Pershing Drive was opened to the public.

"The Pershing Drive, now paved its whole length, will be thrown open to travel on Wednesday (January 17th). Subscribers to the fund, through which the paving was made possible, by a big majority voted against heavy trucking being allowed on the drive."

– *San Diego Daily Transcript*,
January 15, 1923

At first, private citizens' opposition to use of the convenient new roadway by commercial vehicles led to lengthy discussions among Park Commissioners, Councilmen and members of the Pershing Drive Committee. After several months of debating the issue of truck traffic through the park the Board of Park Commissioners upheld the ordinance that prohibited trucks over one-ton from using roads through Balboa Park. Throughout the 1920s, 30th and 32nd streets continued to be the primary routes for heavy commercial traffic into North Park from downtown.

"The city traffic commission has taken under advisement the petition of citizens protesting against the violent traffic noises on 32nd Street used by motor trucks."

– *San Diego Daily Transcript*,
November 11, 1929, page 2

In April 1923, the City Council granted a petition for changing the name of the portion of Oregon Street from Balboa Park to University Avenue to be called Pershing Drive, "of which it is practically a continuation" (*San Diego Daily Transcript*, April 3, 1923).

The citizens committee continued its interest in the roadway, pressing for landscaping improvements in 1924.

"Charles A. Small and his committee, whose efforts resulted in the paving of Pershing Drive, has asked the City Council to appropriate $20,000 to beautify the Drive."

– *San Diego Daily Transcript*,
December 14, 1924

An Early Boom on the Avenue, 1922

The dynamic rhythm of general expansion that emerged in the closing months of 1921 exploded into an unprecedented boom along the business avenues and in the neighborhoods of North Park. In the summer of 1922, the San Diego Union in a series of full-page articles on the community said of it:

". . . the section lying east of Park Boulevard and north of and including Burlingame is the fastest growing section of this city today. Property that for years has been vacant today is dotted with beautiful homes."

– *San Diego Union*,
June 18, 1922

After a decade of growth and development, North Park was becoming a suburb of major proportions and significance. The next few years witnessed the emergence of a commercial center that matched the residential neighborhoods in its expansion.

San Diego Public Market & Produce

West of 30th Street on University Avenue, several infill structures, built during the period 1921-23, added to the inventory of buildings and businesses on the Avenue. At 2905 University, on the southeast corner of 29th Street, in the autumn of 1921, the Radford Building Company (Ray Radford, president, residing at 3024 Palm in North Park) began construction of a tile and brick building for Max and Hyme Rabinowitz. The Rabinowitz brothers operated a prominent food store on Broadway Street downtown: the San Diego Public Market & Produce. Like many other downtown businessmen in the early 1920s, the Rabinowitz brothers were aware of the unprecedented and dynamic growth of residential neighborhoods in the northeast section of the city. They saw in this growth a potential for lucrative expansion of their business.

The Granada Building

One block farther west at the corner of University Avenue and Granada Street, two important new commercial structures were erected. On the corner at 2875 University, a two story building of steel and concrete tile, surfaced in white glazed brick veneer, was built in 1921 for William P. McCloskey. McCloskey used the lower floor for his plumbing shop while the upstairs spaces were rented to doctors and dentists. The Granada Building was of a very modern style that used the exposed steel structure as ornamentation. On the ground floor, a patterned, Art Deco mosaic tile surfaced the base course at windowsill level.

The North Park Furniture Company

In the same year, a smaller shop was constructed next door to the Granada building for Frank J. Crover, proprietor of the North Park Furniture Company. Two years later in the spring of 1923, Crover had contractor Charles M. Williams enlarge the shop for an estimated $11,600. The larger shop accommodated an expanding demand for furniture on the part of the many new residents of the district. The parapet façade of the expanded building was of an elaborate Spanish Revival style. The furniture business failed in the early 1930s and the building was remodeled for the Pekin Restaurant, one of North Park's oldest businesses.

The Granada Building and adjacent furniture store, circa 1922
Photo courtesy of the San Diego Historical Society
(#Sensor 8-194)

Hartley Row & Other In-fills

With the influx of new businesses and new buildings to house them, the Hartley brothers saw the need for an organization of business owners for the purpose of improving and developing the district. In 1922, Jack and Paul Hartley organized the first North Park Business Men's Association. Jack Hartley was elected the first president of the organization.

By the summer of 1922, the row of buildings on the south side of University Avenue begun by Jack Hartley in 1912 had been extended east of 30th as far as Ray Street. The result was a series of seven frame and reinforced concrete buildings including several new businesses for the district. With only two unimproved spaces, the Hartley Row included Kimpton's Kash Grocery, a mom-and-pop store managed by Joseph and Minnie Kimpton at 3001 on the corner of 30th Street. Next door at 3005, The North Park Market offered a Charles S. Hardy butcher shop, which became a long-time award-winning operation.

> "Charles Hardy of this City, one of the largest meat packers in the State, has again, for the tenth consecutive year, won first premium at the State Fair in the Baby Beef, Hereford and Durham Class."
> – *San Diego Daily Transcript*,
> September 6, 1929

A branch of Heller's Grocery Store followed at 3009. In the middle of the block, shoemaker Glenn Dutton managed the North Park Shoe Shop at 3011 University. Toward Ray Street were a restaurant; the Coast Market; a poultry store at 3019 that became John Demetre's Washington Fish Market in 1926; and Mr. Friedman's billiard hall, the North Park Pool Room, at 3021.

On the corner of Ray Street was one of the oldest buildings on the Row, the first bakery in North Park. In the early 1920s, that establishment was operated as the Ideal Bakery, one of the Merritt Baking Company stores. With two brick ovens, the shop produced all its goods on the site and maintained a fleet of delivery trucks. The company was one of the biggest employers on the Avenue with several bakers, sales staff, office managers and delivery men on its payroll.

East of Ray Street, next door to Fire Station #14, a post-World War One development phase in the commercial blocks of Hartley's North Park began with the construction of a large wood-framed structure. A building permit issued to Frank Swain in February 1923 called for an $11,500 structure to house the Swain & Poe Furniture Company at 3041 University Avenue.

Hartley Row with Merritt Baking Company (Ideal Bakery) Deliverymen and Their Trucks, 3000-block of University Avenue, circa 1923

Photo courtesy of the San Diego Historical Society (#7200-2)

Merritt Baking Company (Ideal Bakery) Bakers, Deliverymen, Sales Staff & Managers, 3027 University Avenue, circa 1923
Photo courtesy of the San Diego Historical Society (#7200-1)

This Little Piggly Went to Market

The branch of the San Diego Public Market & Produce was not the only major market to open in the 30th and University center in 1922. Piggly Wiggly stores, a modern concept of grocery shopping begun in Memphis, Tennessee in 1916 by Clarence Saunders, opened two stores in San Diego in 1922. The first was at Seventh and Broadway downtown, the second at 3829 30th Street in North Park. Both stores were managed by Dudley D. Williams, who helped to open the first Piggly Wiggly store in Memphis, Tennessee.

Dudley Williams found San Diego was "due for big growth," and was so impressed with the dynamic business district in North Park, he bought the franchise for the 30th Street store. During his first few years in San Diego, he and his wife Elma lived at 3781 Goldfinch. In 1926, he resided in North Park at 3675 31st Street. That year, he commissioned a house at 3594 28th Street from builder Joseph Kelley. The home was completed January 24, 1927. That property was his family home from 1928 until his death January 8, 1949.

> "It has been my good fortune to visit every city in the United States of more than 10,000 population and things look right to me in San Diego."
> – Dudley D. Williams, *San Diego Union*,
> October 15, 1922

Prior to Piggly Wiggly, North Park housewives shopped for groceries in small "mom-and-pop" stores where clerks brought requested items from behind the counters and the variety of products was limited. The large chains that began to reform merchandising in the USA during the war years introduced modern concepts of sales and service to consumers. The Piggly Wiggly chain applied the principle of "step in and help yourself" shopping. Old fashioned practices of taking orders by telephone, putting charges on monthly accounts and delivering purchases to customers' homes were replaced by cafeteria style shopping and cash-only purchasing. Customers were provided with baskets upon entering the store and served themselves from open display shelves. On the way out, the customer paid for purchases in cash, and bundles were wrapped.

The North Park location was opened December 9, 1922, preceded by a three-column advertisement rich in social commentary announcing:

"The Piggly Wiggly Store at 1040 Seventh Street has been a pronounced success. The Housewives of San Diego have evidenced, by their continuous patronage, their unqualified approval of the PIGGLY WIGGLY System. This store has been visited by the society class—the banker class—the wage-earner class—and by the PLAIN American class—all of whom have said that they liked the PIGGLY WIGGLY way—that they saved money—that they find a most comprehensive assortment of food products of the best nationally known brands. The location of the SECOND PIGGLY WIGGLY store which opens Tomorrow Morning, was chosen because of repeated solicitations from that neighborhood that we establish a PIGGLY WIGGLY store in that part of San Diego. . . A PIGGLY WIGGLY STORE WAS MADE FOR YOU. It was made for her who is just a plain woman. It was made for her who goes about in silks. It was made for her who walks. It was made for her who rides in an automobile. It was made for her who uses a gingham apron, while she gets ready an evening meal for the homecoming of her man. It was made for her who lets the cook prepare the meal for the lord of the house. A PIGGLY WIGGLY was made for everybody."

– *San Diego Union*,
December 8, 1922, page 15

The Piggly Wiggly concept was highly successful, not only in San Diego but across the country. The modern concepts applied by Piggly Wiggly became instantly popular with shoppers, resulting in nearly 2,000 stores in 340 cities in 42 states by 1922.

"Piggly Wiggly stores have succeeded because of the low operating cost which is obtained by the customers helping themselves, bringing their purchase to the checking counter, paying cash and taking their purchase with them – unnecessary clerks, bad debts and delivery cost are eliminated."

– *San Diego Union*, April 4, 1925

Getz & Grant Realty

In September 1922, a local real estate partnership opened its office in the 2900 block of University Avenue. Principals of the Getz & Grant firm were Fred B. Grant of Mission Hills and Thomas B. Getz whose family home was at 3946 Oregon Street.

The small structure built for the Getz & Grant office was "a unique class of building" and said to be so peculiar in form that even the anonymous architect was unable to identify its style. The partners chose the form of the building in order to attract attention of passers-by on University Avenue. The building remained as a curiosity on the Avenue until replaced in 1941.

Getz and Grant reported that they had searched through various parts of San Diego prior to choosing North Park for their headquarters. The reason given for the choice of the 30th and University district was that ". . . we found this the fastest growing section, and consequently the best business possibilities." The business survived the difficult years of the 1930s in North Park.

By autumn of 1922, 52 businesses were reported to be serving the 30th and University district including eight real estate offices.

Getz & Grant News Article
San Diego Union, September 17, 1922

Getz & Grant Realty Office, circa 1925

". . . This office of ours has, because of its odd structure, produced a much larger 'punch' than we expected and daily we are receiving calls with an inquiry 'why'. . ." (Thomas Getz, September 17, 1922)

Photo courtesy of the San Diego Historical Society (#S-590-1)

North Park Goes to the "Picture Show"

Thomas A. Edison's invention of moving pictures, a curiosity in the early years of the century, by the early 1920s had become a major American industry producing a steady flow of popular entertainment vehicles. Elaborate, downtown motion picture palaces that showed first-run Hollywood productions were followed by smaller neighborhood houses that offered re-runs. Admission prices in the neighborhoods were, on the average, 20 cents for adults and 10 cents for children. On November 15, 1921, the following announcement was made in the local press:

"Of interest to residents near Thirtieth and University avenue is the announcement that E. C. Wills will erect a theatre on University avenue, north side on the site east of the oil station. A sign is being erected calling attention that the theatre will be built at once. Stevens & Hartley closed the deal for Wills."

– *San Diego Daily Transcript*,
November 15, 1921, page 8

Euclid C. Wills was the owner of the Hillcrest Theatre on Fifth Avenue, a neighborhood house that had brought motion pictures to that community in the period before World War One. The Ramona Theatre, an early example of the Art Deco style, opened at 3012 University Avenue in the autumn of 1922. The builder of the theatre was Joseph Beck, a carpenter who lived with his family at 3736 Ray Street in the 1920s. Flanking the lobby of the theatre were two small retail rooms that in the early years were occupied by a watchmaker's shop and a tobacco store.

Ramona Theater, circa 1926
Shops: E. E. Starr, Watchmaker, and
R. J. Wilson, Cigars
Photo courtesy of the San Diego Historical Society (#20015)

Reconstruction of the Street Railway, 1922-1924

By 1922, the extreme and rapid increase in population and growth of both residential as well as commercial construction in the vicinity of 30th and University put a great strain on the popular street railway system. It became apparent that an increase in service would soon be necessary.

The #7 line not only served the expansion of population in North Park but also that of East San Diego. The #2 line along 30th Street had to serve the expansion in the older neighborhoods of West End, Lynhurst, Blair's Highlands and Burlingame as well as the new tracts just opening up to the east.

John D. Spreckels, president of the San Diego Electric Railway Company, announced on June 25, 1922 that the Company would soon begin a major rehabilitation of all the railway lines in the city. Spreckels considered work on the University Avenue line to be the most urgent. However, opposition to his plans by some council members forced the schedule to begin with reconstruction on other lines.

Spreckels announced that an order had been placed for 1,000 tons of 93-pound rails. The order for steel ties, bars and special accessories for the #7 line alone was estimated to cost $50,000. The project called for a total replacement of the original line #7 (1907) and line #2 (1909) as well as the double tracking of each. In June 1922, Spreckels said, ". . .you will have a car service that you'll never need to be ashamed of." Construction began late in 1922 and was completed at 30th and University in autumn of 1924. Following completion of the rehabilitation, the two lines remained in service to North Park until all streetcars were removed from city streets in 1949.

New turns at the junction of #7 and #2 car lines at the intersection of University Avenue and 30th Street, June 1924
Photos courtesy of the San Diego Historical Society
(#20254-106 above, and 20254-112 below)

Double track being laid for the #2 car line on 30th Street south of University Avenue, June 1924
Photo courtesy of the San Diego Historical Society (#20252-62)

A #2 Trolley rolls down the new double track line on 30th Street and Kalmia, Burlingame, circa 1925
Photo courtesy of the San Diego Historical Society (#14028)

Looking West on Upas at the Junction of 30th Street, Lynhurst Building on the left, September 1923
Photo courtesy of the San Diego Historical Society (#20254-118)

1920s Residential Neighborhoods

Several new North Park residential tracts were placed on the real estate market in the immediate post-war years. In the early 1920s, five were opened: Altadena, Carmel Heights, Montclair, Balboa Square, and Kalmia Place. The first two were contiguous tracts located east of 32nd Street and west of Boundary Street, with Altadena south of Upas Street and Carmel Heights south of Redwood Street. Both were subdivisions created by the Pacific Building Company.

Architecturally, these tracts displayed the mixed architectural character of post-war neighborhoods. They included shingled bungalows of the late Arts & Crafts movement, columned dwellings of the American Colonial style, and stucco cottages of the Spanish Colonial Revival. These last reflected the 1915 Exposition buildings in Balboa Park with the latest Mediterranean designs in arched portals, terra cotta tiled roofs, round turret entries and colorful faience trimmed patios. After 1923, the predominate style in domestic architecture was some variation upon the Mediterranean themes.

Altadena Tract

Altadena was a pre-war tract planned by Oscar Cotton's Pacific Building Company, the firm that had introduced North Park's first housing tract a dozen years earlier. The tract extended from 32nd to Boundary streets on the west and east, and from Upas to Redwood streets on the north and south. Subdivision map #1663 was filed March 15, 1915, showing 40-foot by 117-foot lots. Although streets were graded and blocks and lots were surveyed, the shortage of materials and labor and the government controls on construction in the 1917-1919 period prevented home building there until 1920. Altadena was subsequently re-opened for public investment in 1921.

Historically significant builders and contracting companies active in this tract included the Pacific Building Company, David Owen Dryden, William Gibb, and Hurlburt & Tifal. During the period from 1920 to 1922, the Pacific Building Company obtained building permits for nine homes, including 3314, 3328, and 3348 33rd Street (1920); 3101, 3357, and 3369 Bancroft Street (1921); and 3219 and 3345 33rd Street, and 3130 Felton Street (1922). David Dryden obtained permits for 3340 and 3344 33rd Street in October and November 1922. William Gibb received the permit for 3309 Gregory Street in October 1924, and Hurlburt & Tifal obtained the permit for 3236 33rd Street in September 1924.

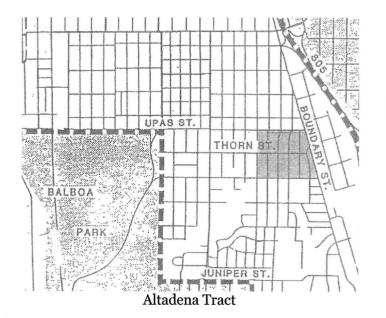

Altadena Tract

Carmel Heights Tract

Carmel Heights, another Pacific Building Company tract, lay immediately south of Altadena, extending from 32nd to Boundary streets on the west and east, and from Redwood to Nutmeg streets on the north and south. Subdivision Map #1736 was filed September 8, 1922, showing 25-foot by 117-foot lots. The tract was opened in 1922 but attracted little construction until after St. Augustine school was opened in the autumn of 1923. Advertisements for lots in the joint Carmel Heights and Altadena district of North Park identified the area as "The Cream of the Burlingame West End District." That attention-getting realtor's ploy was used to attract buyers by association with two of North Park's most successful pre-war tracts. Additional efforts at association with nearby successes in land and real estate development included references to Pershing Drive and St. Augustine school.

"The lots we are now selling comprise some of the cream of this entire district and will be brought even closer to town by the paving of Pershing Drive."
– Oscar Cotton, President Pacific Building Company, October 1922

"Two entire blocks have been purchased by the Order of Saint Augustine from the heart of this beautiful property for high school and college purposes. Beautiful mission style buildings are to be erected. . ."
– Pacific Building Company, November 1922

Subdivision Map #1897 for the Carmel Heights Extension tract was filed March 22, 1926, showing irregular lots. The extension of the tract was advertised by the Pacific Building Company in 1926 as:

". . . lying directly east of one of our most popular subdivisions, Carmel Heights, and south of another spectacular subdivision success, Altadena. It is just north and east of Burlingame, right in the very center of home building activity . . .If you ever want to own a close in lot in a good, highly restricted district where all street improvements are to be put in and everything is high class, where you can get to the center of town in eight minutes, come out immediately and see these lots that we are now selling at Carmel Heights Extension. Don't delay, come at once."
– *San Diego Union*, May 2, 1926

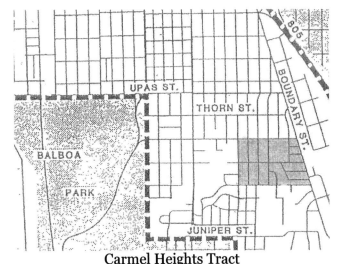

Carmel Heights Tract

Carmel Heights Extension

Carmel Heights Extension is that new tract comprising only about 130 lots, lying directly east of one of our most popular subdivisions, Carmel Heights, and south of another spectacular subdivision success, Altadena.

It is just north and east of Burlingame, right in the very center of home building activity, a district where lot values have jumped again and again in the last two years, and yet the prices for which we are now selling big 50-foot lots

in Carmel Heights Extension are actually less than the prices of similar sized lots in other districts nearly twice as far from Fifth and Broadway.

Carmel Heights Extension is laid out with contour streets. Nearly every lot has 50-foot frontage or more. All streets are to be paved and other improvements installed, such as sidewalks, curbs, sewer, et cetera. All street work is to be done under the 10-year bonding plan, which means minimum cost to the purchaser.

While they last you can buy these $900 splendid 50-foot lots in this tract for

Some of the very best for $1000 to $1200
And a few not so good for considerably less

If you ever want to own a close in lot in a good, highly restricted district where all street improvements are to be put in and everything is high class, where you can get to the center of town in eight minutes, come out immediately and see these lots that we are

now selling at Carmel Heights Extension. Don't delay, come at once.

For your convenience we will have salesmen on the tract all day today to show these lots or we will take you out Monday or any day next week by appointment.

Phone Main 4913

Come Today

How to Come

Drive out Broadway, Pershing Drive, or University Avenue to 30th Street, turn east from 30th on Thorn to McKinley Street, then south, following our direction signs, to Carmel Heights Extension.

Pacific Building Company
WE BUILD SAN DIEGO
Note New Address
426 "C" Street

Carmel Heights Extension Advertisement
San Diego Union, May 2, 1926

Montclair Tract

The third of the Pacific Building Company tracts to be placed on the market in 1922 was Montclair. This was a thin parcel of land between the city boundary and the eastern line of Altadena/Carmel Heights. Montclair was land that the company had owned for several years before World War One. Subdivision Map #1684 was filed March 20, 1916, showing irregular lots. When subdivided, the tract had contained some lots in the canyon bottom lands. Less desirable than view lots on the edge of the mesa, these portions were offered for as low as $35 to $50 each. Larger sloping lots were priced at $100 to $150 each and were described as being

". . . half acres partly on top and partly in the bottom with fine rich soil. . ."

"Last month was the biggest month in point of numbers and amount of real estate sales that the Pacific Building company has had in any single month since 1914. . . The opening day of the Montclair sale called very vividly to our minds the opening days of the company's subdivision sales in 1910 and 1911. . ."

– Oscar Cotton, *San Diego Union*, July 16, 1922

115

Montclair

Beautiful high view property right adjoining one of San Diego's finest residence districts at the most marvelous prices and terms of any similar tract offered in years

In all the twenty subdivisions we have marketed and built up in San Diego there has been none finer than Montclair; it is just the kind of property in the kind of neighborhood the people you like want to own —and will own. It is the kind of property that grows into value and then keeps on growing.

This beautiful property has been held intact by us for

years with the expectation of developing and marketing it as we do other properties at $500 to $1500 per lot.

Past plans have been changed, and it has been determined to sell the entire north half of this property —more than two hundred lots and half acres— immediately.

Today we will start our opening sale of this fine property at prices and terms absolutely astounding

$90 per lot for fine high level lots in the heart of the tract

This does not mean the first payment, but it means that this is the full purchase price.

When you have paid $90 you have paid all there is to pay and the lot is yours. You have never seen a proposition like this since San Diego was a small town. The only reason we can do it is because we have owned the property since San Diego was but a village.

Other fine lots, but not so good as these, will be sold for $60, others for $40, half acres at $150, and some at slightly higher prices. This, without any question, is the biggest real estate opportunity you will ever see in San Diego, and terms are within the reach of all. Actually during this big sale you can purchase these fine lots as low as

$5 Cash $1 per Week

Now is the time to lay the foundation for the nest egg you have always wanted

You have heard of the big profits that have been made in real estate in growing cities by buying when it was cheap and holding; well here is your opportunity! This is the property, it is good, close in, and so cheap that it will double again and again as the city expands.

Come out today and come early before the crowds —and get the first selection.

If you can't come out today, come into our office Monday, or any day this week, and we will take you to Montclair in fifteen minutes—or phone Main 4913 and we will send our auto for you.

How to Get There

Take No. 2 car marked 30th and University and get off at Thorn Street, our autos will meet all cars today. By auto, follow yellow signs East on Thorn street from Thirtieth to our tent.

Pacific Building Company
We Know How And Do It

334-338 "C" Street

Come Out Today

Take No. 2 car marked 30th and University and get off at Thorn Street, our autos will meet all cars today. By auto, follow yellow signs East on Thorn Street from Thirtieth to our tent.

Montclair Advertisement
San Diego Union, June 11, 1922

In August 1922, South Montclair was announced. The advertisement noted:

"When we opened our North Montclair subdivision we announced that those who wanted some of the best lots had better come out early before the best were gone. That was on Sunday, June 10th, and before the following Sunday practically every level lot in the entire tract had been sold."

"Every purchaser of North Montclair lots is perfectly delighted with his or her purchase; some are already building their homes; others are making plans and all will make big profits on their investment. The soil in Montclair is rich and red; there are loose cobble rocks on part of it, but to clear it we had to cut heavy sage brush six feet high. From some of our $75 lots there is a better view of the bay and ocean than any other lots north of Juniper Street in the West End district, and the view of the mountains is wonderful and permanent . . ."
– *San Diego Union*, August 20, 1922

Balboa Square Tract

The smallest tract to be developed and offered to the public in 1922 was Balboa Square, an abandoned and nearly forgotten citrus ranch on the east side of the former Hartley lemon grove. In the 1890s, an Australian native, John M. Highett had purchased 20 acres within the Park Villas tract and planted lemon and orange trees in the hopes of producing a lucrative business in citrus fruits.

Water was always a limited commodity before the 1900s. Whenever water was directed his way, Mr. Highett tried storing the excess in improvised tanks for use in those times when it flowed less freely or not at all. Those times came more and more often during the drought years of the late 1890s. By 1900, it had become necessary for water to be purchased in town and brought up the narrow and steep "big grade" (later Pershing Drive) by wagon to the ranches on the mesa.

Highett finally gave up the life of a dry-land rancher in 1905 and moved to England. Nearly 20 years passed, and in 1922 he returned to San Diego to find that his abandoned and remote 20-acre ranch was surrounded by urban development. A well known Los Angeles real estate development firm, Welsh & Campbell, was aggressively moving into San Diego at the time and persuaded Highett to sell them the ranch for a residential subdivision. The 20 acres became four blocks divided into lots of 50 feet by 125 feet. Selling price of the lots was $450 with 10% in cash. The four blocks of the tract were bordered by 32nd and 33rd streets on the west and east; and Landis and Myrtle streets on the north and south.

In November 1922, the tract was opened to the public as Balboa Square, one of the last remaining residential developments in North Park. Mr. Welsh, the Los Angeles developer, reported to the *San Diego Union* that the city was "on the eve of great expansion."

"This splendid residential tract is wonderfully well located in the fast-growing Thirtieth and University section, near good stores, schools and other conveniences. No part of San Diego is expanding and improving in comparison with this thriving district of charming homes and paved streets. You know what your money is buying at Balboa Square!"

– Welsh & Campbell, Realtors,
San Diego Union, November 1922

The block of 32nd Street, east side, between Myrtle and Dwight Streets was the first to be built up. Between October and December 1923, ten homes were under construction on that block indicating with what intensity the real estate market was moving in the far northeast section of the city. All of those homes were small stucco bungalows in variations of the Spanish Colonial Revival style.

In order to serve the daily needs of the many new residents who were moving into that far northeast corner of North Park, a new commercial center began to develop at the junction of University Avenue and 32nd Street. In 1924, on the southeast corner of that junction, a business structure was built to house a grocery store, meat market, pharmacy, furniture store and real estate office.

This was followed in 1925 by a $12,000 structure to house other stores and apartments. In January 1924, *San Diego Union* said of the bustling little suburb that it had ". . .taken on the appearance of a metropolitan business mart. . ."

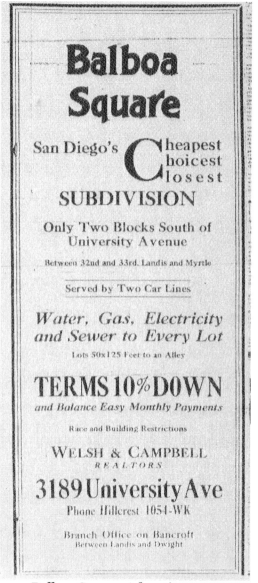

Balboa Square Advertisement

Burlingame's New Growth

Phenomenal growth was not apparent in the new tracts alone. Those neighborhoods that had gotten their start before World War One exploded with new growth in the early to mid 1920s. The McFadden & Buxton showcase tract, Burlingame, (1912) is a prime example of that post-war growth in the older neighborhoods.

"Burlingame has during the last few months been getting a large part of the building and real estate activity. Scores of beautiful homes have been built this year. This is one of the residence sections of the city, having the most stringent restrictions as to buildings. . ."
– *San Diego Union*, October 29, 1922

The new interest in property in Burlingame began in the second half of 1921. From June until Christmas that year, nine new houses were built. Then in 1922, the greatest resurgence of construction took place with 36 new starts made. J. P. Hymer, a local realtor, reported in October that in one month more than $30,000 in sales had been transacted in the tract.

In the next year, 1923 continued the trend with 29 new starts in construction followed by 21 in 1924 and 17 more in 1925. Then, as the Burlingame began to be built out, interest in the contiguous new tracts of Kalmia Place and Burlingame Manor took the lead. Between 1926 and 1930, only 14 new houses were built in Burlingame. The wild-fire of home construction had moved on into other North Park neighborhoods.

Kalmia Place Tract

At the western end of Kalmia Street overlooking the municipal golf course in Balboa Park, a new tract was opened in January 1923: Kalmia Place. Lewis P. Delano, a member of the City Planning Commission and realtor with the John W. Snyder Company, created the small subdivision as an architecturally controlled environment. Delano envisioned a small and highly individual community of artistic houses designed around the theme of "modified types of Spanish or Mission architecture."

In order to assure a high level of quality in the 20-parcel tract, Delano commissioned Cmdr. Lincoln Rogers and F. W. Stevenson to lay out the ground plan and specify the landscape materials for the entire project. Rogers and Stevenson were also retained as supervisors of the project to assure a harmonious development of the individual lots. Lincoln Rogers, a New York City architect, had been sent to San Diego in 1920 by the U.S. Government to design and supervise the construction of the Navy projects. The Naval Training Center was his design as was the Army and Navy YMCA building in downtown San Diego.

Kalmia Place was situated on one of the more spectacular plots of ground overlooking the east border of Balboa Park. A promontory that projected out into Switzer Canyon, it offered a view of the canyon slopes with their indigenous chaparral, the new municipal golf course and in the distance, the domes and towers of the exposition grounds.

"Twenty remarkable homesites" were advertised in the *San Diego Union* on January 21, 1923, "each of which offers splendid opportunity for characteristic individuality in fashioning the home you want amidst an

irresistible environment affording an exquisite beauty of panorama unsurpassed within our city."

Descriptions of the view site by the local press, while enthusiastic, lost sight of reality and bordered somewhat on fantasy.

". . . sweeping down the canyon, the eye quickens with interest as it takes in the business district, the harbor and an entrancing vista of North Island, Point Loma and the open sea."

– *San Diego Union*, January 21, 1923

". . . Kalmia Place, a semi-circular tract that slopes gently toward the wide expanse of park mesa providing a number of splendid sites for distinctive dwellings of the better sort. Already several attractively designed homes have been completed in the tract and others are now in process of construction. A quiet restful atmosphere, undisturbed by any annoying features, is combined with an attractive view of rolling mesa and both comfort and architectural beauty together with every modern device for convenience have been built into the various residences completed or under way in this restricted tract of homesites."

– *San Diego Union*, May 11, 1924

Delano had a great appreciation for canyon side view lots. He and his wife lived in a house on the east side of Panorama Drive above the slope of the canyon overlooking Mission Valley. Ironically he met a premature death on the cliffs of the Pacific Ocean.

"Coroner S.C. Kelly is preparing to hold an inquest over the death of Lewis P. Delano, who was fatally injured Saturday when he accidentally backed his machine off an embankment on Point Loma. Delano died shortly after the accident."

– *San Diego Daily Transcript*, August 2, 1926

"Kalmia Place . . .the artistic realization of an ideal"(Lewis P. Delano, *San Diego Union*, January 21, 1923)
Photo taken October 1, 1957, courtesy of San Diego Historical Society (#92:18835-349)

Burlingame Manor Tract

Burlingame Manor, a small tract in the Eastern Addition contiguous with the Burlingame tract, was a project of San Diego "builder, real estate expert and financier" Godfrey L. Strobeck. The tract, bordered by 32nd Street, Maple Avenue, Felton Street and Juniper Street, was opened in 1925. Many of the homes built there in the mid-1920s exhibited northern European historic themes, such as Tudor Revival and French Normandie. The tract was advertised as being "San Diego's Last Close-in Home Subdivision." Its advantages were said to be proximity to McKinley Grammar School, Saint Augustine School, Trinity Methodist Church, and the Burlingame shopping district.

Godfrey Strobeck (1879-1937) came to San Diego from North Dakota in 1918. He had been a banker and lumberman in that state. Following his arrival in San Diego, he developed an expertise in property values and real estate, and founded the Continental Building and Loan Co. He was also the owner of the Cuyamaca State Bank of El Cajon. Burlingame Manor was one of his more successful San Diego real estate ventures before the market crash of 1929 diminished his fortunes. In November 1934, Strobeck moved to San Francisco where he died in 1937.

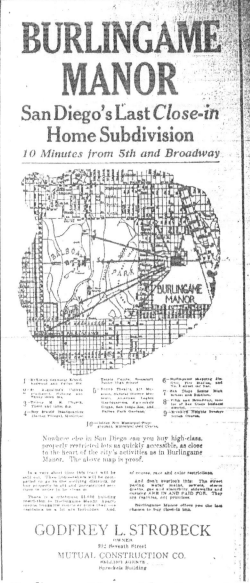

Burlingame Manor Advertisement
San Diego Union, January 24, 1926

Chapter 9
Expansion of the Ecclesiastical Community

The expansion of population and prosperity within the local community in the early 1920s affected religious institutions as much as commercial ones. In the period 1922-1924, five congregations built impressive facilities in North Park:

Plymouth Congregational Church
Trinity Methodist Church
North Park Baptist Church
Saint Luke's Episcopal Church
Saint Augustine School, Saint Patrick's Parish

Plymouth Congregational Church

In 1922, the pioneer church of the 30th and University district, the Park Villas Congregational Church, made plans for a new church building. Under the direction of the pastor, Rev. G. A. Charnock, it was determined that the church could not expand without a move from its 28th Street home. The congregation purchased a 100-foot by 125-foot plot on the corner of University and Pershing Avenues. The architect, William H. Wheeler, was commissioned for a building complex that included a parish house and auditorium. Space was reserved for a future sanctuary for services. A contract was signed with T. M. Russell, builder, on August 22, 1922. Estimated cost of construction was $17,000. The church was dedicated on Easter Sunday, April 20, 1924.

The complex included space for meeting rooms including a stage and movie projection equipment to be used by community groups. Several local organizations were assigned regular space in these rooms: the North Park Business Men's Group, the University Heights Mothers Group, and the North Park Improvement Group. There was also a large room facing University Avenue that was set aside for North Park's first branch library with over 3,000 books. The first librarian there was Genevieve Hopkins.

Such an ambitious project was too taxing for so small a congregation without committing to heavy loans. These were secured through the Southern California Congregational Conference and agreement that the local church would become affiliated with the San Diego First Congregational Church. The congregation studied the matter and voted to change the name of the church to the "Plymouth Center of the First Congregational Church – the Community Church." The name change was accomplished July 17, 1922. George Marston, who had supported the establishment of the Park Villas church in 1912, offered to pay off the remainder of the loan if the congregation would meet the first $1,000 of it. Between 1923 and 1927, George Marston paid off the major part of the $6,500 loaned by the Conference. North Park gained its first community center and library.

Plymouth Center, William H. Wheeler, architect; T. M. Russell, builder, 1924
New Plymouth Congregational Church, 2717 University Avenue
Photo courtesy of the San Diego Historical Society (#2344)

North Park Baptist Church

The North Park Baptist Church was officially recognized as a member of the Southern California Baptist Convention on October 15, 1923. Forty-two charter members of the congregation celebrated the event. The new Church was under the temporary supervision of L. P. Valentine in whose home at 3092 University Avenue the first organizational meeting was held on January 4, 1923. At a subsequent meeting of April 12, a little group of ten members resolved to take on the large task of official recognition and the construction of a sanctuary and accessory church buildings.

In the summer of 1923, ten members of the congregation were appointed as the building committee charged with the mission of having a building by the Christmas season. In the meantime, the new church held services in a tent pitched at the corner of University Avenue and 32nd Street. The Baptist Convention had purchased the 150-foot by 125-foot plot for $3,800. The architect, Erwin T. Banning, was commissioned and an elaborate design in Mediterranean Baroque style was prepared for a group of church buildings to be constructed in phases. The first phase was planned for a Sunday School and office building.

Ground breaking ceremonies took place on October 30, 1923 with Reverend F.O. Belden wielding the first shovel of earth. The first phase of the project, a lath and stucco structure, was completed in time for the Christmas service. Reverend L. P. Valentine served as the first pastor for the congregation. He officiated at the church dedication on February 24, 1924.

Phase One of the church project, which cost over $12,000, served the growing congregation well throughout the 1920s. The final phase, the ambitious main auditorium, was never built due to a combination of unfortunate events including a catastrophic fire on July 14, 1930 that destroyed the wood-framed roof and attic. The decision was made to not re-build at the present site but to find a new one in an area of less traffic and noise. The plot chosen was on the corner of Wightman (North Park Way) and Bancroft Streets.

The new building, an Art Deco style structure, was built of reinforced concrete as a precaution against fire. The building, a first phase in the project, was a three-story wing that held the Sunday School rooms, social rooms and offices. It was dedicated on November 8, 1931. Although it was said at the time that the main auditorium would soon follow, the intervening Great Depression and World War Two prevented construction until the autumn of 1948.

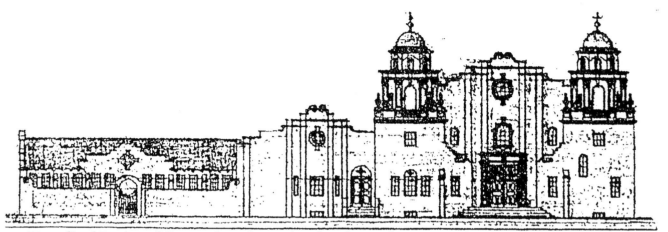

Unrealized Design of the North Park Baptist Church, October 1923, Edwin T. Banning, Architect.

North Park Baptist Church Nears Completion at the Northwest Corner of University Avenue and 32nd Street December 1923
Photo courtesy of the San Diego Historical Society (#UT 1647)

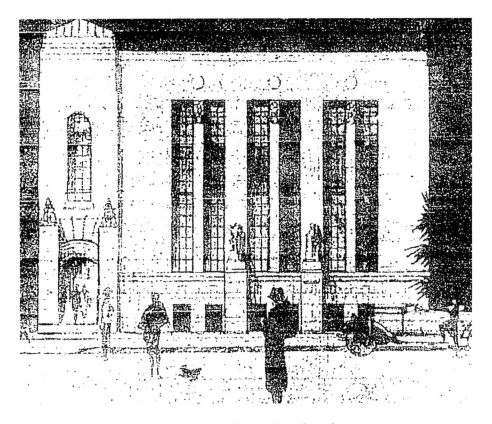

New North Park Baptist Church
J. S. Groves, Architect

Trinity Methodist Episcopal Church

In 1915, one of the many visitors to the Panama-California Exposition in Balboa Park was a young minister from Kansas, Rev. Walter Grant Smith. Like many other visitors that year, Rev. Smith determined to stay in San Diego. As a Methodist minister, Rev. Smith needed a congregation and a church to make transferring into the Southern California Conference a possibility.

With the help of his friend, Rev. Dorah W. Wilt, pastor of the Normal Heights Methodist Church, Rev. Smith determined that the growing residential center around Upas and 30th Street was a potential site for a new congregation. On January 24th, the two reverends met with a group of people in a private residence at 3237 30th Street and established plans for a rally to form a new congregation.

That public meeting took place in February and by March a small chapel measuring 20 feet by 42 feet had been built on borrowed land near Upas and 30th Streets. This chapel was later moved to a lot that the congregation purchased at Grim and Thorn streets. As the congregation expanded, two side wings were added to the little chapel.

A new pastor, Rev. Daniel Dundas was assigned to Trinity Methodist Church in October 1922. By that time, the little chapel with its added wings had become inadequate for the burgeoning congregation. Rev. Dundas announced to his new congregation that his special mission was to see that a new church building was constructed. Such a grand scheme seemed impossible to many of the congregation, but with Rev. Dundas leading the way, the small group of faithful members set out to raise the necessary funds.

Rev. Dundas and his small flock of congregants eagerly took on the task of raising enough money and pledges to assure the success of the project. Many times the task of fund raising seemed impossible. But each time, a small "miracle" would revive spirits and the fund raising went on.

Many benefactors such as the Hage Ice Cream Factory, Bishop Cracker Company, and anonymous donors helped to keep the project moving along. The congregation's Boy Scout troop and the Ladies Aid Society were also constant contributors to the project.

Finally, in the spring of 1924, it was determined that there was enough money in the building fund to begin the project of construction. Somewhat less than $10,000 in cash and pledges could be accounted for against a project estimated to cost $50,000.

A tent was set up on a nearby corner of 30th Street for services, and members of the congregation began the task of tearing down the old chapel and clearing the plot at Thorn and Grim streets. Plans were drawn by E. Tuttle, architect, and a contract was made with a builder.

Construction continued through the summer and fall of 1924. Finally, two years after Rev. Dundas had first announced to his new congregation that his mission was to acquire an appropriate building for the congregation, his mission was accomplished. The new home for the Trinity Methodist Episcopal Church was dedicated on November 2, 1924. At that ceremony, $12,000 was pledged to be applied to a $32,000 debt.

Trinity Methodist Episcopal Church
Photo courtesy of the San Diego Historical Society (#UT 1688)

Saint Luke's Episcopal Church

Until the post-World War One period, the nearest place of worship for North Park Episcopalians was All Saints' at Sixth and Pennsylvania Avenues. From 30th and University by streetcar, the journey required two transfers. This was considered by the rector, Rev. Charles T. Murphy, and the vestry of the church to be unacceptable for children attending Sunday school.

Plans were begun for solving this problem by establishing a mission of All Saints' for its rapidly expanding North Park congregation.

In October 1923, Rev. Murphy received permission to establish the North Park mission. The first meeting of the organizing committee was held in the private residence of Henry R. Lewis on Pershing Avenue. As the first meeting was held on the day following the Feast of St. Luke's, it was decided to name the mission church St. Luke's. With the prospect of a quickly growing local congregation, the organizing committee was faced with obtaining an immediate place of worship. That problem was solved when Euclid C. Wills offered his Ramona Theatre as a temporary facility for all services of the new mission. All expenses of the theatre were assumed by Dr. and Mrs. Wills. The first Sunday school services were conducted in the theatre on November 11, 1923.

A more permanent solution for St. Luke's was obtained in 1924 when All Saints' responded to its own need for greater space to house its growing congregation. The architects Richard Requa and Frank Mead were commissioned to design a new complex of sanctuary, vestry hall, rectory and chapel for the plot at Sixth and Pennsylvania. The chapel of the former complex was at that time offered to the North Park congregation. The chapel, a part of a larger design by Hebbard and Gill was built in 1897 in their typical Mission style of the period.

In May 1924, All Saints' bought a lot on the corner of Gunn and 30th Streets in North Park. The wood lath frame and hardwood floor was then moved from the Hillcrest lot and the chapel was re-built on the new site. The stucco building features gothic pointed windows and door set into an asymmetrical Mission style façade with espadana parapet over the main body. The entrance to the building is set in a short tower with sloping walls topped by a pyramidal hip roof. The contractor for the reconstructed building was John Love, an architectural designer with other North Park projects.

The first service in the little chapel was held on August 17, 1924 with All Saints' rector Rev. Charles Murphy giving the sermon. Rev. William F. Dawson, first Vicar of the church, celebrated Holy Eucharist. Two services were offered that day and a total of 98 congregants were in attendance.

Drawing From the 50th Anniversary Book of St. Luke's Episcopal Church (1978)

Saint Augustine School, Saint Patrick's Parish

The extraordinary growth of population in the North Park area during the immediate post-World War One years created a need for an additional Catholic parish beyond the six belonging to the Diocese of Monterey-Los Angeles. Bishop John Cantwell of that diocese appointed one of his priests, Father Gregory Ashe, to the new Saint Patrick's parish in October 1921.

A search was made for an appropriate site for parish church, rectory and hall. That site turned out to be a block in the West End tract bordered by Dwight, Ray, 30th and Landis Streets. A framed board-and-batten parish hall facing Ray Street was the first completed in February 1922 and was temporarily used for services. The first Mass was said on February 5, 1922. The rectory, a Craftsman style two-story house was next completed in October 1922. The third structure, a parish church, had to wait until the end of the decade.

Beyond the requirement of church buildings and rectory, Bishop Cantwell realized that there was a great need in San Diego for a boys' high school. In February 1922, he invited the Augustinian provincial of Villanova to visit San Diego to suggest a response to that need. The result of that visit was the assignment of Father Alphonse Martel, a chemistry teacher at Villanova College in Pennsylvania to the position of principal and teacher of new Augustinian boys' day school in San Diego. The temporary quarters for the school were on Stockton Drive in Mission Hills. The first classes for 19 boys opened on September 18, 1922.

St. Patrick Parish Hall, February 5, 1922

"The moral, physical and spiritual welfare of the boys who attend this school will be carefully attended to and their instruction along these lines will be equally as important as their training in the arts, sciences and professions."

– Father Gregory Ashe, *San Diego Union*,
September 17, 1923

The search for a permanent school site in North Park turned up a ten-acre lot bounded by 32nd, 33rd, Palm and Nutmeg Streets in the newly opened Carmel Heights tract. The prestigious San Diego architectural partnership of Mead & Requa was hired to design the school complex. Richard Requa assumed the role as principal designer and a contract was awarded to Keyes Construction Co. The contract with Arthur Keyes, signed on April 5 1923, called for a brick & tile building estimated at cost of $64,000.

Saint Augustine's High School opened on September 4, 1923 and was dedicated on September 16th. There were four teachers including Father Martel and 59 students. At its opening, the building was said to be of great importance ". . . a monument of architecture embodying the most perfect type of Spanish Old Mission style." The complex included large classrooms for art, science and professional training; as well as a chapel, a library and physical exercise facilities.

Bishop Cantwell stated at the dedication ceremony, "the Catholic Church is sponsoring such schools as this so that the young people who will be our future citizens may go out into the world thoroughly equipped spiritually and with a full knowledge of their chosen pursuit."

In 1924, it was reported that:

"Covered archways, quaint porticoes, hidden recesses and enclosed courts remind the visitor of ancient Spain or quaint Mexico."

– *San Diego Union*,
January 1, 1924, page 6

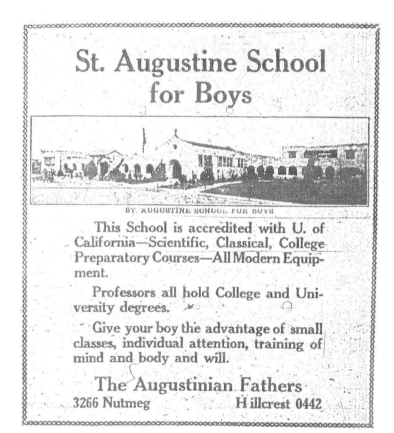

Saint Augustine School Advertisement
San Diego Union, January 1, 1929

Saint Augustine High School, 1923
Richard Requa, Architect
Photo courtesy of the San Diego Historical Society (#8333)

St. Patrick's Parish Church, 1929
Frank Hope Jr., Architect

Chapter 10
"A City of Our Own" ~ 1925-1929

The Business Boom Peaks

The momentum of growth along University Avenue and 30th Street that began with a flourish in 1922 became more dynamic with each passing year. In April 1925, it was announced that the building permit record for San Diego in the first quarter of the year showed a two-million-dollar increase over the same period of 1924. On January 1, 1926, the previous year was considered to be the "biggest year for building permits" with a total in excess of $18 million. Then, in January 1927, the year just ended was declared the record-breaking year in building in San Diego. The record number of buildings and their costs of construction in 1926 would not be matched in the City of San Diego as a whole until the post-World War Two years. In North Park, however, the peak years in commercial building construction that began in 1926 continued with major annual projects until the early 1930s.

As the projects grew larger and more ambitious, it appeared to many of the businessmen in the district that the status of the community was surpassing the suburban stage. By 1928, many would have agreed with Emil Klicka that the urban seeds sown in the fertile soil of the 30th and University district in the previous decade would soon sprout a new city on San Diego's horizon. As Klicka himself said:

". . . Balboa Park, as you know, separates this business section from the downtown districts, and only recently a banker from San Francisco called my attention to this fact. . . In the last few months I have visited San Francisco and Los Angeles many times. At San Francisco the big men have their eyes on San Diego. They believe that it has a great future. . . As to North Park, I believe that within a few years we are going to have a city of our own in this district."

– Emil Klicka

In the five final years of the 1920s, North Park's expansion brought with it the need for a wider Pershing Drive; and a new road for truck traffic through Balboa Park on Florida Drive. It became necessary to provide a large San Diego Gas & Electric Substation, an Electric Railway substation, a new water filtration plant, and an increased water supply. A system of street lighting for University Avenue and semaphore traffic controls for the junction of 30th and University were also added safety conveniences.

By 1928, when Emil Klicka made his quoted remark about having a "city of our own," North Park, with a population greater than many of California's small towns, was beginning to possess most of the daily living requirements and amenities of an urban community.

A Booming Demand for Grocery Markets

In the commercial district of North Park, there were 11 major commercial projects either under construction or completed in 1926. These 11 were estimated at just under $140,000 in construction costs. Six of those 11 were for grocery markets, including a new facility for Piggly Wiggly at 3829 30th Street. That building was ordered by Jack Hartley. A reinforced concrete structure, it was estimated to cost $12,000. William E. Gibb, a contractor associated with the Hartley firm and a notable North Park builder, was responsible for the project.

Two markets opened back to back with a continuous façade on Wightman Street (now North Park Way). One of those stores with an entry on 30th Street was a reinforced concrete structure built for George Walter Hopkins. The contractor for the job was Charles M. Williams, a prolific North Park builder and resident responsible for several of the commercial buildings in the 30th and University district. The building housed the Wig Wag Grocery from 1927 to 1931.

The building that backed onto Mr. Hopkins' store opened onto Ray Street at 3804. This building, also constructed by Charles M. Williams, housed the Ideal Grocers branch franchised by George B. Wittman, who lived next door with his family at 3812 Ray Street. Wittman was president of the Ideal Grocers Inc.

Farther down 30th Street at its intersection with Upas Street, another building to house a grocery store was constructed for Waite & Archibald by W. W. Brunson & Son, contractors. The building on the northwest corner of Upas and 30th was of brick construction at an estimated cost of $20,000.

An Upgrade on Hartley Row

Another Hartley/Gibb project of 1926 was the remodeling of four of the stores of Hartley Row on the corner of 30th and University. One of those, 3005, was leased to Heller Grocery and Charles Hardy meats. Both stores were reputable, citywide markets that had held a presence in North Park from its beginning. Another space in the three-building complex, at 3001 University Avenue, was a real estate office for Mayer-Krumholz on the southeast corner of 30th and University. The complex was a remodeling of four individual stores that unified the facades in a classic Mediterranean style, tripartite design. Following the 1926 remodel, 3009 University Avenue became the real estate office for Jack Hartley after the break-up of the Stevens & Hartley Real Estate Company. The middle space in the plan, 3007 University Avenue, was leased by Emil Klicka for his latest venture, the San Diego State Bank. The Mayer-Krumholz firm remained on the corner. The organizing of individual shops into one integrated architectural unit was a new design concept for North Park in the mid-1920s. Once it was established, it took several innovative directions.

A New Type of Shopping Center

One of the earliest of the multi-unit shopping centers was an annex to the 1913 Stevens/Hartley building on the northwest corner of 30th and University. The Thomas Carter Construction Company, the same firm that had built the original building, was the contractor for the Stevens Annex at 2926-36 University Avenue. The Annex was in a Mediterranean style based on ancient Roman Villa traditions with an arcaded façade ending at each end in a tower unit. The central four arcade units were built with a mezzanine overlooking the sales floor while the two end units were two-story.

With the break-up of the Stevens & Hartley firm in 1927, Will J. Stevens moved his real estate office into 2932 University within the Stevens annex. In the west end tower unit at 2926, Henry Leighton opened a café. Above the restaurant, Henry and Daisy Leighton made their home. Next door at 2928, Mrs. Joe Head ran a confectionery shop. At 2930, Lee Milikan maintained a men's haberdashery. Next to Will Stevens at 2934 was the Citizens Thrift Company, and in the east tower, two prominent North Park businessmen, Dan Harmer and Robert Dent, operated a shoe store that grew into a small department store by the end of the decade.

The Hurlburt & Tifal Retail Center

Three months after the beginning of construction on the Stevens Annex, another multi-unit retail center was begun at 2849-2863 University Avenue. The reinforced concrete structure featured six shops with facades that alternated between Spanish Colonial Revival and Pueblo Revival styles. One of the most interesting architectural designs in North Park during the 1920s, the façade design was lost to modernization during the 1950s. The building was a product of the Hurlburt & Tifal Company, Architectural Designers and Contractors. Ralph Hurlburt, the architectural designer, and Charles Tifal, the builder, had been a team since the early years of the decade.

Remodel of 3009, 3007, 3005, 3001 University Avenue, 1926
Photo courtesy of the San Diego Historical Society (#UT 84)

The retail center was built for M. B. Boys, whose real estate office was in the center of the building at 2859. On the west end at 2849 was the Markle and Fearnley "Town Pub" restaurant. On the ground floor of the tower at the east end was the Mattingly Tire Company, with a second floor studio for the *North Park Leader,* a community newspaper published there in the late 1920s.

University Motor In Market

The most innovative of these mid-1920s retail centers, and one that had the most resonance in later development, was the University Motor In Market. Designed for the convenience of the newly emerging automobile culture of the suburbs, the Market straddled the corner of Arizona Street and University Avenue.

The Hurlburt & Tifal Retail Center at 2849-2863 University Avenue, a Mix of Spanish and Pueblo Revival Styles, 1926
Photo courtesy of the San Diego Historical Society (#Sensor 8-194, detail)

The V-shape building at the rear of the corner lot allowed for auto parking on the outer segment. The building was composed of nine retail spaces with one larger central hall flanked by two wings of four spaces each. The larger central space was occupied by a Humpty Dumpty grocery store. The retail center, under construction in the winter months of 1926, opened to the public in January 1927. It was built by Charles M. Williams for Waite & Archibald. The University Motor In Market was North Park's first response to the emerging automobile culture of the 1920s. It was also one of the earliest designs in San Diego's mid-city suburbs reflective of later shopping malls.

Dixie Retail and Office Building

The growth of construction in North Park and other mid-city communities had brought increased activity and prosperity to the two local lumberyards, Klicka Lumber Company and Dixie Lumber Company. By the mid-1920s, Dixie needed additional office space.

The Stevens & Hartley building in 1913 had offered the first business offices. The Granada Building with its upstairs offices and ground floor retail spaces followed that in the early 1920s. Most construction projects otherwise had been for small retail shops, leaving the North Park commercial district with a shortage of professional offices by 1926. The new Dixie retail and office building on the corner of Ohio and University helped to amend that shortage. The building permit for frame stores and office at 3911 Ohio Street and 3050 University Avenue was issued January 4, 1926. The first occupants to show up in the City Directory in the Dixie Building (listed at 3913 Ohio Street in 1927) were George

Murison, O. L. Brown (dentist), Browning & Browning (chiropractors), and H. L. Jones (physician). The following year, T. S. Christopher (lawyer), Ruth E. Felt (music teacher), and Trude Phillips (dressmaker) joined O. L. Brown in the Dixie Building.

North Park Furniture Company (Stern's Gym)

Between 1921 and 1923, Frank J. Crover had two one-story buildings constructed at 2877 and 2879 University Avenue for his North Park Furniture Company. In 1926, Crover moved his furniture store around the corner to a new two-story building at 3829 Granada Avenue. Like the Granada Building of 1922, the structure of the building was brick with a steel frame. Until the mid-1930s, the lower floor of the red brick building housed the Crover furniture store. Upstairs, Frank Crover and his wife maintained an apartment for a few years before moving into a house on Utah Street.

From the late 1930s through the 1950s, the lower floor was occupied by three successive poultry shops operated by Nathan Raitzas (1938-1945), L. J. Summers (1950-1952), and West Coast Poultry & Egg (1952-1960). In 1961, the New Life Chinese Laundry moved into the ground floor, where it remains to this day. Upstairs, a billiard parlor existed until 1948. At that time, it was succeeded by a weight lifting gym that Leo Stern operated until the late 1980s. The gym is still in operation under the same name. Some of the notables who have worked out at the gym are Steve Reeves, the movie's "Hercules;" Arnold Schwarzenegger; Bill Pearl, Mr. Universe from 1953 to 1971; and Lou Ferrigano, TV's "Incredible Hulk."

University Motor In Market, University Avenue at Arizona Street, 1926-1927
Photo courtesy of the San Diego Historical Society (#6763)

Dixie Building, circa 1926
Photo courtesy of the San Diego Historical Society (#9196)

U.S. Post Office, North Park Branch

Prior to 1927, postal service in North Park was limited to over-the-counter purchases of stamps. These counters were part of the service area in local drugstores. The one longest in use was the Robertson Drugstore in the Stevens & Hartley building. Delivery of mail came directly from the downtown post office and later the Hillcrest branch. Then on October 11, 1927, a permit was issued to Hostetter, Goss & Norris, contractors, for a $7,000 stucco and tile store at 3830 Ray Street. This site became a full service Post Office Branch office from 1927 until 1951, when it was moved to a new building at 3791 Grim Avenue.

SDG&E Substation F on El Cajon Boulevard

The booming expansion of population and its accompanying construction of dwellings in the first half of the 1920s put a great strain on the power sources of the city. At the beginning of 1925, the San Diego Consolidated Gas & Electric Company was serving electricity to over 46,000 customers, an increase of 13% over 1924. The northeast section of the city, including North Park, especially put an unprecedented demand on the company. Plans were made during 1925 for a new substation to serve the newly expanded neighborhoods of the northeast sections.

On April 15, 1926, a permit was issued to the San Diego Consolidated Gas & Electric Company for a tile and stucco substation at 3169 El Cajon Boulevard. Construction cost was estimated at $38,000. When the facility opened in February 1927 it served approximately 6,000 households and businesses. The design of the building attempted to harmonize with the contemporary architecture of the immediate neighborhood. The street façade presents a formally balanced two-story building in the restored style of a Spanish Renaissance villa. Busts of Thomas Edison and Benjamin Franklin are on the façade.

A Carnival of Light

Advancement of the commercial center in North Park had reached a mature stage by the early weeks of 1926. Evening uses of University Avenue for business and pleasure brought a desire for a well-lit environment. In the residential neighborhoods, good street lighting had been an element of the sales pitch from the very earliest times. In 1912, Joseph McFadden promoted his North Park tract with references to its illuminated streets in his "Afraid to Go Home in the Dark" advertisements.

In April 1926, The North Park Business Club began an aggressive campaign for street lighting in the 30th and University district. Cost, estimated to be between $30,000 and $35,000, was funded by subscription on the part of property owners, most of them among the eighty-four members of the Business Club. On May 28th, conduits were beginning to be installed on University between 28th and 31st Streets. Ornamental poles carrying 600 candlepower lamps were soon to follow.

By August 7, North Park was ready to throw the switch on its own "Great White Way," and it did so during a major carnival and street dance at Kansas and University. The affair was held under the auspices of the North Park Business Club headed by Frank Vavrock.

San Diego Gas & Electric Substation F on El Cajon Boulevard
Photo courtesy of the San Diego Historical Society (#2000.56.3563)

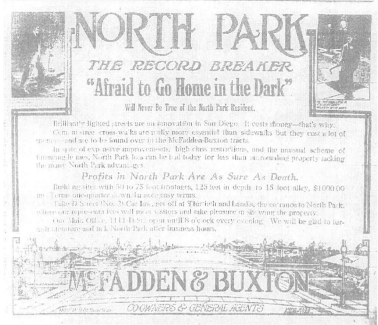

McFadden & Buxton "Afraid to Go Home in the Dark"
Advertisement, 1912

Preceding the celebration in North Park, 18 decorated floats paraded through downtown San Diego promoting the carnival and the merchants of the 30th and University district.

"The switch was turned on, and the illuminated white way shone forth in all its brightness and beauty."
– *San Diego Union*, August 7, 1926

During the evening carnival, $1,000 in merchandise was given away by lottery; 35,000 pieces of candy and 3,000 noisemakers were given to children. Entertainment under the direction of Tommy Getz of Getz & Grant Realty included bagpipers, choral groups, piano soloists, and a ladies brass band. At 8:00 P.M., street dancing began to the music of the George Nagel band playing from the temporary bandstand at Kansas and University.

"The final event in the city's annual San Diego Week took place in the 3900 block of Kansas Street in North Park on the night of August 7, 1926. The gathering of an estimated 10,000 persons attended from all parts of the city to aid in the celebration of the first illumination of University Avenue."
– *San Diego Union*, August 7, 1926

North Park Business Club

The parade, carnival and street dance held to celebrate the street lighting of University Avenue was one of the most extravagant affairs arranged and funded by the merchant members of the North Park Business Club. With general improvement of the community as a goal, the club members developed a strong sense of civic pride and duty. They not only sought to increase trade in the business district but organized community entertainments as well. The club was formed in 1922 by Jack and Paul Hartley, when the brothers saw the need for an organization of business owners to improve and develop the growing district. Under the leadership of Jack Hartley, the first President, the club strengthened its role as the catalyst for community action during the 1920s. Jack Hartley estimated that 10,000 people attended the celebration and that the cost of the event was $2,000. The North Park merchant group paid the bill for the affair. Picnics at the beach or in the mountains were sponsored by the Club, as were monthly ballroom dances.

> "The annual picnic of residents of North Park will take place on Sunday May 29, at El Monte Oaks. Preparations are being made to entertain 2000 people."
> – *San Diego Daily Transcript*, April 1928

North Park Lions Club

Another community association first led by Jack Hartley was the North Park Lions Club, which was formed on May 18, 1926. In 1949, Pappy Vestal recalled the club's origins:

> "Early in 1926, Phiny Packard, a Charter member of the San Diego Lions Club and known as the Father of Lionism in San Diego, had the idea that the growing community of North Park was fertile ground for a new Lions Club. The idea resulted in a Charter from the National Association of Lions Club being presented to 27 active business and professional men of the District the evening of May 29, 1926."

At the time it received its charter there were 29 members. Jack Hartley was elected the first President of the club with his brother Paul following him in that position a few years later. The club met at several locations including the Nordberg Building and the Plymouth Center. In 1940, the club purchased the old Park Villas Congregational Church on 28th Street. After that building burned in 1943, the group had no regular meeting place until 1949. In that year, a new hall at 3927 Utah Street was built with funds collected from member donations.

Many charitable organizations have profited from the generosity of the North Park Lions Club, especially the Braille Club. The Lions Club began its service to the blind with a party for members of the Braille Club and the donation of 29 volumes of Braille books to a library for the blind in 1927.

In 1976, the club observed 50 years of good deeds, when it was noted in the *San Diego Union* that:

> "There may not be a single charity or disadvantaged group that has not benefited either through services or donations from the generosity of the North Park Lions Club, formed 50 years ago. The list is endless – the blind, orphans, the impoverished, students, the unemployed, Boy Scouts and Girl Scouts, crippled children, tuberculosis victims, the Salvation Army, YMCA and YWCA, Neighborhood House, the San Diego Boy's Band, Children's Home Society, San Diego Society for the Hard of Hearing, the American Red Cross, servicemen, the blood bank, Boys' Clubs, the March of Dimes, the polio fund, Community Chest, exchange students, mentally retarded children, schools, and Junior Achievement – just to name some. . . .Dedication is what has kept the North Park Lions Club going – a dedication that began with the club's first president, Jack C. Hartley. The list of Hartley's descendants who have been members of the North Park Lions Club has included the late Paul Hartley, a former

club president and San Diego city councilman; the late William Hartley, another former councilman; and Richard Hartley, a realtor who is a current member of the club."
— *San Diego Union*, May 23, 1976, page B-4

The Ku Klux Klan, an Uneasy Neighbor

The national paranoia that followed the September 1920 Wall Street bombing in New York City by alleged Bolsheviks resulted in the rise of "patriotic" groups. Several of those organizations considered themselves to be defenders against the post-war wave of anti-American rabble.

The threat to national stability presented by many of those groups resulted in counter-action by the U. S. Government. The Attorney General authorized raids on groups purported to be subversive. Some states, including California, outlawed organizations that threatened violence. One group investigated by both the U. S. and California Governments was the Ku Klux Klan.

For decades, the Klan had been a scourge on southern civil society. In the era of World War One, it had begun to flourish throughout the U. S. In the early 1920s, the Klan surfaced in California communities including San Diego.

"Mysterious cards setting forth the principles of the Ku Klux Klan and making an appeal for members are being circulated in this city."
— *San Diego Daily Transcript*, August 6, 1921

In order to disarm negative opinions concerning the Klan, the organizer of the local group in October of 1921 published a statement in the local press that outlined the purposes of the group. Those principles were: to exemplify pure patriotism, to uphold the chastity of womanhood, to prevent intermingling of races, to maintain free public schools, and the separation of church and state.

The first public appearance of the Klan in San Diego occurred during the Christmas season 1922. On Christmas Day the group hosted a dinner for over 100 of the city's "needy aged" who would otherwise have been without a holiday meal.

When the Park Villas Congregational Church moved into its new Plymouth Center on University Avenue in the autumn of 1923, it vacated the little wooden structure that it had built on 28th Street. The Ku Klux Klan, which had never had a local meeting hall, was the next tenant. The existence of the organization in the community was not without controversy, however. On Friday night, November 19, 1926, residents of North Park were awakened by an explosion reportedly heard throughout the city. A charge of black powder tore into the stage and rear of the hall, partially demolishing the structure. As no one was in the building, there were no casualties.

"A reward of $1000 has been posted for the apprehension and conviction of the person responsible for the bomb explosion which partly wrecked last Friday night the local Ku Klux Klan Hall."
— *San Diego Daily Transcript*, December 23, 1926

Membership in the local Klan dwindled during the 1930s but the organization remained in the community until 1943.

Traffic Control for University Avenue

In 1926, the city of San Diego became aware of a severe traffic problem. The increase in motor cars and trolleys had brought with it a growing hazard to both motorists and pedestrians. Therefore, for the first time, control at busy intersections became necessary.

> "The report of the U.S. Department of Commerce, just made public, in connection with automobile fatalities in cities throughout the country, shows that San Diego again leads all. . ."
> – *San Diego Daily Transcript*,
> September 1928

After several weeks of deliberation over alternative solutions, a system was agreed upon. The busiest intersections in the city would have semaphore traffic signals at each of its four corners. A study of city intersections indicated six to be the most hazardous due to the intensity of vehicular traffic. North Park's junction of 30th and University was one of those six. Fifteen years after Jack Hartley had dubbed the junction the "busy corner," it was verified by a city traffic study.

> "The six new semaphore traffic signals decided upon by the city Council will be located at fifth and B, sixth and C, fourth and C, and three on University Avenue at Park, Thirtieth, and Fifth."
> – *San Diego Daily Transcript*,
> January 1927

The semaphore signals adopted were ones newly acquired by the city of Pasadena. A large disk mounted on a pole had mechanically rotating arms marked with "STOP" and "GO." Flashing red and green lights at the base of the disk added to the attention-getting effect. These signals were mounted on the curb at the street crossing. The signals were in place in February 1927.

The Nordberg Building

The most significant construction project of 1926 in North Park was the one commissioned from the Nordberg Company by Mary Jane Hartley. Once built, it became the headquarters of the building contracting company and offered professional offices on the second floor to other firms. The ground floor of the two-story building at 3043 University Avenue was composed of eight individual retail spaces.

Beyond the building's commercial importance for the business environment on the Avenue was its greater significance to the community in the large space at the rear of the second floor, the ballroom. Here, the ceiling rose to one and a half story with tall windows at floor level and small clerestory windows above.

The ballroom was quickly discovered by the business and citizens groups of North Park as it offered an ideal space for community centered activities.

The "Tent," as the ballroom was popularly known, had a ceiling draped with gossamer fabric illuminated from above to produce a dream-like fantasy inspired by Hollywood "sheik" movies of the Valentino era. It was a larger space than the only other community rooms of the Plymouth Center (1923) and made possible larger functions such as political meetings, civic celebrations, community dances and banquets.

"Great preparations are being made by the Greater University Avenue Business Association for the get-together banquet on Thursday evening at the Tent at Grim and University."
– *San Diego Daily Transcript*, May 3, 1927

"The first of a series of community dances this fall and winter, planned by the North Park Business and Civic Club is to take place in the Tent Ballroom, Thirtieth and University, on October 21st."
– *San Diego Daily Transcript*, September 24, 1927

"A meeting has been called of taxpayers for next Tuesday, November 8th at the Tent Ballroom, University and Grim, for a discussion by both sides of the proposed bond issue."
– *San Diego Daily Transcript*, November 5, 1927

Throughout the 1930s, these affairs were held there regularly by the North Park Business and Civic Club, the Greater University Avenue Business Association and numerous other groups. The ballroom functioned as a community center from its completion in 1926 until it was re-structured as apartments for military families during World War Two.

"The Tent" circa 1928
Photo courtesy of the San Diego Historical Society (#1654)

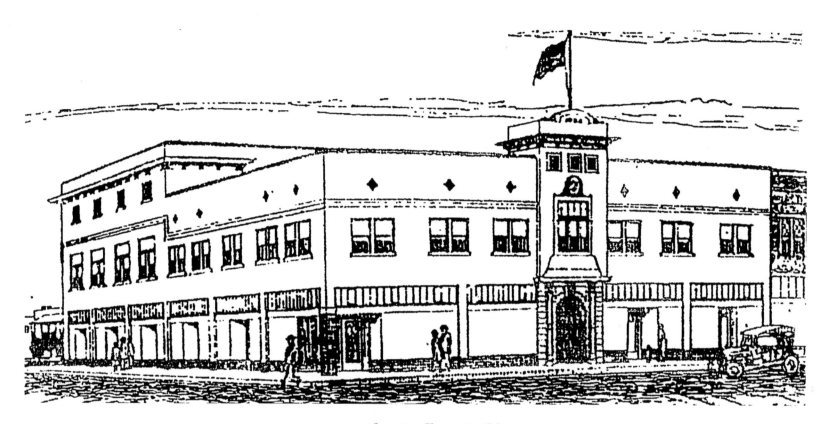

The Nordberg Building
Building Contract: March 26, 1926
Owner: Mary Jane Hartley
Contractor: Siguard G. Nordberg & Company
Designer: J. E. Norbeck
Estimated Cost: $40,000

The Broadcast Era Begins

When on November 2, 1920 Pittsburgh's radio station KDKA took to the airwaves with the results of the presidential elections, the event was entered into history books as the first commercial use of the very new communication device. The innovative system of entertainment and information spread rapidly across the land, altering every aspect of the culture. By 1923, more than 500 broadcasting stations had been established in the USA. One of those was KDPT in San Diego.

KDPT, *San Diego Union Tribune's* pioneer station, began citywide broadcasting from the top of the Pythian Building downtown on April 17, 1922. North Park residents who had one of the primitive receivers were able to enjoy the brief musical concerts of the early transmissions.

Those first local musical programs were followed on April 30, 1922 by Reverend Roy Campbell who gave the first broadcast sermon. Reverend Campbell was a North Park resident and pastor of the First Congregational Church. These concerts and sermons proved so popular with the growing number of San Diegans who had receiving sets that by November there were four stations competing for the local airwaves.

Greater North Park entered the wireless era on April 18, 1922, one day following the initial broadcasts. On that day, building permits were issued to Henry Stacey for the construction of two apartment buildings on the east side of the 3600 block of Park Boulevard. The contractor for the buildings was Edward F. Bryans, a notable North Park designer/builder who lived at 3022 Upas Street across from the Lynhurst Building. The design of the two apartment buildings called for all residential units to be equipped "with radio apparatus" so that all tenants might receive the new broadcasts.

Another new type of business establishment that emerged with the coming of wireless communication was the radio shop that sold and serviced the new receiving sets. The United Radio Electric store that opened its doors at 2807 University in 1926 was only one of several North Park shops of the type.

The Machine

The "machine," as the automobile was referred to in the early years of the century, became big business after World War One. By the mid-twenties, it was no longer a mere toy for the affluent and bachelor playboys. It had assumed the status of every family's necessity.

In the post-war era, the popularity of the automobile not only created oil shortages but also spawned a new type of business: the general service garage. The earlier oil station that offered only required fluids, lubricants and limited maintenance was replaced by the full service garage. North Park in the 1920s supported several of those new businesses.

In March of 1925, a building permit was issued to L. D. Selmser for a tile and brick building on the southeast corner of 28th and University estimated to cost $18,000. When completed at 2803-09 University Avenue, it housed the Public Service Garage that not only offered the service of a mechanic but also shared space with J. A. Dick Radiator Repair and Grant Hiatt Auto Repair. The Western Oil and Supply Company offered fluids and tires. Also included within the building was the Bottled Gas Company of San Diego and the United Radio Electric. (In the twenties, almost any service was more marketable if it included "radio" in the business name.)

Another garage of the new all-purpose type was the North Park Garage at 3029 University Avenue purchased by Paul Hartley in 1927. The Harmon brothers, John and Arley, had operated the garage throughout the post-war years maintaining an upstairs apartment above the service area. In October 1927, Hartley had the apartment removed and modernized the garage to include battery and tire service along with the full service of a mechanic.

Development in 1928-1929

Following a rather quiet period in the waning months of 1927, the building boom resumed in North Park with an increasing intensity and pace in the early months of 1928. By year's end, the 30th and University district had four major new commercial centers in place. Several years in the 1920s produced a greater number of important projects but none could match the sophistication of design and innovative planning as those four projects completed in 1928. They were Miller Brothers Service Inc. service station, the First National Trust and Savings Bank, the North Park Theatre/Klicka Building (discussed in Chapter 11), and the United Stores Shopping Center. Added to that group of major projects in 1929 were the Newman / I.O.O.F. building, the Home Supply Company Grocery, the third and final segment of the Jefferson Elementary School, and St. Patrick's Church complex.

Miller Brothers Super Service Inc.

The most elaborate and largest of all the North Park full service garages was that operated by the Miller Brothers, Charles and William, at 3171 University spanning the block between Herman and 32nd Streets. Automobile service by Bill and Charley Miller was not new to North Park in 1928. The brothers had first purchased the oil station at 30th and University from Albert Winter in 1923. It was there that they began the expansion of automobile services by investing in a $1,500 renovation of the premises. One of the notable facilities added to the property for the convenience of North Park residents was an ice station with a capacity of 18,000 pounds. In the days before residential refrigeration, block ice was a daily requirement for the proper operation of home kitchen "ice boxes." The commercial ice house was a necessary fixture within the retail district of every community.

In the spring of 1928, the brothers moved their operation to the larger site farther east on University Avenue at 32nd Street. The steel and stucco station was built by Lowerison & Wolstencroft at an estimated cost of $28,000. Gas for four post-type dispensers had to be manually pumped from underground storage vats to glass receptacles on top of the posts. The feeder hose then emptied the gasoline into the auto tank by gravity. Associated Gas was sold by the firm at each of the sites. Along with the gas and oil operations, Miller Brothers offered full garage service, battery and brake service, tire re-treading, headlight-testing, and wheel alignment.

Checking Wheel Alignment and Testing Brakes, 1932
Photo courtesy of the San Diego Historical Society (#Sensor 6-319)

Miller Brothers, circa 1932
Photo courtesy of the San Diego Historical Society (#Sensor 6-317)

They also provided steam-cleaning, washing, waxing, polishing, painting, paint removing, body repair, and a parts department stocked with Ford and Chevrolet parts. The firm offered free pick-up and delivery to the customer's home.

In the 1920s and 1930s, the station was an example of the most advanced automotive service then available at a single site. It also carried one of the largest payrolls of any business in a suburban San Diego district in that era.

First National Trust & Savings Bank Building

In February 1928, permits were let to the First National Bank for two shops and a bank building on the southwest corner of 30th and University. The architect for the project was Richard Requa, one of San Diego's leading architects. The contractor was builder Arthur E. Keyes, who a few years before had worked with Requa on another building with a Spanish theme, the Saint Augustine school project. The bank building design was one of grace and elegance, a result of Requa's recent study tour of Spain. An example of the architect's mature period, the First National Bank building was the first to develop an air of cosmopolitan sophistication on Jack Hartley's "busy corner" at 30th and University.

As a draftsman in the offices of architect Irving Gill, Requa had served his apprenticeship in the early years of the century. Following his association with Gill, Requa had established his own practice, and by the mid-twenties was a recognized local authority of the Spanish Revival style of architecture. A memorable tour of Spain in the mid-1920s had afforded him numerous sketches and photographs of authentic Renaissance buildings.

Among those was a civic palazzo in the quaint old town of Toledo.

Requa's design for the North Park branch of the First National Bank, like its predecessor in Toledo, was a classic combination of Spanish and Moorish architectural details. Sand colored stucco walls of the exterior were supported at sidewalk level by a deep band of green-veined black marble. Carved wooden beams that were richly polychromed supported a terra cotta tile roof with deep overhangs. Deep set panels on the two street facades containing the windows and entrances were built of warm toned brick. Exterior doors were of bronze and windows were crested with intricate wrought iron screens. Colorful glazed tiles in Moorish fashion decorated the window bays.

The interior of the building was as richly furnished and decorated as the exterior, with colorful ceramic tile walls and floor, wrought iron teller cages and lighting fixtures, polychromed beamed ceilings and renaissance styled furniture.

On the afternoon of September 22, 1928, a reception hosted by the bank celebrated the opening of the building. A popular orchestra furnished music, and hors d'oeuvres were served to the local public. It was said at the time of the opening that "neither expense nor thoughtful effort were spared in providing a building which will be a permanent and beautiful feature of San Diego." Permanence, however, was less than a half century as the "beautiful feature" was replaced in the early 1970s by a bank building in the minimal, functionalist style of corporate modernism.

First National Bank, North Park Branch, October 1953

United Stores Shopping Center

On June 22, 1928, two days after the building permit was issued to Emil Klicka for the North Park Theatre, another was granted to the United Realty Company for the construction of a major shopping center on the northeast corner of 30th and University. The Orndorf Construction Company estimated the project of brick and concrete stores to cost $20,000. On December 21, an additional permit with an estimated cost of $2,000 was issued to the Owl Drug Company for remodel of the corner store space at 3002 University Avenue. The drug store opened on February 9, 1929. By 1930, most stores were occupied and included a florist, a beauty shop, a gift shop, a restaurant, a millinery shop and a furrier. As the national economic troubles became more extensive, some retail spaces on 30th Street remained vacant throughout the early years of the 1930s.

The Newman / I.O.O.F Building

In July 1929, a permit to build a four-story steel and concrete department store at 2906 University on the northeast corner of Kansas Street was issued to Edward W. Newman and William E. Gibb. Newman, who had purchased the four corner lots in 1926, was a pioneer builder in University Heights, Normal Heights, and Kensington, as well as North Park. He and his wife Fanny lived in North Park as early as 1912. In those early years, Newman built several houses in the residential neighborhoods, occasionally experimenting with concrete construction. By 1929, at age 65, he was culminating a successful career.

William Gibb (1880-1939), an early house designer/builder in the community, came to San Diego in 1912. He had greater experience in design and construction of small, reinforced concrete commercial buildings in the vicinity of 30th and University. Many of those structures were built for Jack Hartley. In the late 1920s, Gibb and Hartley shared office space at 3009 University Avenue in Hartley Row. Gibb, a member of the North Park Lions Club, retired in 1936.

The building on the corner of Kansas and University was planned in June of 1929. By early autumn, a full basement with reinforced concrete and steel foundation had been completed to support a four-story structure. Then, sometime during the later weeks of construction, plans were changed and the building turned out to be a two-story one. Why the change was made is unclear. However, it is reasonable to suspect a loss of financing following the October Wall Street crash as the cause.

The exterior of the building, a modified Mission Revival style, featured a prominent series of round arched windows mimicking a glazed Roman arcade with towers and red tile roof. Modernization in the 1950s covered over transom windows in the arches, and other original features were also lost. However, the full arches and decorative features re-appeared in the restoration design of Richard Bundy and David Thompson, a Main Street sponsored project of the 1990s.

The interior of the original building was divided into two large retail spaces. The corner space featured a mezzanine overlooking the atrium of the ground floor. In 1930, North Park's first department store occupied this space. The E. N. Mudd Department Store shared the building with the Norman F. Maw Music Company that

156

moved its facility from downtown to the Newman building. As well as musical instruments, the Maw Company stocked Frigidaire refrigerators and Brunswick radios. At the public opening of Norman Maw's new store, representatives of the Frigidaire Company served frozen desserts "to illustrate the advantages of electrical refrigeration in the home." Entertainment was offered by the 30 voices of the Treble Clef club, and the San Diego State College Men's Glee Club. Several ukuleles and banjos were given away during the grand opening.

The business of those first two tenants of the Newman Building foundered during the darkest months of the Great Depression, and in September 1932, Edward Newman sold the building to the Independent Order of Odd Fellows (I.O.O.F.). A remodeling project began immediately under the direction of Lee Brendt, a Marine officer and member of the I.O.O.F. fraternity. The project resulted in lodge facilities facing Kansas Street and four business spaces on University. In 1933, these four spaces were leased to new tenants.

Edward Newman also owned the four lots directly across Kansas Street. In the summer of 1930, he leased those lots to James Truax who promptly laid out a "midget golf" course, the North Park Golf Club, on the property. With the Maw Music Company, and the new North Park Theatre and vaudeville house directly across the avenue from the miniature golf course, the corner of Kansas and University functioned as North Park's first center of entertainment for the local community in the early 1930s.

The 1931 panorama photograph on the next page shows this entertainment section at the junction of Kansas Street and University Avenue. An elegant late 1920s town-car is parked in front of the Maw Music

Company marquee. Two men stand on the street side of the motor car as though in conversation. One of them is dressed in the formal black suit and cap of a chauffeur. The other, in summer white dress shirt, trousers and shoes, appears to be giving instructions. Could this gentleman be Norman Maw, the proprietor of the store? Mr. Maw was a very prominent businessman and musician. In 1925, he had been elected a director of the Western Music Trades Association. Before moving his business to the Newman building in 1930, he had maintained a reputable music business downtown.

The close-up below shows the admissions shack and equipment office of the North Park Golf Club, a small reinforced concrete building. The four corner pillars were decorated to resemble golf bags. After the golf club closed in the mid-30s, the building was moved farther west to 2890 University Avenue where it now houses a local fast-food operation.

North Park Golf Club Admissions Shack, circa 1931
Photo courtesy of the San Diego Historical Society
(#80:2789, detail)

Kansas Street and University Avenue, Looking West, 1931
Photo courtesy of the San Diego Historical Society (#80:2789)

Home Supply Co. Grocery

In September 1929, a building permit for a concrete and steel market building at 3794 30th Street on the southwest corner of Wightman (North Park Way) was granted to owner Alfred Williams Jr. The permit was for a $10,500 concrete and tile store building. When completed, the building was leased to Home Supply Grocery that included L. C. Canfield, baker, J. P. Healey meats, and H. Y. Kondo, fruits. The builder was Joseph C. Kelley.

Burlingame Court and Shops

The Burlingame Court offered not only small affordable rental housing but several retail shops as well. These businesses were a part of the neighborhood shopping center that in the 1920s began to emerge at the crossing of Juniper and 30th Streets immediately south of the Burlingame tract. Construction began on this site in late September 1927. The shop portion was completed just before New Year's Day 1928 at an estimated cost of $27,000. The owners of the properties were the Bauman brothers, Isidore and Samuel, proprietors of a pawn shop on Fifth Avenue in downtown San Diego.

The earliest tenants for the shops in 1929 were a florist, a small café, and the offices of building contractor J. H. Lovett. The façade of the shops was a rather elaborate Spanish Plateresque design with low relief plaster panels in the frieze. The contractor for the project, Francis Young, founded F. E. Young Company in 1926, a year after moving to San Diego from Los Angeles to accept employment as a designer for contractor A. M. Southward. From his early work in Burlingame as an independent contractor, Young's firm was destined to become a multi-million-dollar international contracting company in the 1950s and 1960s, completing such major projects as the San Diego Civic Center and the San Diego Public Library.

Jefferson Elementary School

Construction of the third and final wing of Jefferson School was permitted in June 1929. A two story building opening onto Gunn Street, the building spanned the block between 28th and Utah streets. It closed the gap between the two earlier wings which faced Utah (1914) and 28th (1921) streets, respectively. Construction costs were estimated at $18,436 and $1,000 for an alteration of the Utah Street wing. The style of the building continued to follow the Mediterranean Baroque theme set by the original 1914 building. A notice of completion was filed on November 5, 1929.

St. Patrick's Parish Church

On October 19, 1928, a building permit was issued to St. Patrick's Church for the construction of a concrete building at 3597 30th Street. Although it was estimated to cost $37,000, the final cost was just over $60,000. The builder of the structure was M. H. Golden. The elaborate church was considered by the Southern Cross publication to be "one of the most beautiful in southern California." The design of the building was the first major project by a young architect, Frank Hope, Jr. It was completed late in March 1929 in time for Easter services. The church was in Romanesque Revival style and featured a west facing rose window with saints depicted in stained glass. Pews were constructed of the finest Philippine mahogany. Bishop John Cantwell of the Monterey-Los Angeles Diocese dedicated the church on September 8, 1929. The collapse of the stock market not two months later would have a long-term effect on the parish.

> ". . . the thunderous economic collapse of black Tuesday, three thousand miles away, was to create waves even on the far distant California coast, and Saint Patrick's would struggle an entire decade to liquidate its parish debt."
> – John R. Sanders, O.S.A. <u>Before All Else,</u>
> Augustinian Press, 1987

Saint Patrick's Church, 1929
Photo courtesy of the San Diego Historical Society
(#Sensor 18-103)

Chapter 11
North Park Theatre/Klicka Building

The North Park Theatre Opens

On Thursday, January 17, 1929, at 6:00 p.m., the doors of North Park's newest motion picture palace opened to the public. Emil Klicka's vision of the 30th and University district as the core of a new town on the northernmost border of Balboa Park came ever closer to reality with the opening of this link in the chain of William Fox's West Coast Theatres.

In June 1928, at an expected cost of $350,000, a two-story reinforced concrete structure had been planned to house an elaborate new motion picture theatre, a bank, a street-level shop, and medical offices on the second floor. Funded by Emil Klicka, the building was designed by architects Charles and Edward Quayle. Bernard O. Larsen, an acquaintance of Emil Klicka, was the general contractor on the job. The design of the building featured a Spanish Renaissance facade with a prominent arabesque frieze on the University Avenue side. The frieze in Plateresque style was modeled and cast by Ray Anderson, master plasterer. Other plaster sculpture gave elegance to the structure that echoed the Exposition buildings on the Prado in Balboa Park.

The Spanish Renaissance theme of the exterior of the Klicka Building was accompanied by a theatre foyer interior that introduced touches of Byzantine and Moorish details in marble and tile wall panels, a painted and coffered ceiling, decorative fountains and plush, brilliant-hued furnishings and carpets.

At a price of $120,000, Emil and George Klicka had purchased four 50-foot by 100-foot lots in block #3 of the West End tract for the major new project. The theatre, as planned by the Quayle brothers, was the first large, elaborate structure of its type to be built outside of downtown San Diego. In June 1928, the Klicka brothers and Fox West Coast Theatres Inc. agreed to a 20-year lease of the showhouse portion of the Klicka building. Fox planned to exhibit "newly developed movietone talking screen plays" as well as vaudeville performances.

The design of the theatre included an orchestra pit, dressing rooms below stage level, and a fly-loft above for manually raised and lowered stage scenery. The proscenium stage was flanked by two Wurlitzer sound projection units. The auditorium had a seating capacity of approximately 1,200 persons in a 144-square foot space. The chief significance of the project was that it broke new ground in theatre design in San Diego. The North Park Theatre was the first one in the city to be built specifically to project the latest in synchronized sound and moving pictures. The new "talking pictures" were revolutionizing the industry. In 1929, most of the San Diego cinema houses were converting their theatres to sound projection.

At 6:30 on the evening of January 17, 1929, the dedication ceremony began with a performance by Jamie Erickson on the theatre's console organ, which rose hydraulically from the orchestra pit. The New California Music Masters led by Ted Mack, the Director of the California Theatre downtown, followed Mr. Erickson's performance with a musical stage production.

The opening night ceremonies included several films that demonstrated the new synchronized sound system. The main feature, "Win That Girl," was one of

William Fox's experiments in the media. It was followed by several short subjects including Mack Sennett's first efforts at a talking comedy, a Movietone newsreel, a travelogue of Hawaii, and a special George Dewey Washington sing-a-long recital.

A newspaper article announcing the dedication of the theatre praised it for "its deeply-cushioned seats, the silent, thick carpeted aisles, the restful lighting, the spacious beauty of the design." It was further declared to be "one of the most modern, comfortable, pleasantly appointed and delightful motion picture theatres to be found anywhere." It was predicted that the theatre would become an integral part of its community (*San Diego Union*, January 17, 1929, page 7), a prophetic remark in relation to the theatre's role as a food-collecting and fund-raising center for the unemployed during the early 1930s.

The ambitious North Park Theatre/Klicka Building project, criticized by some as being too grand for a suburban community, was indicative of Emil Klicka's faith in the continuing development of North Park. Klicka envisioned it becoming a satellite town within a rapidly growing San Diego metropolitan district. It was a futuristic vision shared by other community leaders in the closing months of the 1920s. Within nine months of the opening of the North Park Theatre, however, the New York Stock market had collapsed and the national mood was mirrored by the Great Depression that followed.

Detail of Frieze
Photo courtesy of B'hend & Kaufmann Archives

North Park Theatre, circa 1950
Photo courtesy of B'hend & Kaufmann Archives

North Park Theatre Lobby

North Park Theatre, circa 1930
Photo courtesy of B'hend & Kaufmann Archives
(San Diego Historical Society #7092-D)

North Park Theatre, 1930s
Photo courtesy of B'hend & Kaufmann Archives

Klicka Building

The major occupant of the retail space in the new Klicka Building was one of the branches of the new Bank of America. In 1926, Emil Klicka had organized the San Diego State Bank, engaging Jack Hartley as one of the Directors. As President of the bank, Klicka managed the North Park branch that opened at 3007 University Avenue on Hartley Row.

At the time that the Klicka Building was being designed in the summer of 1928, it was planned that the San Diego State Bank would occupy the corner retail space of the building. However, by the time the bank was completed in December, all of the branches of the San Diego State Bank were purchased by L. M. Gianini's Bank of Italy and the name changed to the Bank of America.

"The San Diego State Bank this evening became a branch of the Bank of America of California. The consolidation takes in all the branches, four in number, of the local bank."

– *San Diego Daily Transcript*,
December 10, 1928

At that time, Emil Klicka became Vice President of the Bank of America under the administration led by his friend Gianini as President. At 4:30 in the afternoon on Saturday December 29, 1928, the new Bank of America opened its North Park branch. Emil Klicka retired from the Bank in 1947. The Bank remained in the Klicka Building until 1950 when it moved to a new building on 30th Street.

Bank of America Building, 1942
Photo Courtesy of B'hend & Kaufmann Archives

North Park Theatre and Bank of America, September 30, 1942
Photo Courtesy of B'hend & Kaufmann Archives

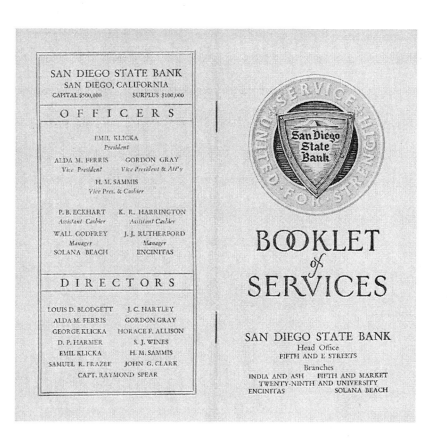

San Diego State Bank Pamphlet

Brochure courtesy of Robert Klicka Archives

Part Four
Decline and Recovery ~ 1930s & 1940s

"The oft-berated depression has accomplished one new step in carrying to a conclusion the intricate Nolen plan of city development that a decade of prosperous years was unable to bring about ~ the building of a swimming pool and recreation center at the foot of Texas street in Balboa Park."

– San Diego Union, October 9, 1932

Chapter 12
Depression ~ 1930-1934

Following the October 1929 failure of the New York stock market, there were some local predictions concerning "the worst is over:" and that "the economic situation will soon return to normal."

North Park was described as the "population center of San Diego." It was said to be "one of the fastest growing residential and business sections in the city. The Business Men's Club of North Park was quick to assert that most of the needs of everyday living could be acquired in the business center of the district, which was served by three of the city's street car lines and nearly 300 firms. The community also claimed the distinction of having unexcelled educational facilities and "the finest ventilated theatre in San Diego County, conforming to the highest standards of the entertainment field." (*San Diego Union*, January 1, 1930)

In spite of the boosterism and brave talk, however, records of real estate activity for 1930 indicate a deteriorating status in the local construction industry. Comparisons of building starts reported for North Park in the *San Diego Daily Transcript* reveal that only 14 building permits were issued in the first quarter of 1930, compared to 36 in the first quarter of 1929.

By 1934, in spite of the first-year success of the National Recovery Act (NRA) in national labor relations and large scale engineering projects, construction was slow to respond to the stimulus at the local community level. After a lackluster spring season, local construction projects were meager. In the third quarter of 1934, North Park could count only two housing starts, two residential completions, and one small commercial building.

"Progress of recovery generally has been disappointingly slow. The new federal bureaus, including the NRA, have not been able to accomplish as much as was hoped."
– *San Diego Daily Transcript*,
July 31, 1934, page 8

Still, there were bright spots. Some contracting firms remained active, and several of North Park's enduring landmarks were constructed in this period.

The Dennstedt Company

One of a few contracting firms that weathered the financial storms of 1929 was the Dennstedt Company. Albert L. Dennstedt and his family arrived in San Diego in April of 1926 from Davenport, Iowa. A fellow Iowan living in San Diego sent Mr. Dennstedt a copy of the *Union-Tribune* newspaper of January 1, 1926 that extolled the booming local economy and real estate activity. The paper arrived in Iowa during a snowstorm, doubling the impression it made upon the Dennstedt family. Once in San Diego, Albert was followed by his brothers, Chester and Edward. The two brothers joined Mr. Dennstedt in creating the contracting company. The first office of the firm was at 2861 University in the shopping center built in 1926 for Mason B. Boys by Hurlburt & Tifal. The first building permit recorded in the name of the Dennstedt Company was for a home at 3322 Gregory Street in Altadena for W. Nordstrom. In December 1926, Albert Dennstedt began construction on a home for his family at 2511 32nd Street in the Burlingame Manor section of North Park. By 1930, the company had built 20 homes in the neighborhoods of North Park and had moved the office to downtown San Diego.

One of three major residential projects in the spring of 1930 was a single house at 3117 28th Street (*San Diego Daily Transcript*, May 28, 1930). Construction was valued at $13,000 by the Dennstedt Company with plans drawn by Sam Atkins. Owners of the home were Mr. and Mrs. Antoine Frey. A "modified" Spanish style design, the house was said to be one of the largest single residence plans seen at City Hall in some time. The house had eight rooms and four baths. A luxurious two-story residence, the home was described as having a red quarry tile walk and stoop which extended "into the entrance hall with massive arches leading to the spacious living room and dining room which have oak, plank-effect floors, with beamed ceiling in the living room and coved ceiling in the dining room." (*San Diego Daily Transcript*, May 29, 1930, page 1). The Dennstedt Company confidently reported to the *San Diego Daily Transcript* that it had eight other house projects lined up in May 1930. These projects existed in suburban neighborhoods from Point Loma to Casa de Oro.

The *San Diego Union* covered the company in a January 26, 1930 article headlined "Building Concern Sees 1930 as Home Construction Year." The article read:
"Practical assurance that 1930 will be a home building year is offered by the Dennstedt company which continues to announce the beginning of the construction of new homes.

These builders renew their invitation of previous years and invite all home lovers to inspect their work. This week homes were started at 1206 Pennsylvania avenue for Mrs. M.L. Miller and Casa de Oro for William Keller.

Officers of the organization point out that the rapidly increasing scarcity of desirable rental houses coupled with the fact that hundreds of families are discovering the world's best climate will contribute to San Diego's civic beauty by making new homes and better homes a necessity.

It has been one of the intentions of the company to dispel the notion that California homes are cheaply built, and they point with equal pride to a four-room Spanish bungalow or a $20,000 Point Loma mansion, both their products.

One of the building permits obtained by the company this week calls for the wrecking of one of the older types of board houses to be replaced by a modern structure, the value of which will be in proportion to the value of the lot. Executives of the organization, who understand San Diego property values, predict that this will have to be repeated many times where buildings unworthy of their sites and no longer desirable will have to be replaced with modern and more substantially built homes.

At present many of San Diego's best residential sections present a patchwork appearance because of inferior structures. The history of population growth in many other American cities has shown this process to be necessary. Dennstedt officials believe that San Diego has reached the stage where the weeding out of older types of houses must come and that 1930 will do much to swell the civic pride.

The company is trying in every possible way to adapt its organization to the specific needs of the city. Its service is the more remarkable because it may be as complete as the home builder likes, and has in some past work included everything from the selection of the lot to interior decoration.

The success of the company is said to be due to its insistence on friendly personal service and the fact that three brothers are actively engaged in its work, devoting their full time to the business. Although the work is efficiently departmentalized, the homes are not standardized and the individual's problem is always considered."

– *San Diego Union*, January 26, 1930

The company ran an optimistic advertisement on December 28, 1930, saying:

"YOUR HOME SHOULD COME FIRST Build now while building material prices are still low."

"We have ample funds to do your financing."

"This is one of our very latest ideas in modern architecture and one that will be in vogue for many years to come.

Our only wish is that you could walk through this wonderfully planned home and note the many unique and attractive features. We predict there would be very few changes.

Our many years of experience in the construction of homes places us in a position to give you valuable information in the selecting of your home site; the designing of your home and the arranging of your finances, so as not to be a burden.

Begin the NEW YEAR with a firm resolution to own your own HOME, which will afford your children unrestrained play and happiness and does reflect an air of prosperity, comfort and independence."

– *San Diego Union*, January 26, 1930

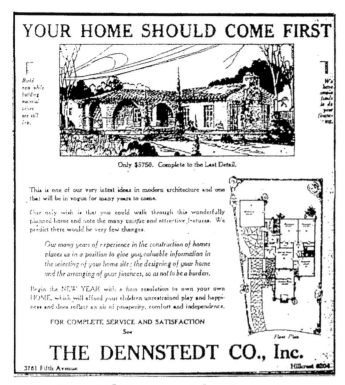

Dennstedt Company Advertisement
San Diego Union, January 26, 1930

The company remained busy and optimistic throughout the depression. On November 9, 1932, the *San Diego Daily Transcript* reported "DENNSTEDT COMPANY HAS HIGH RECORD," noting, "According to figures at City Hall, the Dennstedt Company, local building firm, constructed 83 percent of the total cost of all apartment buildings erected in the month of June and 15 percent of the cost of building permits taken out for dwellings for the month of August. (Out of 200+ licensed contractors in the city.) This is regarded as a marvelous record. . ."

In January 1933, John G. Clark, president of the San Diego Realty Board, published the results of his exhaustive research into local real estate cycles. According to Clark, those cycles since 1900 had approximated seven year swings from cycles of property accumulation and growth to cycles of liquidation. By his calculations, 1926 was the last peak of growth, making 1933 the bottom of the bear market in real estate. Clark's prediction: the current shortage of desirable homes in the city had established the base for the beginning of a new upswing soon to come.

"It is believed that if we did not have families doubling up, that is two and three families living in one home or one flat, we should have in San Diego today a real shortage of housing facilities."
– John G. Clark, *San Diego Union*, January 15, 1933, section 2, page 1

Following the first six months of Franklin D. Roosevelt's administration and operation of the National Recovery Act, a turn-around in the economic condition seemed to be at hand. The last quarter of 1933 began to show signs of new confidence in the national marketplace and on the avenues of commerce, but not in the building industry. In North Park, with the exception of small repair and remodeling jobs, there were only three building permits issued in November and December, two for homes and one for a store building at 30th and Redwood for the Newton Brothers grocery. Contrary to all other local reports, on December 31, 1933, A. L. Dennstedt declared that home building in San Diego was on the uphill side. Dennstedt, with approximately

$27,000 worth of current construction underway, believed that prosperity was just around the corner (*San Diego Union*, December 31, 1933, section 2, page 6).

The Dennstedt Company was on the forefront of the recovery wave. In the second half of 1934, the newly established Federal Housing Administration established the Better Housing Act which was meant to encourage greater home ownership on the part of the American family. The Act made possible, for the first time, long-term loans at low interest with payments meant to be not larger than rental rates. The qualified buyer could purchase a new home offered at a maximum of $16,000 with the new 20-year loan at five percent interest (*San Diego Union*, December 1, 1934, page 3). In October, residents of North Park, along with merchants of the district and the North Park Business Club, established a committee with the purpose of locally supporting the national campaign for establishing the Better Housing Act in the community (*San Diego Daily Transcript*, October 23, 1934, page 8).

The first house in the city constructed with a loan secured under the Federal Housing act was at 3525 Felton Street in the Park Villas section of North Park. The house was built for Mr. and Mrs. C. D. Sparks by the Dennstedt Company under a permit dated November 21, 1934 (Dennstedt ad, *San Diego Union*, December 9, 1934, section 3, page 9).

Other Residential Construction

The Dennstedt Company was an exception in an otherwise slow residential building period. In 1930, besides the Frey house, the only residential projects underway in North Park were a $25,000 ten-unit bungalow court at 2814-32 30th Street overlooking Switzer Canyon from the north, owned by Verne M. Robinson (*San Diego Daily Transcript*, August 11, 1930 Notice of Completion, apartment court and ten garages: Aurora Heights lots 3, 4, 13, 14); and a bungalow court and two houses at 4165, 4171, 4181, and 4185 Utah Street by the team of Cooley and Torgerson (*San Diego Daily Transcript*, January 2, February 21, and March 10, 1930).

Continuing into 1931, most of the North Park building permits were for residences, with a large number of them for lots in the newer neighborhoods of Carmel Heights Extension. Costs of home construction were greatly reduced from those of the previous decade. Among the most successful builders in North Park residential construction for the year were the firms of Cooley & Torgerson with seven jobs, and Robert R. West with five.

From mid-September to the final days of 1932, there were only five permits recorded for North Park houses, and residential development in 1933 was even less. In the fourth quarter of 1934, one new house in North Park was completed and three others were started. No new non-residential buildings were planned or under construction. The lack of local construction projects dried up the market in lumber and other building materials. In order to compensate for this lack, Dixie and Klicka lumber companies had to resort to sales of other household goods, such as the new electrical home service equipment.

The Healy House

The inactivity in construction during 1930 created a pool of available skilled labor. In December, the

National Association of Real Estate Boards (NAREB) published a bulletin urging owners of unimproved lots to build new homes immediately. Funds for home building had accumulated in savings institutions during the preceding year and were available for the prudent investor. The NAREB stated that "today a home that normally would cost $6000 to build can be built for $4200" (*San Diego Daily Transcript*, December 5, 1930).

But newly constructed houses in 1931 were not the only bargains available. Existing homes that were put on the market were offered at a greatly reduced price. The luxurious home at 2711 28th Street had been built for the real estate developer, Martin J. Healy, at a cost of $10,000 in the late fall months of 1927. When it was offered for sale in the highly inflated market of 1928, the price was $42,500. In February 1931, Healy offered the house for resale at the price of $19,500. The two-story stucco house in Spanish Colonial Revival style had been built in the fashionable hill area of North Park overlooking Switzer Canyon, with a distant view of the civic center and San Diego Bay (*San Diego Union*, February 15, 1931, section 2, page 7). The two-story, ten-room house had four bedrooms and three tiled bathrooms. Aside from the usual living rooms downstairs, there was also a servants' quarter. One of the unusual features prominently advertised was "electric refrigeration."

Martin Healy had become a prominent builder of large scale, quality homes in the Blair's Highlands addition of North Park in the late 1920s. His stated reason for resale of the 28th Street house was that he needed cash for his current building project, a 22-unit apartment building in the Bankers' Hill area of San Diego. Healy was intent upon taking advantage of the current low cost of building. Government estimates of building costs in 1931-32 indicated that houses could be built at rates that averaged two-thirds their cost in 1928-29. Cheap labor and the reduced prices of materials accounted for the difference in rates.

2711 28th Street
San Diego Union, February 15, 1931, section 2, page 7

North Park Business Men's Association

In spite of the declining economy, the North Park Business Men's Association continued to act as an unofficial Chamber of Commerce for the community and promoted a generally positive air of "business as usual."

It was announced that the annual picnic which the association sponsored would be held on July 20th at Crystal Pier in Pacific Beach.

> "Over 200 prizes will be given. One of the features of the day will be a scramble after 30 chickens, each of which will belong to the catcher."
>
> – *San Diego Daily Transcript*,
> July 15, 1930, Local Notes, page 8

For the annual community picnic in 1931, arrangements were made for an outing to El Monte Park in the foothills on June 28, 1931. A prize was awarded the best-decorated "conveyance" in the procession of automobiles that carried the community revelers from 30th and University to the mountain picnic grounds (*San Diego Union*, June 25, 1931, Local Notes, page 8).

The "Club" initiated monthly Dollar Days in spring of 1930, continuing through the deepening economic depression. For the April 4, 1932 event, many stores participated with special bargains including: 200 pairs of women's and children's shoes at $1.00 a pair by Harmer & Dent Company; low priced lawn mowers by Berger Hardware Store; and discount-priced Philco automobile radios by Miller Service Incorporated (*San Diego Union*, April 4, 1932, page 3).

Charity was not the only focus of the group. Upkeep and traffic safety in the business district were major concerns. On May 4, 1933, it was reported that:

> "The North Park Business club will ask the City Council for traffic signals at Wightman (North Park Way) and Grim Streets. Attention of the street superintendent has been called by the Club to the 'unsightly condition' in the neighborhood of University Avenue and Thirtieth Street."
>
> – *San Diego Daily Transcript*,
> May 4, 1933, Locals, page 8

Christmas on the Avenue

The North Park Business Men's Association sponsored their first of many annual Christmas celebrations on December 22, 1930. On that day, the North Park Christmas tree was dedicated by the mayor of San Diego at the corner of Kansas Street and University Avenue. The district merchants gave away $1,000 worth of gifts, and every child received a bag of candy from "Santa." For two weeks in advance of the event, North Park's Santa had been sent out all over the city wherever requested to talk to children and to receive their Christmas wish list (*San Diego Union*, December 19, 1930, page 8).

In November 1931, during weekly meetings of the North Park Business Men's Association at John Carter's café on University Avenue, the main topic of discussion was the annual community Christmas festival and how to pay for it in an era of declining business profits (*San Diego Union*, November 25, 1931). The merchant club had never before asked the city or county for help in funding their sponsored community events. However, in a year of diminishing revenues, the time had seemingly come to request help. G. F. Cunningham, North Park electrical contractor, made a formal request of both the county and the city for $300 to help in offsetting costs of the annual Christmas events. He based his request on the traditional sum allowed downtown businessmen for their seasonal activities. His rationale was that there were "thousands of youngsters in North Park who never will see the Plaza." The county denied the request for fear that if it were granted, Escondido, National City, Chula Vista and Coronado would make a similar request (*San Diego Union*, December 1, 1931, page 7). On December 7th, the city council appropriated $300 to the North Park Business Men's Association with the stipulation that the funds be spent under direction of city officials (*San Diego Union*, December 8, 1931, page 10). The local association then raised approximately $1,000 for the events.

A queen was chosen to reign over the 1931 festival and was awarded a valuable fur coat. The streets were decorated and a community Christmas tree was placed at the junction of Kansas and University where the festival party was held. In the three days prior to Christmas, merchants awarded many gifts to shoppers.

In December 1932, the city council voted not to allocate the usual funds for street decorations for the Christmas season. Instead, it was decided to allocate the sum of $1,000 to the City Welfare Commission for the purchase of food for the needy. A like move was made on the part of the North Park Business Men's Association, leaving it up to individual merchants to decorate shop fronts for the season.

The hard pressed were similarly treated the following year, when "approximately 1800 needy families in this city were given baskets containing clothing and toys, distributed through the Community Chest Christmas Exchange since Saturday" (*San Diego Daily Transcript*, December 25, 1933, Locals, page 8).

Charity continued in the fall of 1934, with "pound dances" and "can movies," where admission was a can or pound of any food. At Thanksgiving time, the North Park Junior Lions Club collected from local residents and distributed to the poor 542 cans of food. The cans of vegetables, fruits, soups, pork & beans, and milk were combined in care packages which also contained bread, meat and flour (*San Diego Union*, December 1, 1934, page 3).

In spite of the continuing malaise in the construction industry in late 1934, some consumer confidence in the local economy began to return and businessmen of the 30th and University commercial district became hopeful that the approaching Christmas season would be a more lucrative one than that of the past five years. As the holiday season drew nearer, timid hope turned into firm optimism and plans for a colorful avenue of decorations became more elaborate. Wishing to restore the shopping avenue to the festive days prior to the market crash and economic disasters that followed, the North Park business club announced plans for "gaily festooned Christmas trimmings, dozens of trees" (*San Diego Daily Transcript*, November 22, 1934, Locals, page 8).

What resulted from these exuberant new holiday plans by the North Park merchants was "one of the most attractively decorated districts in the city" (*San Diego Union*, December 25, 1934, page 5). The junction of 30th and University was crisscrossed overhead by cypress streamers. White fir trees were attached to light poles and all decorations were illuminated each night from 5:00 to 11:00 p.m. in what was said to "present a blazing bit of holiday incandescence."

The crowning event, opening the holiday shopping season, took place on Tuesday night, December 11. Christmas lights were turned on for the first time to welcome a parade of decorated automobiles, theme floats and four bands. The North Park Santa Claus led the parade, which was viewed by several thousand people. The crowd included several merchants from the downtown district who "praised the community spirit that makes the North Park district a leader in civic enterprises." Following the parade, a street dance was held in the roped off block of Kansas Street at its intersection with University Avenue (*San Diego Union*, December 12, 1934, page 10). The merchants' cost for the lighting and decorations was in excess of $500, but at the end of the holiday season the North Park Business Men's Association declared business, at last, was "exceptionally good." Better times, it seemed, were just around the corner. The 1934 event established the tradition of a North Park Christmas parade performed annually thereafter with a few exceptions during the war years of the 1940s.

Food Drives at the North Park Theatre

In an effort to improve conditions for those without work, traditional institutions of charity were joined by movie houses that often pledged proceeds earned at special showings or traded theatre tickets for donations of food (*San Diego Union*, November 18, 1931, page 7). The North Park Theatre frequently held special showings and food drives for the indigent residents of the local community. The first charitable event took place in November 1931 as part of a national unemployment relief effort. Every theatre in San Diego held a "midnight" showing of a major feature with revenue from ticket sales turned over to the local agency for unemployment relief. A member of the planning committee for the event was Emil Klicka, owner of the building that housed the Fox West Coast Theatre in North Park (*San Diego Union*,

November 15, 1931, page 6). These special food-drive matinees were scheduled frequently by the North Park Theatre during the early 1930s.

> "Mayor Austin has issued a proclamation making Wednesday, November 25 National Motion Picture Day for San Diego, urging residents to patronize movie theatres on that day on behalf of the unemployed, for whose benefit extra performances will be given."
> – *San Diego Daily Transcript*,
> October 29, 1931

In the years of the Great Depression, admission prices for first run movies at the North Park Theatre were 30 cents for adults, 10 cents for children and 40 cents for loge seats. In spite of the difficult economic conditions for most local business houses, the North Park Theatre never closed due to lack of attendance or operating funds.

Commercial Development Weathers the Storm

Boosterism aside, the shopping center at 30th and University lost several businesses in 1930. Establishments dealing in luxury items were the first to be affected by the failing economy and loss of employment opportunities. Two of the three auto showrooms failed and a like number of cigar stores closed their doors. By 1933, in the depths of the Great Depression, it was no longer possible to buy a new automobile in North Park. There were, however, seven auto repair shops and a used car lot.

Food Drive at the North Park Theatre, 1932

At the same time, the North Park business district gained two new shops specializing in radio receivers for the home and one that specialized in car radios. Vacuum tube radio receivers became the popular commodities of the late 1920s, and in 1930 two additional North Park establishments offered the new improved devices for the modern home. At Christmas 1930, these newly improved receivers, set in elaborate cabinets of pseudo-historic design, were being advertised as the preferred gift of the season. Meanwhile in December, the Maw Music Company at 2912 University Avenue had 16 repossessed pianos for sale (*San Diego Union*, December 9, 1930).

"The Radio Manufacturers Association estimates that between this time and Christmas, $150,000,000 to $200,000,000 will be spent on radio receivers, radio tubes and accessories."

– *San Diego Daily Transcript*,
December 8, 1930

There were no major commercial building projects under construction in North Park in the first half of 1930. Nevertheless, by June, four additional stores were under construction at 29th and University (*San Diego Daily Transcript*, June 28, 1930), and a start was made on a frame-and-stucco store building at 3209 Thorn Street, on the southeast corner of Thorn and 32nd Streets. This $4,000 project for N. Fares by J. D. Manseau continued the development of a small neighborhood strip-mall in the heart of the Altadena neighborhood.

Competition from the new Fox West Coast theatre in Emil Klicka's building down the avenue combined with the growing numbers of out-of-work residents caused the Ramona Theatre to close in 1930. After being converted to sound, the theatre re-opened as the New Ramona in 1933.

The Plymouth Center of the Congregational Church continued to be the site of community forums. In May, the topic was "Unemployment;" in November the subject discussed was "Restoring Business Confidence." In 1930, both topics were growing concerns locally as well as nationally. R. A. Mathewson, director of the San Diego free employment bureau, led the May discussion, while E. K. McCormick presented the latter topic.

Emil Klicka's boast in June 1928 that "within a few years we are going to have a city of our own in this district" must have struck a chord of sympathy with many local residents. In September 1930, 2,000 residents of the North Park District petitioned the City Council for an adjunct city hall in the 30th and University neighborhood (*San Diego Daily Transcript*, September 29, 1930). On October 6, 1930, City Manager Fred M. Lockwood reported to the City Council that if a branch city hall were established in North Park, the cost of maintaining it would be approximately $345 a month (*San Diego Daily Transcript*, October 6, 1930, Local Notes, page 8). Later that autumn, Mr. Lockwood stated that there was no need for branch city halls in San Diego, not a surprising statement in a fiscal year of severe budget cuts in the operating divisions and other municipal departments including police and fire units.

In 1931, Jack Hartley converted the old bakery ovens on Ray Street into a new storeroom and apartment at No. 3836. Another new store building with an Art Deco zigzag façade was built by contractor J. C. Kelley at 3793-95 30th Street. That building immediately became the grocery store for the Great Atlantic & Pacific Tea Company. Three other commercial building projects got under way in 1931. Two of those broke new ground in April at the intersection of 30th and Lincoln Streets, expanding the local business area. One of those on the northeast corner of the intersection at 4001-15 30th Street was a super service station (*San Diego Daily Transcript*, April 1, 1931, Building Permit). The other, on the southwest corner at 3990-94 30th Street, was a store building of hollow tile construction built by Alexander Schreiber (*San Diego Daily Transcript*, April 3, 1931, Building Permit). Upon completion, the building was occupied by the Staple Cash & Carry Wholesale Grocery. The last commercial building start of the year was at 3925 Ohio Street, an office and warehouse for Dixie Lumber & Supply Company. The $5,000 permit was issued to builder G. D. Martin on the 11th of December. When completed, the frame and stucco building reflected an older residential style with third story dormer windows on the roof.

In November 1933, the nation voted to repeal Prohibition, and on December 5, the sale and consumption of liquor became legal again. For the next several months, the State of California was faced with the task of issuing licenses to retailers who wished to take advantage of the new liberal period. Early in 1934, five new businesses were opened in the North Park commercial district. Two retail liquor stores opened on 30th Street and one on University Avenue. One billiards room and beer bar set up shop on University Avenue and one restaurant that sold beer opened on 30th Street. These businesses were:

- W. A. McKee Liquors, 3395 30th at Upas (southeast corner)
- Charles Cohen wines and liquors, 3793 30th (shares building with A & P)
- Eugene Lawler Liquor, 2859 University Avenue
- Henry De Bus billiards and Ostrander & Baugher beer, 3034 University Avenue
- A. W. Porter, beer and Sypher & Duffy restaurant, 3056 University Avenue.

In July 1934, a frame building was started at 3015 Wightman that became the produce market for Matsui & Couchman fruit sellers. The light wood-frame store was built by O. E. Mark, and was removed in 1939 for the construction of a larger, steel framed building for Piggly Wiggly grocery. Matsui was one of several Japanese fruit sellers who operated produce markets in North Park, who included Y. Oihara fruits (1929) at 2561 University, and H. Y. Kondo fruits (1929) at 2901 University (with Liberty Food Co).

Mudd Department Store

North Park got its first comprehensive department store following completion of the Newman/IOOF Building in the winter of 1929-30. The E. N. Mudd Company that occupied the retail space on the corner of Kansas and University offered a complete stock of ready-made clothing for the entire family as well as a dry goods department. The unfortunate timing of its opening must have brought a year of disappointing sales as the North Park shopper grew more and more conservative with the deepening economic depression and expanding unemployment.

After little more than a year in operation the Mudd Company was forced to close its ready-to-wear department and find less extensive quarters for its dry goods section. In 1932, it opened in a small space on 30th Street as E. N. Mudd Dry Goods and by 1933 it was no longer a part of the North Park business environment.

At the clearance sale in February 1931, many bargains were offered the customers. Among the many advertised reductions were men's pure wool sweaters, $5.79; women's fur trimmed dress coats, $39.00; boy's wool knickers, $1.00; and girl's sweaters, $2.35. No other department store followed in the 30th and University district until the J. C. Penney Company opened the first segment of its store in 1942.

E. N. Mudd Department Store Advertisement
San Diego Union, February 15, 1931, page 13

Silver Gate Masonic Lodge

One of the most significant building projects in North Park began in the drafting room of the Quayle Brothers' architectural office in June 1930. There, plans were being drawn for a major Masonic temple for the Silver Gate Lodge to be located on the corner of Wightman and Utah Streets, in the heart of the North Park commercial district. It was reported that:

"The campaign of The Silver Gate Lodge for funds to erect a temple on Wightman Street will be under direction of Ed Fletcher. It is to continue for ten days beginning June 2. The amount to be raised is $75,000."
– *San Diego Daily Transcript*,
May 17, 1930

A building permit for the Silver Gate Masonic Lodge was issued to the builder, B. O. Larsen, on April 21, 1931, and cornerstone-setting ceremonies followed on April 24th. The three-story building was estimated to cost $52,000 in the Building Permit. The contract for the building projected a completion date in August. However, by August a public announcement stated that "work is progressing satisfactorily," and that the building would be dedicated in October (*San Diego Daily Transcript*, August 10, 1931, Local Notes, page 8). The actual completion date for the project was December 2, 1931 (*San Diego Daily Transcript*, December 2, 1931, Notice of Completion), with occupation of the building occurring on December 28th. Final cost of the building furnished was in excess of $75,000.

"Judge Clarence Harden will be the orator Saturday afternoon at 2 o'clock at the ceremonies incident to the laying of the cornerstone of the new Masonic Temple at Wightman and Utah Streets. Several hundred Masons will be in attendance."
– *San Diego Daily Transcript*,
April 24, 1931

Dedication of the lodge building was a spectacular event for North Park in the spring of 1932. Present at the dedication ceremonies were the grand master of the Masonic order of California, Robert Brainerd Gaylord, six grand lodge officers, all officers of the eighteen county lodges, R. P. Wakeman, master of the Silver Gate lodge, and other local dignitaries. Dinner was served in the banquet hall to 200 members and guests. The dedication ceremonies were attended by more than 500 people (*San Diego Union*, April 20, 1932, page 10).

The reinforced concrete building was described as "modern throughout." The architects had been asked to design the temple to resemble King Solomon's Temple in Jerusalem (to which the lodge members trace the beginning of their lodge). The Quayle brothers hypothesized that the modern temple should resemble a blending of Mesopotamian Ziggurat and Egyptian Temple, which were features already found in the highly fashionable Art Deco style of the 1920s to 1940s. Popularized by the *Exposition International des Arts Decoratifs et Industriels Mondernes* held in Paris in 1925, by 1929 Art Deco had become the favored style for detailing buildings from skyscrapers to gas stations. Art Deco zigzags, chevrons, and other stylized and geometric forms grace the Masonic Temple façade. Outstanding features of the building include the entryway, third floor lodge room decorated with elaborate Egyptian motifs, an auditorium, kitchen, library and committee rooms.

Silver Gate Masonic Temple, 1931
Photo courtesy of the San Diego Historical Society (#Sensor 11-70)

Municipal Golf Course

On January 15, 1931, it was announced that the San Diego City Council had asked Balboa Park superintendent John G. Morley to present the council with an estimated cost for a nine-hole grassed municipal golf course. It was emphasized that the city was not interested in "a luxury expenditure" but only in "unemployment relief" (*San Diego Union*, January 15, 1931, page 1).

Superintendent Morley's requested budget of $30,000 for a nine-hole course was appropriated from the general fund by the city council at its meeting of January 21st. It was noted by the council that the appropriation was "an emergency measure to aid the local employment situation" (*San Diego Union*, January 22, 1931, section 2, page 1). Park commissioners estimated that the project would afford work for approximately 40 men employed three days a week. Employment was limited to men with families only. In order to apply the funds solely to workers' salaries, the city council suggested that private citizens who had been prominent in obtaining a municipal golf facility cover the architect's fee.

William Bell, the notable golf architect of Pasadena, was chosen to complete the design for the nine-hole course. The mayor and councilmen requested that the course be designed in such a way that it could be expanded to a full 18-hole course in the future. A special fund was established to receive profits from the new course for the purpose of the future expansion. Work on the grounds began February 2, 1931 with a scheduled completion date of August 1. The chosen site bordered 28th Street in the far southeast corner of Balboa Park (*San Diego Union*, February 2, 1931, section 2, page 1).

The golf course affected roadway planning. A major commercial route into the North Park commercial center, 32nd Street, continued to present problems of congestion and the hazards that accompanied heavy use. Stop signs were removed in an effort to improve traffic flow and a speed limit of 20 miles per hour was enforced. A new road was proposed by the city council to connect Pershing Drive with 32nd Street in order to improve traffic flow into North Park from downtown. The proposed road would have traveled through Switzer Canyon under the 30th Street Bridge emerging at Thorn and 32nd Streets. However, the new municipal golf course planned for Balboa Park made that traffic link untenable and Redwood Street became the link instead (*San Diego Union*, November 13, 1931, page 9).

Improvements were also made to Pershing Drive, which had remained the 30-foot wide, two-lane road first improved in the early 1920s. As traffic increased, so did the hazards of travel up the steep grade with its precipitous canyon-side drop. An improvement project in the spring of 1931 widened Pershing Drive to 50 feet and brought a renewed measure of safety and comfort to the well-traveled road (*San Diego Daily Transcript*, May 18, 1931, Local Notes, Page 8).

Morley Field Recreation Center

Offsetting the decline in residential and commercial building activity in the first half of 1932 was another city-sponsored project in Balboa Park. At North Park's back door, the northeast corner of the park had historically lacked the development given to the central and western mesa areas. The rough chaparral-covered corner of the Park had "remained in practically the same condition as it was when Cabrillo sailed into San Diego bay" (*San Diego Union*, October 9, 1932, section 2, page 1). In 1931, the city's special project for unemployment relief that had resulted in a municipal golf course on the eastern park boundary began to shift that focus. The city was eager to continue creating municipal projects that would offer temporary jobs for the unemployed. In the winter of 1932, the city council, under the leadership of third district councilman Joseph J. Russo, began discussions with the North Park Business Men's Association concerning the development of a recreation center in the northeast region of Balboa Park.

"City Manager Gregory is making preparation for the construction of the $72,000 recreation area in Balboa Park, one of the projects to be financed with the $300,000 unemployment relief bond issue. Mr. Gregory expects to put men to work on Monday, April 4th."

– *San Diego Daily Transcript*,
March 24, 1932, Local Notes, page 8)

In March 1932, at a special election, San Diego voters approved a $300,000 bond issue for unemployment relief. On March 29th, a project committee of North Park residents including William Miller, president, George Klicka, Paul Hartley, Arthur Jenson, E. C. Ryan, Horace May, and city manager Robert Gregory, revealed plans for a center of approximately ten acres (*San Diego Union*, March 30, 1932, page 3). The plans included a swimming pool, heating plant, clubhouse, two baseball diamonds, eight double tennis courts, ten shuffleboard courts, children's

wading pool and sand pits. The swimming pool was planned to be 130 feet long by 65 feet wide with depths of 2 ½ to 9 feet. A budget for the construction of the center was estimated at $75,000. Following approval of the project by the city council, a crew of 25 men began grading the site on Monday, April 4th, 1932 (*San Diego Union*, April 2, 1932, page10, and *San Diego Union*, April 6, 1932, page 7).

The recreation center had been a plan of park superintendent John Morley since 1914 in his early days of responsibility for park development. In that year, Morley had set aside the northeast corner of the park for major outdoor recreation grounds. Supported by public desire to provide relief work for the growing number of unemployed families in San Diego, Morley's project was finally funded by the City Council. Plans for a summer opening of the center had to be postponed as completion of the large pool kept being delayed. Finally, plans were made for a spectacular public dedication to be held on New Year's Day 1933 (*San Diego Union*, April 27, 1932, page 6, and *San Diego Union*, October 9, section 2, page 1).

"The oft-berated depression has accomplished one new step in carrying to a conclusion the intricate Nolen plan of city development that a decade of prosperous years was unable to bring about – the building of a swimming pool and recreation center at the foot of Texas street in Balboa Park."

– *San Diego Union*, October 9, 1932,
section 2, page 1

"Exhibition tennis matches by teams of prominent champions will be one of the

189

features of the dedication ceremonies of the new municipal swimming pool in Balboa Park on New Year's Day. The games will be played in the new courts at the recreational center in the park."

– *San Diego Daily Transcript*,
December 27, 1932, Local Notes, page 8

"Councilman Joseph J. Russo, vice-mayor, next Sunday will dedicate the new municipal swimming pool in Balboa Park. The ceremonial will be in charge of the North Park Business club. A feature not heretofore mentioned will be the beauty contest to select 'Miss San Diego'."

– *San Diego Daily Transcript*,
December 28, 1932, Local Notes, page 8

January 1, 1933 was a warm, sunny day well suited to the dedication ceremonies of the municipal pool and its elaborate recreation grounds. Thousands attended the ceremonies which included a parade, drill teams of the Veterans of Foreign Wars, a concert by the Sciots band, and a beauty pageant of 13 competing young women (*San Diego Union*, January 1, 1933, page 1). Dave Millan, president of the Chamber of Commerce; Albert V. Goedel, city manager; and Joseph J. Russo, city councilman, judged the competition for beauty queen. The winner was Alberta McKellop.

The ceremony and program events were under the direction of the North Park Business Men's Association with its president, William Miller, the chief sponsor along with councilman Russo. One week later, on another warm and sunny weekend, the pool was so crowded with swimmers that the dressing rooms became overcrowded and admissions had to be cancelled three times. On Saturday, January 7th, nearly 1,000 swimmers crowded the facilities. Accurate count of participants was not known as the cash register was so overtaxed that it became inoperable after registering 761 admissions (*San Diego Union*, January 9, 1933, page 1).

At its regular meeting the following Tuesday, the city council heard William Miller present a request for additional funds to expand the facilities. Miller overcame some of the councilmen's opposition by asserting that more than 100,000 residents lived within three miles of the pool and playgrounds. The council voted 5 to 2 an appropriation of $3,000 to fund additional tennis courts, shuffleboard courts and another baseball diamond (*San Diego Union*, January 10, 1933, page 5).

When completed, the new landscaped recreation center and municipal golf course turned the former undeveloped northeast section of Balboa Park into North Park's backyard playground. For the following two decades, many of the municipal events, including the annual opening of the pool, were planned and sponsored by the North Park Business Men's Association.

The annual picnic sponsored by the North Park Business club in 1933 was held on June 25th in the eucalyptus grove by the Balboa Park municipal pool. All San Diegans were invited to attend by the local merchants. Hal Royle of the local branch of the First National Bank was in charge of the events. Royle was assisted by William Miller (Miller Super Service), Fred McSpadden (North Park Theatre) and William Cowling (Dixie Lumber Company) (*San Diego Daily Transcript*, June 22, 1933, Locals, page 8). No admission was charged and free coffee and lemonade were offered the revelers. Those who attended were urged to bring their own lunch. A crowd of more than 12,000 was in attendance at the day-long festival. The opening event was a scramble for balloons carrying theatre tickets to the North Park Theatre. Shoe and sack races for various age groups followed. At the conclusion of the races, a concert was given by the 85-piece Fox North Park Theatre band led by C. E. Romero (*San Diego Union*, June 26, 1933, page 5).

Dances were held on the tennis courts to music by the Clark Brothers' orchestra. A capacity crowd of swimmers enjoyed the pool and free style swimming races for children and adults were held throughout the afternoon. A special event was the exhibition diving by three of the 1932 Olympic swim team members. Closing the afternoon activities was a beauty queen parade and competition which resulted in three winners: Alice Bradley, Alberta McKellop, and Betty Jackson (*San Diego Union*, June 26, 1933, page 5).

Following the festival at the pool and tennis courts, an exhibition game was held on the new baseball diamond (*San Diego Union*, June 26, 1933, section 2, page 4). The city's championship North Park Grays defeated the Old Town team with a closing score of 13 to 2. The North Park line-up included Carlson, Misner, Hunt, Villarino, Holt, Harrett, Rowe, Luscomb, and Robinson.

> "Gathering 15 hits, five of which went for extra bases, the North Park Grays thumped Old Town, 13 to 2, in a seven-inning game yesterday at the new municipal baseball field in Balboa park."
>
> – *San Diego Union*, June 26 1933, section 2, page 4

The North Park Grays

Three exhibition games were held in June to raise money for bleachers for the new municipal baseball diamond. It was reported that approximately 2,000 watched the first game on June 11th (*San Diego Union* June 12, 1933, section 2, page 3). Although the North Park Grays had been the 1932-33 champions of the new city baseball league, they finished third in the following season.

The area was named Morley Field in honor of John G. Morley, Park Superintendent of all City parks from 1911 to 1938, by adoption of the following resolution of the Park Commission on June 28, 1934:

> "NOW THEREFORE, BE IT RESOLVED that the Recreation Area in Balboa Park along Upas Street from

Alabama to Arnold Streets be, and it is hereby officially named 'Morley Field.'"

In December 1934, the Morley Field recreation center in Balboa Park received twelve new roque and shuffleboard courts. These were dedicated on Sunday, December 9th, in a ceremony sponsored by the North Park Business Club. The North Park Theatre boys' band under the direction of C. E. Romero entertained. Public addresses were given by Hal Royle, president of the Business Club, and John Morley, superintendent of Parks. An exhibition tournament followed (*San Diego Union*, December 8, 1934, page 6).

The year in sports ended in controversy over which baseball team had home rights on the field at the University Heights playground. The North Park Grays, champions in the city's league, claimed the rights but were turned out by the city recreation department and all week-end amateur games at the contested playground were cancelled. The North Park team withdrew from the city league in protest (*San Diego Union*, December 22, 1934, section 2, page 3).

Emil Klicka & the Consolidated Aircraft Corporation

On January 1, 1933, the day of the big celebration at the recreation center in Balboa Park, the city of San Diego was also celebrating the announcement that Consolidated Aircraft Corporation of Buffalo New York would be moving its factory and administrative offices to San Diego's Lindbergh Field. The firm, under the leadership of Major Reuben H. Fleet, was one of the most important aeronautical plants in the United States at the time. With a current investment of $3 million and 1,000 employees, Fleet's operation represented a rich industrial prize for San Diego. The deal between the city and Consolidated Aircraft had been closed by the Harbor Commission. One of North Park's leading citizens, Emil Klicka, had represented the Commission and the city in the negotiations at Buffalo. In a *San Diego Union* report concerning the success of the negotiations, Klicka was cited as being San Diego's chief representative in the successful completion of the deal with Consolidated Aircraft.

"A warm tribute was paid by (T. C.) Macaulay, manager of the chamber of commerce, to the splendid work of Klicka who is a member of the harbor commission and also chairman of the chamber's industrial committee. Klicka represented the civic organization and the harbor commission in deliberations at Buffalo."

– *San Diego Union*,
June 25, 1933, page 10

Chapter 13
Expo Years ~ 1935-1936

The tremors of renewed prosperity that were felt up and down the commercial avenues of North Park at the close of 1934 began to intensify in the early weeks of the new year. After months of no activity in the local real estate market, a turn around began in the spring of 1935. In April, the director of the State Employment Relief Association reported that "it is becoming difficult to find experienced workers in many lines of trade" (*San Diego Union*, April 14, 1935, page 12, "Building Trades Gains Point To New Prosperity"). The Better Housing Act sponsored by offices of The Federal Housing Administration (FHA) was making home ownership easier for the average citizen by offering long-term loans with minimal monthly payments. The director of the local Better Housing Act declared in April that prosperity "seems at last to be a coming reality."

At the end of the first half of 1935, the city planning commission advised that North Park was the leader in home building activities with 63 new residences at a total construction cost of $163, 345 (*San Diego Union*, Sept. 6, 1935, page 3: "North Park Sets Pace In San Diego Residential Construction Activity"). This record was followed in the third quarter by 25 housing starts and 16 completions. On September 30th, an announcement by the Federal Bureau of Labor Statistics revealed that "expenditures for residential buildings were more than three times as great in August 1935 as in the same month of the preceding year" (*San Diego Daily Transcript*, page 1). The fourth quarter ended with 21 residential building starts and 11 homes completed in North Park.

In the first quarter of 1936, North Park had 20 new permits for residences, 2 for apartments, 3 for store buildings and 13 notices of residential completions. Those numbers indicated that the revival of construction, cautiously begun in the spring of 1935, was vigorously continuing. At the time, credit for that revival of home building was ascribed to the enactment of the Better Housing Act. With a low down payment, low interest rate, long-term loan guaranteed by the FHA, a family with a low to moderate income could again afford to own a home (*San Diego Union*, December 27, 1936, section 2, page 1). The problem now became finding a home in that affordable category. Several years of little or no construction had left San Diego with an extreme housing shortage (*San Diego Union*, September 27, 1936, section 2, page 3).

The Klicka "Studio Bungalo"

The economic revival was especially good news for George Klicka, manager of the Klicka Lumber Company, as he had lost his family home in the downturn.

A 1935 advertisement for the company declared,
"Busy Days Are Here Again!
Carpenters are busy!
Trucks are busy!
We are busy supplying materials for the Exposition buildings and new housing facilities for Exposition visitors."

– *San Diego Union*,
April 28, 1935, section 2, page 9

Perceiving the combination of abundantly available financing, improved employment offerings, and a shortage of appropriate houses for sale as an opportunity to rescue the Klicka Lumber Company from economic catastrophe, George Klicka developed plans for a low-cost kit house. To create a more affordable home for the wage earner of modest income, Klicka and his company of designers and builders simplified the costly construction techniques and design styles of the 1920s. The result was a pre-fabricated package of wooden frame-and-panel construction offered in several price ranges beginning as low as $2,222.22. The design reflected George Klicka's personal slogan that "to own a home and fireside is every man's ambition and every family's heritage."

In January 1936, after months of refining the plans and construction techniques, the Klicka *Studio Bungalo* was readied for public introduction at the California Pacific International Exposition in Balboa Park (*San Diego Union*, April 1, 1936, page 5).

A Klicka kit bungalow was set up in the Model Town exhibit at the Federal Building in Balboa Park. On April 11, 1936, this exhibit was dedicated by officials of the Federal Housing Administration. At the dedication

ceremony, it was announced that Labor Day, September 7, would be "Klicka House Day."

It was planned that on that day the $2,500 model *Studio Bungalo* would be awarded to a lucky attendee of the exhibition. That person was Mrs. Annie Ball of Coronado (*San Diego Union*, September 22, 1936, page 2).

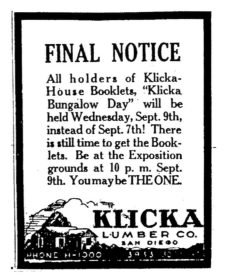

– Klicka Advertisement
San Diego Union,
June 21, 1936

In June 1936, the FHA approved the house design for guaranteed low cost loans (*San Diego Union*, January 31, 1937, section 2, page 6).

The structure of the Klicka bungalow rested on a regulation concrete foundation and footings. Redwood mud-sills and seasoned lumber including kiln-dried Ponderosa pine were included in all models. In order to keep costs low, economy of materials, equipment and space was incorporated in the design and construction. The house was described by George Klicka as follows:

"The construction of this home is of California knotty pine, with a two-tone El Rey Nu-Art composition shingle roof; complete sanitary plumbing fixtures, automatic water heater, modern electric fixtures in every room and large casement windows throughout. Beside the two bedrooms, there is a kitchen of ample size, with tile sink and built-in features, large and modern breakfast room, hall and linen closets and a commodious living room. Each bedroom also has its own large clothes closet.

The wall construction, which is a detailed flush wall, incorporates studs. This treatment of the walls has now reached the very highest degree of perfection and is recognized as one of the greatest achievements of modern building by lumbermen all along the Pacific coast and across the South as far as Florida. The new wall treatment, known as the Monterey finishes, consists entirely of oil paints."

The photograph caption notes "Studio bungalows built by Klicka Lumber Co. to provide a real home at moderate cost, with their owners, are 1-I.O. Swigart, 3211 Adams ave; 2-Demonstration house, 3019 Thirtieth st.; 3-Ivy Howe, 3685 Monroe ave.; 4-J.A. Wolff, Fifty-first st. and Monroe ave.; 5-G.T. Morton, 7781 University ave."

– *San Diego Union*, June 14, 1936

The patented Klicka "Studio Bungalo" was advertised in a brochure by the Capital Lumber Company in Sacramento, California, as "Introducing all-wood, plasterless construction, ultra-modern design and detail achieved thru brilliant engineering."

Examples of several of the bungalows were constructed in a Model Town at the Klicka Lumber Company on 30th Street in North Park early in 1937 (*San Diego Daily Transcript*, March 29, 1937).

The bungalow kits were sold up and down the Pacific coast and as far east as Florida. George Klicka's *Job Record Book* documents 1,125 houses constructed in San Diego County between the introduction of the kits in the winter of 1935-36 and the late summer of 1941. Although over 100 of these were built in North Park and University Heights, most of them have been replaced or 'modernized' beyond recognition. However, some still have the curbside image of the original design, including a five-unit bungalow court at 3988 Kansas Street, near Lincoln Avenue (Job #6, built by O. D. Arnold), and 4575 Shirley Ann Place (Job #91, built by C. F. Stephens and started April 12, 1937). Although the façade is stucco, this kit house retains its original wood interior walls and wood trim under the eaves. Other Klicka bungalows retaining their heritage include 3345 Dale Street (Job #90, built by Ben Murphy and started April 5, 1937); and 3666 Alabama Street (Job #725, built by A. H. Ekern and started March 18, 1940).

Two months after the close of the Exposition in Balboa Park, the FHA office in San Diego declared that the exhibition of model homes at the Federal Building had been a success as many of the 56 models exhibited had been duplicated by local builders. Stuart Ripley, manager of the FHA exhibition sent a letter to George Klicka with encouraging news about the popularity of the house which Klicka had designed and displayed as house #26 in the FHA exhibit. Ripley's letter read in part:

"It is interesting to know that 77 designs have been sold of House No. 26, which you designed and known as the Klicka studio bungalow. During the past 30 days we have received four times as many inquiries regarding Model 26 as any other of the 56 homes in this exhibit."
– *San Diego Union*, December 6, 1936,
Building Section, page 4

George's brother Emil was also a part of Exposition success. In 1934, the newly formed Board of Directors of the California Pacific Exposition appointed Emil Klicka Treasurer of the exposition for 1935. On June 3, 1935, the board of directors of the Merchant's Association of San Diego commended the directors of the exposition for their appointment of Klicka and recommended that he be kept on as Treasurer for the 1936 year. In the resolution adopted by the Merchant's Association, Emil Klicka was commended as a "San Diego citizen who commands the community's respect, and who is interested only in the financial success of the Exposition and in San Diego's future" (*San Diego Union*, June 4, 1935, page 2).

Klicka Lumber Company Advertisement

Klicka Studio Bungalo Advertisement

Klicka Lumber Company "Package House" Advertisement

The Dennstedt Company

Residential construction news was not limited to the Klicka "studio bungalo" in 1936. "San Diegans not only built more homes in 1936 than in the last six years, but they spent more money on each home constructed during the year" (*San Diego Union*, January 17, 1937, Building News Section, page 1). That was the statement made by city planning commissioner, Glenn Rick, following his analysis of the home construction data compiled by the county recorder. According to his analysis of the documentation, the 1,712 homes built in 1936 more than doubled the total of the previous year. Furthermore, the average cost of those homes, $3,005, was 12% greater than that of 1935.

In a list of 24 local communities, North Park was credited with the greatest number of residences completed, 284. Average construction cost of those homes was given as $2,540. The average 1936 home in San Diego was said to be "a five-room frame and stucco dwelling with one bath and two bedrooms" (*San Diego Union*, January 17, 1937, Building News Section, page 1).

One of the North Park residential projects that created a measure of interest in the closing weeks of 1936

was a 3-apartment unit at 2828 Upas Street on the corner of Utah Street. The project, designed and built by the A. E. & A. L. Dennstedt Building Company for Henry Landt, was reportedly unique by combining a duplex with an apartment over a double garage (*San Diego Union*, December 13, 1936, section 2, page 4).

An unusual feature was the two-story arrangement of the duplex apartments. Landt, a draftsman for the Dennstedt Company, stated that the project was the first true "studio" apartments built in San Diego with living rooms on the first floor and bedrooms on the second level. A further innovation was large steel-frame windows that rounded a corner in the fashion of international modernism. The exterior of the building was stucco on the lower floor and wide boards on the upper. The entire 'modernistic' exterior was painted white with thin, light blue lines. When completed the building was said to be "modern colonial." The apartments were planned and furnished for the higher rent category. Cost of the building was approximately $10,000. The building was completed in early February 1937 (*San Diego Daily Transcript*, February 9, 1937, Notice of Completion).

North Park Go-Getters

Meeting at the Silver Gate Masonic temple on Utah Street on January 31, 1935, the North Park Business Men's Association installed its new officers for 1935 including Clyde Cahill, president and Daphne Murray, secretary. One of the agenda items for the meeting was the re-naming of the organization. Henceforth, the Association was to be known as the North Park Community Club. In a review of the club's work since 1917, Hal Royle, the past president "paid tribute to Mrs. Mary J. Hartley, mother of Jack and Paul Hartley, well known North Park business men. She was a real pioneer, Royle said" (*San Diego Union*, February 1, 1935). Earlier, the association had established a Women's Auxiliary of the organization. The first president of the Auxiliary was Mrs. William Miller, who played a large part in organizing the fund-raising events for the North Park Sign.

Officials of the Ford Motor Company invited members of various civic business and professional groups to attend, as guests of the company, a musical performance in the Ford Bowl (Starlight Bowl). On July 2, 150 members of the club attended a performance of the Los Angeles Symphony Orchestra. The master of ceremonies announced that the North Park group was the first to accept the invitation of the Ford Company (*San Diego Union*, July 3, 1935).

On December 3, the club held the final monthly meeting of the year and elected new officers for 1936. Fred McSpadden, manager of the North Park Theatre, became president of the men's group and Gertrude Bird was elected to preside over the Women's Auxiliary. During the meeting, J. E. Dryer, one of the new merchants of the district, stated that he brought his new business to 30th and University because of the community's cohesive spirit in civic affairs. "Their efforts out there would do credit to a well-organized group for the entire city. They are up-and-doing folks. I wish that San Diego had more districts like the North Park go-getters," Dryer was reported as saying (*San Diego Union*, December 4, 1935, page 3). Dryer's business was the Standard Furniture Company, located at 3918 30th Street.

The *San Diego Union* later reported that Mayor Percy Benbough praised the group, saying that if the entire city had the progressive spirit of the 30th Street and University Avenue residents and business people, San Diego's population soon would increase to 250,000. "The pull-together spirit of the North Parkers is commendable," the mayor said. "Your cooperation and friendliness well could be copied by every other section of the city." The article also noted that the Women's Auxiliary was complimented on its growth. Started in late 1934 with 14 members, it had 141 members by January 1936 (*San Diego Union*, January 1, 1936).

Christmas Festivals

Less than a week after that meeting, a dramatic example of the community boosterism by what Dryer called "the North Park go-getters" was played out on University Avenue in the form of the city's first community pageant of the holiday season (*San Diego Union*, December 8, 1935, page 8). Begun in 1934, the North Park Christmas parade, in 1935, reached the full-blown form it was to continue as a tradition to the end of the century. Once again sponsored by the North Park Community Club and Women's Auxiliary, the 1935 parade was an extravaganza of gaily decorated floats, musical groups, and nine divisions of parading representatives of every major business in the community (*San Diego Union*, December 10, 1935, page 5). The 1935 and 1936 presidents of the Club, Clyde Cahill and Fred McSpadden, led the parade as Grand Marshals. Val Dage was chief of staff for the entire event. The musical groups included the San Diego Army & Navy Academy band, the V.F.W. Drum and Bugle Corps, the Bonham Brothers Boys' Band, and the Merkeley's Musical Maids. The winner of the first place prize in the musical category was the Army & Navy Academy Band. The Standard Furniture Company was awarded a gold cup for the best float (*San Diego Union*, December 11, 1935, page 3).

Beginning at 7:00 p.m. on Tuesday, December 10th, the three-mile long parade entered the North Park business district at 33rd Street, proceeded west on University Avenue to Idaho Street where it turned north to Polk Avenue, then east to 30th Street and south on that thoroughfare to Landis Street. All trolley and automobile traffic was stopped for the duration of the event as an estimated 30,000 spectators crowded the sidewalks and streets of the district. The parade was halted occasionally to allow police units to force the enthusiastic crowds of people back onto the sidewalks. As the parade approached each new block, the special red and green decorative street lights were turned on by Hampton Stevenson. Telephone poles along the route were decorated with silvered Christmas trees. Cypress boughs and wreaths festooned the cross wires along the streets. In addition, 54 illuminated trees decorated University Avenue (*San Diego Union*, December 4, 1935, page 12).

Following the parade, the illuminated street decorations were turned on every night throughout the Christmas season. The officers of the Club declared the 1935 holiday event to be the "greatest and most successful" one in their many years of outstanding celebrations (*San Diego Union*, December 11, 1935, page 3).

In 1936, the sixth annual Christmas festival centered on the 30th Street and University Avenue business district was even more spectacular than all previous ones. The event was held on Friday evening, December 11th. The two-mile long parade formed at University Avenue and 32nd Street at 6:30 p.m. and ended at Texas Street and University Avenue. It was led by Mayor Percy Benbough on horseback and included more than 60 decorated automobiles and floats. In addition, there were seven musical groups including the 140-member Bonham Boys' Band (*San Diego Union*, December 10, 1936, page 5).

The Avenue was decorated with 64 ten-foot, silvered Christmas trees, innumerable garlands, strings of colored lights, and twinkling illuminated stars strung in canopies across the street. As in the past, the merchants of the Club sponsored the event. The general chairman of the festival was O. H. Stevenson. Paul Hartley was chairman of the parade committee (*San Diego Evening Tribune*, December 10, 1936, page 5).

The North Park Sign

In 1935 and 1936, the business club and women's auxiliary did far more than hold successful Christmas festivities. They were instrumental in the creation of North Park's quintessential landmark: the North Park Sign.

The advent of neon lighting as popular commercial signage in the 1920s grew from a limited market into a booming fad during the 1930s. By 1934, North Park building permits were granted largely for neon signage for businesses on University Avenue and 30th Street. In April 1935, the business club announced the organization's desire to have a great sign mounted across the intersection of 30th and University. It was planned that the sign would have the community name illuminated in neon. The Women's Auxiliary of the Club, under the leadership of Mrs. William Miller, volunteered to spearhead a fund-raising event to contribute to the cost of creating and installing the sign (*San Diego Union*, April 12, 1935, section 2, page 1). On April 24th, the Auxiliary hosted a card party and dance in the Tent ballroom of the Nordberg Building at Grim and University.

> "A series of card parties is to be held by the Women's Auxiliary to the North Park Business Men's Club to raise money for a great neon sign to hang over the intersection of University Avenue and 30th Street. The parties will be held in the Tent Ballroom, University and Grim Avenues."
>
> – *San Diego Daily Transcript*, April 11, 1935, Locals page 8)

A total of $400 was raised by the Women's Auxiliary (*San Diego Union*, December 4, 1935, page 3).

As no structure of the kind proposed by the Club had been erected before over San Diego streets, a new ordinance permitting such work had to be written. On April 20th, the San Diego city manager sent to the city council an ordinance that would allow a community organization to erect an electric sign across a public thoroughfare (*San Diego Union*, April 21, 1935, section 1, page 6). The proposed ordinance forbade inclusion of any signage other than the name of the community. That ordinance was approved by the city council at its meeting on April 24, 1935, clearing the way for the installation of the first sign over the intersection of 30th Street and University Avenue identifying the community of North Park (*San Diego Union*, April 25, 1935, page 6).

On Saturday evening, July 6, 1935, the sign was dedicated in place by Mayor Percy Benbough. The dedication ceremony was preceded by a parade down University Avenue that featured, among other participants, the Bonham Brothers' Boys' Band. Following the festivities, residents continued to celebrate at a community dance held at "The Tent" in the Nordberg Building (*San Diego Union*, July 7, 1935, section 2, page 2).

Prior to the sign dedication ceremonies, North Park was treated to a parade of a different kind. In the morning of July 6, a motorcade of more than 20 1935-model Ford automobiles proceeded down University Avenue on its way from El Cajon to the east gate of the Exposition grounds in Balboa Park. The motorcade was led by the two-millionth Ford V-8 automobile. Henry Ford had sent the car from the factory in Dearborn, Michigan to participate in the automobile exhibition at the Ford Motor pavilion within the Exposition grounds. The motorcade was photographed as it proceeded down University Avenue, co-incidentally, under the new North Park neon sign. The photograph was probably the first one made of the sign that became one of North Park's most cherished landmarks (*San Diego Union*, July 7, 1935, section 2, page 2).

View of the intersection of 30th Street and University Avenue toward the northeast corner.
The Ford motorcade is on its way to the grounds of the California Pacific International Exposition in Balboa Park, passing under the North Park sign and past the Owl Drug Company building and Ramona Theatre on July 6, 1935
Photo courtesy of the San Diego Historical Society (#UT 1379)

North Park Sign and Toyland Parade, December 7, 1958
Photo courtesy of the San Diego Historical Society (#UT 85:9534-1)

Photographs of University Avenue indicate that by late 1949, the rectangular shape of the sign had been modified to the scalloped shape seen in the 1958 picture of the Toyland Parade, taken from nearly the same vantage point as the 1935 photo. Because the sign appears to be hung lower, it is possible that it was modified and reinstalled after the streetcars and their accompanying electric cables were removed. The sign was taken down permanently in January 1967, and the news article noted that "The marker, which cost $3,500 and has become a landmark, will be replaced by a revolving sign. The change is project of North Park Business Club" (*San Diego Union*, January 15, 1967, page A-23). However, it wasn't until 1993 that a modified, and static, reproduction by Wieber Nelson Design was placed near the intersection.

The Pekin Café

The California Pacific International Exposition opened in Balboa Park on May 29, 1935 in time for the start of the revived tourist season. It was a stimulus to the local economy affecting the construction and real estate market, the retail trade, and the entertainment industry. With the growing popularity of nightclubs following the defeat of prohibition in November 1933, many restaurants added alcoholic beverages, music and dancing to their traditional food service. One of those local restaurants that began advertising "Dine and Dance" with meals served in "Exclusive Booths" was the *Cho Book You Restaurant* at 2877 University Avenue next door to the North Park Theatre. This building had started as Frank Crover's expanded North Park Furniture Company in 1923, and became a Chinese restaurant in 1931. The family of Chow Kway Leung and Leo Y. Fong were the original proprietors.

Playing upon the Asian theme and the current popularity of Chinese food, the proprietors of the restaurant remodeled the façade of the building in the spring of 1935 (*San Diego Daily Transcript*, May 24, 1935, Building Permits, page 4). The altered façade was advertised as a "new attractive oriental front." The *exclusive booths* were actually individual dining areas sectioned by Chinese-style paneled screens and illuminated by oriental lanterns. Emphasizing the theme, the name of the restaurant was changed to the Pekin Café.

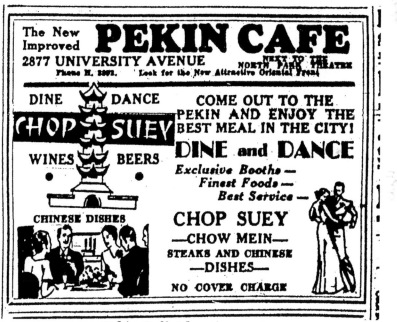

Pekin Café Advertisement
San Diego Union, June 23, 1935

205

Miller Service

The influence of the automobile was felt throughout North Park. Two of the three building permits issued in the first quarter of 1936 were for auto service stations. One was for a new Union Oil station at the intersection of 32nd Street and University Avenue (January 3). The other, at an estimated construction cost of $9,000, was for an enlargement and improvement of the Miller Service Center on the southwest corner of the same intersection (March 21). The improved center covered the entire University Avenue block between 32nd and Herman streets. In September, following the remodeling, William Miller claimed that his North Park business was the "largest independent Service Station in San Diego." At the same time, Mr. Miller announced that "We have just been appointed Firestone Distributor in the University District" (*San Diego Evening Tribune*, September 9, 1936, page 9).

The addition to the Miller Service Center was the work of Lowerison and Wolstencroft, Contractors, the same North Park partnership that had created the first expansive project for William Miller in 1928. John Lowerison and Herbert Wolstencroft were carpenters by trade and lived and worked in the Spanish Revival bungalow court on the corner of Oregon and Lincoln streets.

Miller Service Advertisement
San Diego Evening Tribune, September 9, 1936

Miller Pick-up and Delivery Service, 1938
Photo courtesy of the San Diego Historical Society (#Sensor 5-412)

Morley Field Tennis

The second summer following the opening of the "North Park Recreational Center," re-named Morley Field, witnessed an increase in athletic activities. In May 1935, the second annual municipal tennis championships were announced by the Southern California Tennis Association to be held on the ten courts near the municipal pool (*San Diego Union*, May 1, 1935, Sports Section, page 1). The first tournament in 1934 offered only men's singles, but in 1935 a full nine divisions were featured, including men's singles and doubles, mixed doubles, junior men's singles, junior men's doubles, junior women's singles, boys' singles, and senior mixed doubles. The tournament committee was headed by Rodney McLeod of North Park (*San Diego Union*, June 24, 1935, Sports Section, page 1; and June 27, 1935, section 2, page 4).

Play began on Friday, June 28 with over 120 participants. The first major municipal tennis tournament proved to be popular with both the entrants and the spectators. In the final play on Sunday, June 30, Bob Muench won the men's singles title over Percy Corrin, and Frances Lodge defeated Barbara Gaines for the women's title. Twenty-three silver trophies were awarded to winners in the nine divisions. During the tournament these were on display at the North Park branch of Stanley Andrews sporting goods store at 3006 University Avenue in the Owl Drug Store building. The tournament ended with an exhibition game featuring international tennis stars Alice Marble and Ruby Bishop Bixler (*San Diego Union*, July 1, 1935, section 2, page 2). In addition to the municipal tournament, tennis champion Harper Ink sponsored the first annual junior and senior boys and girls tournament at the Morley Field tennis courts.

The annual mid-winter tennis tourney in 1936, sponsored by the North Park Business Club, was held from December 19th to 24th on the courts at Morley Field. Rodney McLeod, director of the Center, and the tournament committee lined up matches in five categories: men's singles, junior men's singles, women's singles, men's doubles, and senior singles (men or women 33 and older). The tournament committee was made up of five members of the North Park Business Club including the committee chairman, Horace Hay, local building contractor. Instead of the usual trophy cups, the 1936 prize awards were items of merchandise, which were reported to be more popular among the contenders than the previous cups. Patron firms of the event that donated prizes included Folsom Tennis Shop, Miller's Service Center, Dixie Lumber Company, Berger Hardware, Standard Furniture Company, Dent's Shoes and several other North Park businesses (*San Diego Union*, Dec 13, 1936, section 2, page 6).

Maureen "Little Mo" Connolly

Wilbur Folsom would later teach Maureen Connolly, better known as "Little Mo" of the tennis world, who lived in North Park at 3984 Idaho Street. The nickname was bestowed on her by *San Diego Union* sportswriter Nelson Fisher when she was 12 years old. It was an allusion to "Big Mo," the nickname of the battleship Missouri, because her strokes were so powerful and accurate. Little Mo was named America's "Woman Athlete of the Year" three times, and won three straight U.S. National and Wimbledon titles in 1952, 1953, and

1954, by the time she was 19. She was the first woman to win a Grand Slam (Australia, France, Wimbledon, and the U.S.), and she won 12 major international titles before the age of 20. Her career was curtailed by a severe leg injury from a horseback riding accident in Mission Valley. The Championship Court at the Morley Field tennis complex is named after her.

Ted Williams

"Ted Williams, Padre Serra's right handed pitching ace, had a field day yesterday at Central Playground and led his team to a 10 to 0 shut-out over Post 6's junior legion team" (*San Diego Union*, July 14, 1935, Sports Section, page 2). That prophetic statement led a newspaper report about one of the American Legion Junior baseball games played in San Diego County in the summer of 1935. The Padre Serra, Hoover High School men's softball team, was one of the three teams entered in the Legion's playoff series. When not playing for Hoover, Williams could be found on the baseball diamond of the North Park Playground on Idaho Street, one short block from his mother's house at 4121 Utah Street. The Williams family home was on the borderline between the two high school districts. Williams said he chose to go to Hoover rather than to San Diego high school "because I thought my chances of making the baseball team were better than at San Diego High. Hoover was a newer school and I wanted to play on the team" (San Diego Historical Society, Oral History interview by Jim Smith, September 24, 1989).

Ted Williams was five years old when his family moved into their Utah Street home in 1924. He spent many hours at the University Heights Playground swinging the bat under the tutelage of playground instructor Rod Luscomb. Hall of Famer Ted Williams is considered by many to be the greatest batter who ever lived. His mother, Mrs. Envoy May Williams, was called the "Salvation Army Lassie" for her charitable fundraising activities during the 1920s through the 1940s.

In his final term at Hoover High School, young Ted Williams continued to thrill the local baseball fans with his all-around abilities at the plate and the pitcher's mound. His abilities gave Hoover a leading edge in the Bay league in the spring of 1936. In April, he was said to "exhibit too much speed and deception" for the visiting team. His "devastating bat" was said to make him "one of the most dangerous prep school hitters of the year" (*San Diego Union*, April 18, 1936, section 2, page 3).

Williams, the star pitcher of his high school team, won the batting trophy for his two final years at Hoover. His three season batting average of .420 broke all previous records there (*San Diego Union*, March 18, 1937, section 2, page 3).

Following his June 1936 graduation from Hoover High School, Williams was quickly recruited by the San Diego Padres. He signed a $150.00 a month contract and continued to live in the Utah Street house. His first season as a professional ballplayer in the summer of 1936 brought him as much notoriety as he had enjoyed as a high school star athlete. "Ted Williams, Padre rookie outfielder, had a field day all his own in the opening contest and was pretty much a thorn in the side to the Solons all afternoon." So wrote a *San Diego Union* reporter of one of Williams' first efforts for the Padres (*San Diego Union*, September 7, 1936, section 2, page 3).

The caption on the news article photo opposite, from the same date reads:

"T. Samuel Williams, Herbert Hoover High's gift to the San Diego ball club, yesterday made himself very much a pain in the neck to Sacramento's Senators, robbing them of hits with his ball snagging activities in left field, and doing better than well at the plate."

– *San Diego Union*, September 7, 1936

In his first full year as a member of the San Diego Padres, he played a major role in the success of the team. Hailed many times as the hero of a game for his batting strength, he set a Lane Field record in July, 1937 by batting two home runs in the opening game of the Coast Series (*San Diego Union*, July 14, 1937, section 2, page 3). No player before had ever batted more than a single home run in one game.

As a rookie with the Padres, Williams was fortunate in being picked to fill an open position on the team to replace an outfielder who suddenly quit the team at the end of the 1936 season (*San Diego Union*, March 18, 1937, section 2, page 3).

In the 1937 season, Williams was many times praised for his defensive play in left field as well as for his spectacular batting. Lead sports journalist for the *San Diego Union*, Monroe McConnell, often called him the victorious "hero" of a game. In describing Williams' play in his columns, McConnell used such phrases as "sensational sophomore swatsmith," "Hoover High's gift," "hero of the occasion," and "home run king" (*San Diego Union*, July 14, 1937, section 2, page 3).

The San Diego Union Sports

P-3 S-2   SAN DIEGO, CALIFORNIA, MONDAY MORNING, SEPT. 7, 1936

Budge Downs Joe Hunt in Net Tourney

By SCOTTY RESTON

FOREST HILLS, Sept. 6 (A.P.) —Johnny McDiarmid, slender young political science instructor at Princeton university, staged a lion-hearted five-set battle on the wind-swept grandstand court today to defeat Frank J. Bowden, of New York, 8-4, 1-10, 6-2, 7-5, 6-2, in the outstanding match of the national tennis singles championships.

All other seeded players who went to the courts today survived, though there wasn't a brilliant spot in the entire program. Don Budge, the American favorite from Oakland, muddied through a 6-3, 6-4, 9-7 victory over Blonde Joe Hunt, of Los Angeles; Frankie Parker tumbled Charlie Harris, of West Palm Beach, Fla., 6-4, 3-6, 6-1, 7-5, and Gregory Mangin, of New York, and Bernard Destremau and Yvon Petra, of France won easy victories.

Alice Marble Wins

It was the same in the women's tournament with the three seeded players in the lower bracket. Alice Marble, San Francisco; Gracyn Wheeler, Santa Monica, Calif., and Helen Pedersen, Hartford, Conn., all winning without a struggle.

The gallery favorite, blonde, smiling Dorothy May Sutton Bundy, of Santa Monica, whose upset of Mrs. Sarah Palfrey Fabyan, of Cambridge, Mass., is still the outstanding accomplishment of the tournament, defeated Eunice Dean, San Antonio, Tex., 6-0, 6-2, and now will meet Edith Moore, of Montclair, N. J., who today won a hard battle from Florence Lebowitiller, of Westbury, L. I., 7-5, 8-4.

Today's matches completed the third round in the men's tournament and the second in the women's, and finally brought the favorites to within striking distance of one another. Results:

Women's Second Round

Gracyn Wheeler, Santa Monica, df. Theodosia Smith, Pasadena, 6-1, 6-3.

Dorothy May Sutton Bundy, Santa Monica, df. Eunice Dean, San Antonio, Tex., 6-0, 6-3.

Helen Pedersen, Hartford, Conn., df. Helen Fulton, Winnetka, Ill., 6-1, 6-0.

Men's Third Round

Bernard Destremau, France, df. John Law, South Pasadena, 8-4, 6-3, 6-3.

John McDiarmid, Princeton, N. J., df. Frank J. Bowden, New York, 8-10, 8-10, 6-2, 7-5, 6-4.

Robert Harman, Oakland, df. William Robertson, Los Angeles, 6-0, 6-0, 6-0.

Donald Budge, Oakland, df. Joseph R. Hunt, Los Angeles, 6-3, 6-4, 9-7.

M. Eugene Smith, Berkeley, df. Charles T. Mattmann, Forest Hills, 10-8, 6-2, 6-2.

Yvon Petra, France, df. Gilbert A. Hunt Jr., Washington, D. C., 6-3, 4-6, 6-4, 6-4.

NATIONAL RING PROGRAM LIGHT

NEW YORK, Sept. 6 (A.P.)—The lightest program of the summer sea-

Public Enemy No. 1 to Floundering Sacs

SWIMMERS VIE AT OCEANSIDE IN PIER RACE

By KEN BOJENS

Turbulent surf and tricky currents of the Pacific will test the skill of more than 60 men and women swimmers when the sixth annual Oceanside Labor day pier swim is held this afternoon at 2.

An array of the finest rough water experts in southern California, including numerous San Diegans, has registered for the event, and, with entries eligible to sign up to an hour before the races, it is likely that a record-sized field will leave the starting line. The swim, a half-mile affair which will take the paddlers out around the Oceanside pier and return, will get under way at 2 when the women hit the water and, about half an hour later the men will go into action.

26 Prizes at Stake

Twenty cups and trophies, including four perpetual awards, will be at stake with special prizes being given in the following divisions: Men, women, service, junior boys, junior girls, Oceanside boys, Oceanside girls, North San Diego county girls, North San Diego county boys, veterans and organizations. The last named are new classes and a lively battle looms in both of them, especially the organization group, with Pasadena Athletic club, San Diego Rowing club and Vista Athletic club expected to wage a three-way duel for supremacy.

Herb Barthels, one of the west's most adept rough-water swimmers, returns to defend his title in the men's division and to seek his third and last-remaining leg on the perpetual trophy. Undoubtedly he will have to watch such men as Ronald Schofield, another shrewd distance swimmer; Bob Boals, of the Los Angeles Athletic club, and Devere Christensen, tabbed by many as a likely win-

Long Beach Golfers Win Links Title

SAN FRANCISCO, Sept. 6 (A.P.)—Court Randolph of San Jose, and Paul Kreninger of San Francisco, tied for medal honors today in the 36-hole qualifying trials for the 72-hole medal play western public golf championship. Each posted 150 for the two rounds.

Randolph put together a pair of 75s for the two 18-hole rounds. Par for the Harding Park public links is 73. Kreninger shot a 76 yesterday and 74 today.

Record 624 Team Total

The team championship was won by Long Beach with a total score for the 36 holes of 624. Players and scores for the winning team were: Willard McCay, 75-78—153; Delbert Walker, 79-75—154; Walter Larsh, 78-79—155, and Herb Hussey, 84-78—162.

The Long Beach team took over the title won last year by Alhambra. None of the Alhambra players including Pat Abbott, national

T. Samuel Williams, Herbert Hoover High's gift to the San Diego ball club, yesterday made himself very much a pain in the neck to Sacramento's Senators, robbing them of hits with his ball snagging activities in left field, and doing better than well at the plate.

Following his first spectacular year with the Padres in which he led the team in batting 33 home runs, Williams was sold outright by Padres owner, Bill Lane, to the Boston Red Sox for cash and two players. Williams was reportedly disappointed in having to leave the Padres but accepted his sale to the Red Sox as "a great opportunity to reach the top" (*San Diego Union*, December 9, 1937, section 2, page 5).

During a mid-winter city league game in January 1938, Williams was publicly honored by his fans. Several North Park merchants declared January 15, 1938 "Ted Williams Day" and presented him with gifts. In February, Boston Red Sox owner, Eddie Collins, came to San Diego to personally secure Williams' signature on the contract.

The young rookie and his parents, who were not satisfied with the terms of the contract, met with him and Lane. Williams and his parents claimed that Lane had promised Ted a portion of the money received for his sale to the Red Sox. The claim was denied by Lane. After a lengthy two-day negotiation, Williams agreed to accept a bonus of $2,500 and a one-year salary of $3,000 (*San Diego Union*, February 16, 1938, section 2, page 3; *San Diego Union*, February 19, 1938, section 2, page 3). He joined the Boston team at their training camp in Sarasota, Florida, on March 1, 1938.

In September 1938, at the close of his second year in professional baseball, Ted Williams was reported to be the "batting champion of the American association." A .366 batting average easily placed him at the head of the competition. "Williams also led the league in home runs. He smacked 43. He led in runs batted in, having 142. He led in runs scored with 130" (*San Diego Union*, September 13, 1938, section-E, page 2).

In April 1939, "our boy Teddy," as the local news reporters referred to Ted Williams, opened in the line-up of the Boston Red Sox after having been loaned to Minneapolis during his first year under contract to Boston. During the 1938 season, his outspoken remarks and quick temper had made him the darling of the national news circuit. One story passed around that season was of the gangly young ballplayer who, when he attempted to steal third base was instructed by the coach to hang back at second base, replied "I got this far without your help; I can get the rest of the way." His batting average that season, .367, was the best in the American association league (*San Diego Union*, April 11, 1939, section B, page 5). His skill, combined with growing national notoriety, would render him the most famous male athlete to have risen from the playing fields of North Park.

Chapter 14
Recovery ~ 1937-1941

The San Diego record for winter tourism set in 1929 was broken in the winter of 1937. Although a slack condition in business revenues and manufacturing production returned in the early months of the year, most authorities blamed the frequent and lengthy labor strikes. It was generally agreed that the worst of the depression was over and that prosperity and increasing employment were making a strong come back. In April, the Secretary of Labor reported from Washington that "Rapid strides in re-employment of the vast army of jobless during the long years of the depression are being taken each week" (*San Diego Union*, January 31, 1937, section 2, page 1). The administrator of the Federal Housing office in Washington D.C., Stewart McDonald, stated in May that the recent strong increase in residential construction implied that the requirement of "emergency measures passed in 1934" were no longer a necessity, and in California, the state chamber of commerce reported that "conditions are considerably better than they were a year ago" (*San Diego Union*, May 9, 1937, Building News section, page 1). By June, local real estate developer O. W. Cotton, declared "I have never seen conditions for San Diego real estate as stable as they are at the present time" (*San Diego Union*, June 6, 1937, Building News section, page 4).

Although some industries, such as construction and real estate, had made a major turn around in 1937, business in general remained sluggish. By early 1938, general press commentary was identifying the situation in the retail market as a "business recession." Furthermore, that recession was being blamed by many critics on President Franklin Roosevelt and his newly announced policies of business control.

In the early months of 1939, the world beyond the boundaries of North Park began to infringe upon the daily awareness of the community's residents to a larger degree. Militarism in Japan and fascism in Germany, Italy and Spain increasingly threatened a global holocaust. The American response to that threat, even down to the smallest neighborhood, was a reaffirmation of a democratic way of life, and a re-examination of the defenses against aggression. In February 1939, the first National Defense Week was declared and the community's meetings that once were concerned with plans for parades and picnics, now turned to debates of political philosophy and preparedness measures (*San Diego Union*, February 13, 1939, section B, page 4).

At the same time, the worst of the Great Depression was over and another boom in new construction, remodeling and business development was beginning to be felt up and down the commercial avenues. The expansion of business along the new El Cajon Boulevard continued with greater vigor in 1939, giving North Park an additional focus for its commercial life.

Residential Construction Goes Modern

In January 1937, the value of house construction begun in San Diego more than doubled the total reported in the same month of 1936 (*San Diego Union*, January 31, 1937, section 2, page 1). In June, it was reported by the *San Diego Union* that records for construction in the previous month had not been equaled since 1927. In North Park as well, real estate activity reflected the new confidence in the economy. San Diego realtor Will C. Everett moved his main office to a new streamlined modern office building on the corner of El Cajon Boulevard and Illinois Street. Explaining his choice of the site, he stated that "North Park . . . has been the most active of all districts in San Diego in new construction, 84 new residences rising in that district in the last year" (*San Diego Union*, May 9, 1937, Building News section, page 1).

Although construction continued throughout the various North Park tracts in 1937, the greatest concentrated activity took place in the Eastern Addition, the section known locally as Burlingame Manor. One of the new houses in the Eastern Addition, by builder Ben Torgerson, featured several newly developed ideas in convenient, modern living. That house at 2621 Bancroft Street offered thermostat controlled heating, walls painted in "soft modern tones," and a double garage in front of the house "in the modern trend of home design."

The style of the exterior was identified as the most popular of all home designs, the "California Colonial"

(*San Diego Union*, June 13, 1937, Building News section, page 1). The most often represented residential building contractors in North Park in 1937 were Ben Torgerson, John Lovett, Robert West, Hays & Jackson, Dennstedt Company, and Brock Building Company.

In January 1937, the Dennstedt Company, which had become the leader in individual home construction, announced its introduction of standardization in its "quantity production" house. Chester Dennstedt, spokesman for the company, claimed the new plan was "the answer of the Dennstedt Co. to Uncle Sam's plea for lower cost two-bedroom homes" (*San Diego Union*, January 17, 1937, Building News section, page 2). Meanwhile, Klicka Lumber Company was continuing to offer its two-bedroom kit house for $1,800. Klicka also introduced in January a starter "Add A Room" house for $888 (*San Diego Union*, January 17, 1937, Building News section, page 3). After one year in production, the Klicka Lumber Company had sold 32 of its kit houses (*San Diego Union*, July 18, 1937, Building News section, page 4).

Volume production was initiated by the Dennstedt Company in January 1937. The company planned to cut cost of materials by producing six to a dozen homes of the same plan simultaneously. The result of all of these innovative efforts to stimulate the home construction industry was a movement toward entire neighborhoods of small, plain bungalows with few individualized features and serial production. Out of an effort to economize, the elaborate and unique stucco bungalow of Spanish Revival style gave way to the modernized Cape Cod or "California Colonial" house as it was known at the time.

In the early months of the post-Depression period, a new emphasis was placed upon apartment house construction. The Dennstedt studio apartment structure, completed in February at Upas and Utah streets, was followed by a larger apartment project in March. Built by O. D. Arnold on Kansas Street at Lincoln Avenue just off of the commercial district, the project included five two-family, two-story buildings. Announcement of the completion of the project placed strong emphasis upon the inclusion of modern, colored enamel plumbing fixtures and separate stall showers, "now in great demand" (*San Diego Union*, March 21, 1937, Building News section, page 2). In May 1937, the Dennstedt Company built two other apartments on Granada Street in the vicinity of the commercial district, one for $6,000 at 3782-4-6 and one with a flat above a small street-side store at 3788 Granada.

In February 1938, a report of gains in San Diego's residential construction for 1937 was released by the city planning engineer. "Analysis of the report shows the North Park area leading in total units" (*San Diego Union*, February 20, 1938, section 2, page 5).

Dennstedt Company Advertisement
San Diego Union, February 14, 1937,
Building News Section, page 3

For that year, 1,980 new properties were reported with 290 recorded in the North Park community.

With 7,998 total residential units, the district had an occupancy rating of 87.8 percent, a general stimulus for the revived construction industry (*San Diego Union*, May 15, 1938, section 2, page 1).

The trend continued in the spring of 1938 with a great flurry of activity throughout the city. In North Park, the greatest concentration of home construction took place in the Eastern Addition and Carmel Heights Extension. The historic revival styles of the previous decade continued to give way to austere, FHA approved, low cost structures. Tight little boxes with trim rooflines, fewer windows and an absence of verandahs and pergolas set the trend to minimal cost housing. More expensive structures added porthole windows, pipe railings, glass block and streamline corners in an effort to create the superficial effects of Art Deco Moderne. Architectural designers often used European modernism with its emphasis upon minimalist functionalism as the rationale for their current austere designs. R. P. Ruplinger, who often built homes in North Park, left his practice in the hands of assistants when he sailed to Europe in the fall of 1937 with the explanation: "Moderne architecture for both commercial and residential structures has become international and I am leaving for Berlin and Rome this month to further study the popular trend" (*San Diego Union*, September 5, 1937, section 2, page 6).

An example of the local modern style of 1937-38 is the home built for Mr. and Mrs. Earl Poschman at 3375 Gregory Street in the Altadena tract of North Park (*San Diego Union*, Feb 27, 1938, section 6, page 2). The home was designed and built by the Dennstedt Company and was completed in December 1937. With a construction cost estimated at $4,000, the house was well above the average San Diego cost of $3,108 quoted in the city's report for December 1937 (*San Diego Union*, January 2, 1938, section 2, page 1). Dennstedt's design for the house was considered "streamlined in its exterior" with horizontal lines, large corner windows and trim eave lines (*San Diego Union*, February 27, 1938, section 6, page 2).

Structures detailed by San Diego architects under the influence of European international style modernism became the standard in the newer neighborhood tracts of the late 1930s. Such was the case with Richard S. Requa's Burlingame Knolls houses on 33rd Street in the autumn of 1938. These houses adopted elements of the modern style but were identified as "New California Colonial" (*San Diego Union*, September 25, 1938, section F, page 1). The builder of these houses, at 2614, 2630, and 2636 33rd Street, was L. C. Anderson.

Streamline Moderne Style

Completed in December 1938 and opened to the public in January 1939, Sol's Auto Supply Store at 2820 University Avenue brought the modern storefront style of *streamline moderne* to North Park's commercial center. Appropriately, the auto supply store featured aluminum grills over horizontal transom windows above expansive plate glass show-windows and tiled plinth. Sol Goodman, owner of the downtown business, opened the first branch in North Park "for the convenience of our up-town patrons" (*San Diego Union*, February 12, 1939, section B, page 5).

In August 1939, a restaurant at 2633 El Cajon Boulevard installed a sign with its new name STREAMLINER RESTAURANT in brilliant glowing neon. The restaurant, in existence since 1935, prior to 1939 had always carried the name of the proprietor. It re-opened on September 15th with a new façade featuring an Art Deco layered parapet over horizontal windows and decorative stripes reminiscent of the new streamliner trains. Entertainment was provided along with a menu featuring "shrimp and Virginia dinners" (*San Diego Union*, September 17, 1939, section F, page 4).

Homebuilder E. W. Dennstedt made some timely remarks in June 1939 concerning the current fad in naming and shaping the daily environment:

"It is beginning to look as if this will go down in history as the streamline age. Humans today take their first ride in a streamlined baby carriage, and their last in a streamlined hearse. Every modern product, whether a 350-mile-an-hour plane or a desk thermometer which only moves to record temperature exhibits the smooth lines and rounded corners which we describe as streamlining."
– *San Diego Union*, June 4, 1939, section F, page 4

Dennstedt went on to declare that homebuilding seldom reflected the current fashion with its focus upon a "meaningless slicking up the exterior." The A. L. & A. E. Dennstedt Company at the end of the year announced an increase in residential construction of 15% over 1938 (*San Diego Union*, December 31, 1939).

Klicka Model Town

The Klicka Lumber Company took advantage of the new demand for low-cost housing by creating on their 30th Street property, a Model Town. A dozen full-scale constructions of their most popular models of the Klicka "Studio Bungalo" were installed on the grounds. The homes exhibited were "the pick from more than 500 prize home plans" (*San Diego Union*, May 29, 1938, section 2, page 3) which had been exhibited at the 1935-36

exposition in Balboa Park. All of the models were FHA approved for 25-year loans.

"Having seen Model-Town, one appreciates the tremendous advancements achieved in the building of better homes. Treatments and room arrangements eclipse previous displays."
– *San Diego Union*, May 29, 1938, section 2, page 3

Model Town opened to the public in May 1938 and continued through the summer to draw crowds of interested home shoppers. As a promotional stunt in late August, a mock election was held for a mayor and city clerk. For one week, those who wandered the "streets" of Model Town were encouraged to write-in votes for their favorite candidates (*San Diego Union*, August 28, 1938, section F, page 3). On September 4th, after the close of the ballot box, it was announced that the mayor was "Doc" Dayton and the city clerk was Ted Rosenfield (*San Diego Union*, September 4, 1938, section B, page 4). It probably surprised no one that both Dayton and

Rosenfield were Klicka Company employees responsible for the Model Town home sales.

The success of the Klicka Model Town on 30th Street continued into 1939 and stimulated other smaller sites of model houses. In April, construction of two model homes began, one by Getz and Grant on their lot at 2920 University Avenue and another by Home Owners Modernization Company at 3052 El Cajon Boulevard.

Wilshire Terrace

Two new small tracts were carved out of older additions in the spring and summer of 1938: Wilshire Terrace and Burlingame Knolls. Wilshire Terrace was an addition within the westernmost region of the North Park district in the spring of 1938. The Wilshire Terrace Company's tract bordered Balboa Park on the ridge above Florida canyon in the old University Heights addition. It was described as "one of the last of the close-in subdivisions available for building up-to-the-minute homes" (*San Diego Union*, September 25, 1938, section

F, page 2). Several of the first houses on Wilshire Terrace faced east on canyon lots. The company named these houses the "Sunshine Homes" for the abundance of sunlight which flooded their hillside locations.

The first of the Sunshine Homes at 3544 Wilshire Terrace, facing east on a canyon lot, was opened for sale on May 15th (*San Diego Union*, May 15, 1938, section G, page 3). The company had plans to complete 25 homes with one completed each month. The homes exhibited the current popular modern styles including one "hacienda" type at 3535 Wilshire Terrace (*San Diego Union*, July 17, 1938, section F, page 4). That home was furnished as a model by the Benbough Furniture Company and opened for public viewing on August 21, 1938. The house faced uphill toward the west with a 75-foot front façade. The interior was decorated "to demonstrate art in house furnishings and its practical application in a medium-priced home" (*San Diego Union*, August 21, 1938, section F, page 2). The house was offered at $4,950.

Model Town at the Klicka Lumber Yard, 30th Street, circa 1939
Photo courtesy of the San Diego Historical Society (#18244-6)

Burlingame Knolls

In the spring of 1937, the Burlingame Knolls tract was carved out of the northernmost section of the Eastern Addition. The one-block tract, bordered by 32nd and 33rd streets on the west and east, and Nutmeg and Maple streets on the north and south, was a development of the John Burnham Company. Laurence C. Anderson held the building contract for the tract. Several of the first houses were built to the designs of Richard S. Requa, architect. In the late 1930s, Requa's new style was called "California Colonial," perhaps reflecting his earlier California ranch house style. By 1938, however, Requa had absorbed the incoming influences of modernism from Europe and presented the more abstract minimalist style that would endure for the next several decades.

These houses in the 2600 block of 33rd Street lack the romantic, Mediterranean details of Requa's 1920s style. The rambling, horizontal manner of the California ranch house replaced the soft profile of the 1920s adobe-inspired forms with hard-edged, geometric industrialism. Large "picture windows" were balanced by expansive blank walls. Corner windows broke the mass of building blocks. Continuous foundation blocks and eave fascias emphasized the horizontal layers of the building forms.

The first of these Requa houses constructed by Anderson in Burlingame Knolls was completed in September 1938 at 2636 33rd Street at an estimated cost of $4,500 (*San Diego Daily Transcript*, June 17, 1938). It was furnished as a model house and opened to the public on September 25th. To the north of that house on the corner of Nutmeg and 33rd Streets, a competitor of Anderson's, J. M. Taylor, completed a home in January 1939 that exhibited many of the same modern characteristics. Its broad, horizontal sweep of rooms ties the "Taylor-Made" home to the ranch house tradition which became such an important trend in California houses of the late 1930s. Its porthole window and glass block announce its popular modernity.

A new bungalow court, the Casa Bella by the designer Earl A. Lombard, opened at 4355 30th Street in December 1938. Built by H. A. Wolstencroft, the court offered "Fourteen charming modern units" (*San Diego Union*, December 11, 1938, section F, page 4) in Spanish style with red tile roofs. The units faced a palm lined court and featured streamline windows of glass block on the street facades (*San Diego Daily Transcript*, September 15, 1938).

The early work of a young carpenter began to appear in the North Park tracts in 1938. Larry Imig started construction on a house at 4391 Kansas Street in May (*San Diego Daily Transcript*, May 9, 1938). The 2-bedroom, flat-roofed, frame and stucco home was open to the public in November. Its innovative design featured the horizontal bands, rolled corners, strip windows and roof deck of the streamline moderne style in architecture (*San Diego Union*, November 6, 1938, section F, page 3). Lawrence Henry (Larry) Imig would achieve renown as the builder-owner of Imig Manor (later the Lafayette Hotel) on El Cajon Boulevard in 1946.

Although new dwellings were sprinkled across most of the North Park tracts in 1939, the greatest concentration of residential construction continued to be in the area east of 32nd and south of Thorn streets, the Eastern Addition and Carmel Heights Extension. J. C. Anderson, Robert R. West, and the Hays & Jackson firm were the most cited North Park builders as the decade closed.

Beth Jacob and Tifereth Israel Synagogues

Temple Beth Israel, the oldest San Diego synagogue, was established in 1861 as a Reform congregation and was located downtown. Also downtown was Tifereth Israel, a Conservative congregation established in 1905. The Beth Jacob Congregation synagogue began in San Diego in May 1939, when a group of men and women felt they needed an Orthodox approach to their Judaism. Shortly after forming, the group purchased a house at 3206 Myrtle Street for use as a synagogue, and the Beth Jacob Center was at this location under Jacob Margolis, Rabbi, through 1948. The location, which was remodeled several times, included a Talmud Torah and a Religious School. After World War II, the congregation had become so large it decided to build its own synagogue. They purchased land at 4473 30th Street, near Meade Avenue, and on December 6, 1953, the new Beth Jacob Synagogue and Center was dedicated. It had an auditorium with a 600-person capacity, school rooms and a fully equipped kosher kitchen. Beth Jacob broke ground on a new location in 1972, and moved to the new site on College Avenue near San Diego State University in 1977.

Members of Congregation Tifereth Israel Synagogue also felt that 1939 was the year to make changes. From 1906 to 1917 they had occupied many rented locations. While World War I raged, they consecrated a location at 539 18th Street near Market Street and dedicated it to peace. In 1939, a group was formed to locate land, and they implemented the construction of a synagogue on a corner lot at 30th Street and Howard Avenue in North Park. In 1947,

Congregation Tifereth Israel was listed in the City Directory at 2930 Howard Avenue. In August 1953, the congregation built a large two-story brick building as a Synagogue Center, next door to the temple. It included classrooms, a social hall, offices, a gift shop, kosher kitchen and an auditorium that contained a stage and an additional small kitchen. By 1974, the congregation made plans to move, and in 1979 dedicated a new site in San Carlos.

Commercial Development on Ray Street

In the first half of 1937, there was a renewed surge of activity in commercial development. In April, two new concrete buildings continued the conversion of the 3800 block of Ray Street from strictly residential to mixed-use residential and commercial. One, a $5,000 store building by Calland & Eden for the plumbing contractor, Juda Howell, was completed at 3825-27 Ray Street. The lower floor was Howell's plumbing shop. The upper floor was shared by an apartment and a lease space which in 1937 became the North Park branch of the San Diego Library (3837 Ray Street). Prior to its home on Ray Street, the library had for a few years occupied a single room in the Plymouth Center on University Avenue, followed after 1927 by a larger space in the Nordberg Building. The Howells lived next door to their shop, at 3821 Ray Street.

The other 1937 project was at 3809-15 Ray Street, a $6,500 store building for attorney Ovid E. Mark, who lived at 3794 Ray Street. The building permit for concrete and stucco stores was issued April 7, 1937. The initial building was constructed in a late Art Deco style, and Mark's offices were in this building. Apartments were added on a second floor two years later, with a building permit issued August 30, 1939 for Hays & Jackson, contractors.

During the summer months of 1938, commercial development of the 3800 block of Ray Street continued as one of the last houses was removed for the construction of a duplex building at 3818-20-22-24. The building was constructed at an estimated cost of $7,500 for George B. Wittman, president of Ideal Grocers Inc. His home at 3812 Ray Street stood between the new building and his market, built in 1926, at 3804 Ray Street. The contractor for the new building was E. S. Lewis (*San Diego Daily Transcript*, May 9, & May 16, 1938).

Glenn's Market

In October 1937, one of University Avenue's most visible commercial properties was completed on the southeast corner of Utah Street. The building was constructed by Lowerison & Wolstencroft for Edward W. Gaul at a cost of $24,000. Featuring a modified streamline style of modernism, the two-story building had five apartments above a grocery store. Edward Gaul, a meat-cutter, had maintained a grocery store with his partner, James Cathcart, on that corner since 1931. Before Gaul's investment in a new building, the North Park Public Market and Gaul & Cathcart had existed there in an earlier building. With his partner, Frank Rick, Gaul operated a grocery store, Gaul & Rick Grocers, on that corner throughout the 1920s. Gaul named the apartments above his new grocery store the Reba Apartments for his wife. In 1947, Gaul sold the business. Since the early 1960s, through several changes of owners,

the building has been known to North Park shoppers as "Glenn's Market."

Gaul's former partner, North Park Grocer James A. Cathcart, was in the news in February 1938 as the victim of a house burglary:

> "A burglar last night robbed the home of James A. Cathcart on Bancroft Street of $425 in currency but missed $100 in change and over $1700 in checks stored in a different drawer than the currency."
> – *San Diego Daily Transcript*,
> February 7, 1938: <u>Locals,</u> page 8)

Commercial Development around the Avenue

In March 1937, Calland & Eden built a $5,000 addition to the store building at 2901 University Avenue for H. S. Hillowitz. Development of the 30th and University commercial district continued in the late summer of 1938 with the construction of a $12,000 building by Walter Trepte at 3089 University Avenue. The first tenant of the building was a Safeway grocery store. In September, C. F. Gunden began construction on a new stucco store building at 2820 University. When the $3,750 Art Deco styled building was completed in December, its first tenant was Sol's Auto Supply store, a branch of the downtown business (*San Diego Union*, December 15, 1938, page 7).

The year 1939 opened with a major project on Wightman Avenue (North Park Way). In the first week of January, construction began on a $13,000 brick and frame facility at 3015-17 Wightman for the Piggly-Wiggly store (*San Diego Daily Transcript*, January 18, 1939, Building Permits). A great flurry of construction activity in the commercial areas of North Park signaled the return of a booming prosperity. It made itself felt in early summer by way of many commercial projects of new construction, remodeling and expansion of earlier facilities. The pace of new construction of commercial spaces intensified as the year progressed and resulted in the following significant projects:

- 4328-4332 30th Street, Duplex store building, McInerney & Sisson, Bldrs, $3,000, March 29th
- 2926 University, Lions Club addition, Hays & Jackson, $800, May 24th
- 2901 University, Herbert's department store addition, Hays & Jackson, $1,500, May 29th
- 3180 University, Burch & Cotelle, office, Hays & Jackson, $1,600, May 31st
- 2603 University, Harry Graham, shop, $1,850, June 12th
- 3013 University, Hartley & Sons, store addition, Hays & Jackson, $2,000, June 28th
- 2859 University, C. M. Lutes, store remodel, $1,250. June 29th
- 2814 University, Hays & Jackson, store, $7,000, July 15th
- 2890 University, Nigg Engineering Co., service station, $5,000, Aug 30th
- 3829 30th Street, Hays & Jackson, office alterations, $2,000, Oct 10
  (Note: all are Building Permits, *San Diego Daily Transcript*)

The firm of Hays & Jackson accounted for the largest amount of construction work in the commercial district during 1939. Beyond their major work on the Hartley Block (3000-3029 University Avenue), the firm had several other re-model projects and additions on University Avenue, including 2868 (Western Auto Supply), 2901 (Herbert's Department Store), and 3131 (John Demetre's Poultry Shop). The firm also was involved in the remodel of buildings on 30th Street including 3795 30th for the Dr. J. C. Campbell dental office, and 3829 30th Street for the new offices of the firm and the J. C. Hartley & Sons Insurance Company. A new structure at 3712 30th Street was a dental office for Dr. J. I. Knott.

Hartley Block 1939 Modernization Project

The row of ten stores on the south side of the 3000 block of University Avenue, the "Hartley Block," became the site of a major remodeling project immediately following the Christmas sales season of 1938. Tenants of the J. C. Hartley & Sons Company, owner of the block, were relocated in the district while the construction was underway. When completed, many of them were settled elsewhere, as the block became a project of "real estate management" by Fred B. Mitchell, a downtown San Diego real estate planner. Mitchell's approach to planning involved assessing the shopping needs and desires of the local community and creating a list of ideal businesses that together would create a balanced community of shops. Tenants were then found who would establish that harmonious commercial community (*San Diego Union*, March 26, 1939, section G, page 1). Sixty years later, North Park's Main Street revitalization program has taken a similar approach to commercial planning in the entire 30th and University district.

"The day has long since passed when the suburban shopping center was characterized by the man in shirt sleeves behind his counter joking with his neighbors."

– *San Diego Union*, March 26, 1939, section G, page 2

Mitchell pointed out that North Park was an ideal place for the new "managed" shopping center, which he proposed. According to him what made it ideal was the abundant vehicular and pedestrian traffic; a heavily populated residential district within walking distance, as well as "the fact that the neighborhood has been developed by a group of men who have shown an unusual neighborhood spirit" and "the evident willingness of North Park business men to keep abreast of the times."

After the block re-opened in the spring of 1939, the former mix of produce stores, cafes, pool halls, cigar stores, barber shops and realty firms gave way to a cluster of shops specializing in clothing items, home accessories and notions. One of the largest, a store that required the remodeling of two shop spaces into one, was the Ben Franklin variety store under the proprietorship of W. W. Johnstone (*San Diego Daily Transcript*, January 31, 1939, Building Permits). Johnstone had recently moved from San Francisco after a 50-city search for an appropriate place for his franchise business. Within a year, the business had changed from a variety store to Johnstone's department store (*San Diego Daily Transcript*, January 31, 1939, section G, page 2).

The space on the block that the Hartley family firm had occupied from the earliest years, 3005-07 University, was remodeled in the fall of 1938 and opened in 1939 with a new tenant, Mode O-Day women's clothes. The J. C. Hartley & Sons company and its associate, Hays & Jackson, contractors, moved around the corner to a newly remodeled space at 3829 30th Street following

Piggly Wiggly's move to a new building at 3015 Wightman Street.

The architectural elements of the Hartley Block were remodeled to eliminate the unique features of individual spaces and storefronts, thereby creating a continuous "streamlined" block-long structure, in effect, a modern mall. The block had a continuous façade of identical display windows with recessed entrances. The architectural team responsible for the design and construction of the block was Hays & Jackson. That firm, with offices in the Hartley Block, had been associated with the J. C. Hartley firm since the partnership had been established in 1936. By 1939, the firm specialized in modernization projects. Carl Hays had begun his construction business in 1921 and was able to count approximately 600 houses constructed in the community since that beginning. Richard Jackson had joined Hays in 1936 and together they had set up offices at 3005 University Avenue. After the 1939 remodeling of the Hartley Block, 3005 was leased to the Wahlgren Shoe Store and Hays and Jackson shared space with the Hartley firm on 30th Street (*San Diego Union*, March 26, 1939, section G, page 7).

El Cajon Boulevard Upgrades

In the immediate years following the 1912 San Diego-Phoenix race, El Cajon Avenue was the site of several upgrades. Over the years, it was paved and widened. But by the mid-1930s, it was due for a major overhaul and became the site of an important renewal in 1937. In March of that year, recognizing its importance as the entrance into San Diego from the east, the city council voted to change its name from avenue to boulevard. The ordinance to allow the name of El Cajon Boulevard was effective March 12, 1937. As part of the renewal project, the boulevard was widened by 100 feet. Three miles of new pavement from Park Boulevard to Euclid Avenue and new ornamental lights were also added for a total expenditure of $600,000 (*San Diego Union*, February 10, 1937, page 5).

As the project neared the end of reconstruction work in August 1937, the newly formed El Cajon Boulevard Civic Association made plans to celebrate the completion and the official acceptance of the street as the terminus of Highway 80. Announced by James Robbins, president of the association, the celebration was named the El Cajon Boulevard of Progress Festival and was scheduled for an early date in October (*San Diego Union*, August 8, 1937, page 11).

On October 15, 1937, an estimated 40,000 people clustered along the three-mile stretch of newly paved and widened El Cajon Boulevard to celebrate the governmental acceptance of the boulevard as the official entrance of Interstate Highway 80 into San Diego. Honored guest of the Boulevard Civic Association was California Governor, Frank Merriam, who opened the celebration by crowning 18-year-old Katherine Hunter queen of the event. The Governor then led a spectacular parade of floats and decorated automobiles down the boulevard from Euclid Street to Texas Street. After the two hour parade of 80 floats, Governor Merriam cut a golden ribbon across Texas Street officially accepting the boulevard as the final western segment of U.S. Highway 80 (*San Diego Union*, October 16, 1937, page 1).

As the ribbon was cut, a switch was thrown immediately illuminating the 70 ornamental lights along the entire length of highway. Then followed a roller skating race from Hamilton Street to Euclid Avenue. The Ocean Beach rink team was the winner of the race and received a special trophy cup presented by Jessop & Sons. After the race, crowds poured into the Hoover High School stadium to witness the Governor's dedicatory address. In praising the completion of El Cajon Boulevard, Merriam predicted that all highways would soon follow the model of separating the two directions of traffic by a center divider. That arrangement, a modern trend in highway construction, he claimed would reduce the hazards of travel. Closing the celebration, there was a dance on the high school tennis courts (*San Diego Union*, October 15, 1937, page 12; *San Diego Union*, October 16, 1937, page 1).

The celebrations that opened the new El Cajon Boulevard in October 1937 were quickly followed by the development of another commercial cluster around the intersection of the Boulevard with 30th Street. Early in 1938, two constructions were completed on the north side of the 2900 block of El Cajon Boulevard. These two streamline moderne buildings contained new businesses, a diner and a furniture store. Those two boulevard landmarks would remain with few changes of management until the end of the century. The restaurant at 2902 El Cajon Boulevard, a classic streamline diner built by Elmer Kier of Kier Construction Co., opened in the summer under the management of Walter B. Bickerton (*San Diego Daily Transcript*, May 16, 1938). A decade later, the diner obtained the name it would carry for more than a half century. John T. Rudford, proprietor of the Vista Drive-In on Ulric Street in Linda Vista, purchased the restaurant business in 1949, and changed its name to Rudford's.

The larger new building on the north side of the Boulevard, a more spectacular version of streamline moderne style, opened as Gustafson's, a furniture store that operated under that name for the next five decades. A building permit was issued to M. E. Gustafson on September 23, 1938 for a $5,000 concrete store building at 2930 El Cajon Boulevard (*San Diego Daily Transcript*, September 23, 1938). The builder for the project was the Jenkins Construction Company. Next door to Gustafson's at 2944 El Cajon Boulevard, the Archer Realty Company opened an office in a new structure described as "unique and modern as tomorrow" (*San Diego Union*, October 2, 1938, section F, page 2). The white stucco building had a façade of blue tinted mirror and was trimmed in Chinese red. Across the boulevard from Gustafson's on the southwest corner of 30th Street, a brick building housed a series of pharmacies beginning in 1933. By 1939, Meyer Pharmacy was in place there. Another brick store building was constructed at 3019-21 El Cajon by Victor Lind for Robert Gregovich (*San Diego Daily Transcript*, August 11, 1938).

The new broad highway immediately increased automobile use of El Cajon Boulevard. That increase also stimulated specialty businesses that served the needs of the motorist. On the northeast corner of the boulevard, a modern Associated Service Station was opened with full garage service.

Realizing that each year thousands of tourists entered the city from the east by way of U.S. Highway 80, the El Cajon Boulevard Civic Association made plans to erect a large billboard as a welcome to visitors. In September, the sign was erected at 60th Street and El Cajon Boulevard. Several city officials, including Mayor Benbough, joined officers of the boulevard association in dedicating the sign. The purpose of the sign was to greet visitors and bring attention to the northeastern section of the city (*San Diego Union*, September 4, 1938, section A, page 8).

> "At the luncheon meeting today of the El Cajon Boulevard Civic Association a proposal was made to have a large ornamental billboard extending a greeting to tourists and visitors."
>
> – *San Diego Daily Transcript*,
> May 27, 1938, Locals, page 8)

The following month, the boulevard association celebrated its first anniversary. On October 29, 1938, approximately 300 people attended a dinner and dance party. Officiating at that function was the mayor, Percival Benbough, state senator Ed Fletcher, former city councilman Harry Warburton, and Harvey Lewis, president of the El Cajon Boulevard Civic Association. One of the speakers stated that the creation of the Boulevard was "the beginning of bringing the street into its own as a business section." In 1938, 40 new businesses had been established along El Cajon Boulevard between Texas and 60th streets (*San Diego Union*, October 31, 1938, section B, page 5).

Meyer Pharmacy, 2947 El Cajon Boulevard, 1939
Photo courtesy of the San Diego Historical Society (#83:14541-297)

Associated Gas Station on 30th Street and El Cajon Boulevard, circa 1938
Photo courtesy of the San Diego Historical Society (#8012)

In October 1939, the El Cajon Boulevard Civic Association celebrated the second anniversary of the boulevard as the official entry into San Diego of U.S. Highway 80. This year witnessed a continuation of the commercial development of the boulevard with several major projects beginning in February with a major addition to the Cocklin Motor Company at 2644 El Cajon Boulevard (*San Diego Union*, February 5, 1939, section B, page 5). Six months later, the College Motor Company bought the facility from B. L. Cocklin and established the primary suburban dealership in Dodge-Plymouth vehicles (*San Diego Union*, August 13, 1939, section B, page 3).

The 2800 block of El Cajon Boulevard received four major construction projects during 1939:

- 2851- a store building for A. M. Barber ($1,800), May 19th
- 2864- a chiropractor's office and apartment above ($4,500) for Joseph Stream built by A. L. & A. E. Dennstedt contractors, July 8th
- 2877- a brick commercial garage for Alva Davis ($7700), May 11th
- 2895- a brick building for the Balboa Laundry & Dry Cleaning, August 30th

Other 1939 projects on El Cajon Boulevard included a $7,000 addition to the SDG&E substation at 3171, a multiple shop building for Edward J. Carroll at 3037-41, and an addition to Harvey's Restaurant at 2900.

Consolidated Aircraft

In 1939, defense dollars flowed toward San Diego. In "The World This Week," the *San Diego Daily Transcript* reported:

"Millions for Defense – Only: America now prepares to expand her Army air force to 6000 planes. It means a great increase in our military might. . .It means that aggressor nations will think twice before starting any rough-housing in this part of the world."
– *San Diego Daily Transcript*,
March 28, 1939, page 8

The beginning of San Diego's dependence upon an aircraft industry supported by governmental defense contracts that lasted until the 1960s was marked by a contract for army bombers awarded to Consolidated Aircraft the next month.

"Consair Wins $2,880,000 Contract For Army Bombers -
Bringing the total of local orders for Army and Navy bombers to $7,580,000, a War Department contract for constructing a squadron of four-motor planes at a cost of $2,880,000 was received by Consolidated Aircraft yesterday."
– *San Diego Union*, April 28, 1939,
section A, page 3)

Street Improvements

The increase in business on University Avenue created the need for an improvement in traffic control. The city added two new traffic signals in January 1938 for that purpose. One was installed in North Park at the intersection of Utah Street and University Avenue (*San Diego Union*, January 15, 1938, page 1). The other was installed at the intersection of El Cajon Boulevard and

Euclid Avenue in East San Diego to calm traffic approaching the populated areas from the open highway to the east.

In the fall of 1938, improvement projects for two major traffic routes affecting the North Park community were discussed and approved by the city's traffic commission and council. Both were accepted as Works Progress Administration (WPA) projects. One of those was for widening the Pershing Drive connection between 18th Street downtown and Upas Street in North Park. That roadway had experienced a great increase in traffic in the preceding decade. The latest improvements made the roadway a four-lane highway from the intersection with 26th Street and "Powder House canyon rd." to Upas Street (*San Diego Union*, October 30, 1938, section B, page 1).

The other project was an extension of Upas Street across Powder House canyon (Florida Street) on the western edge of North Park. The extension was planned to link the eastern segment of Upas Street with Park Boulevard. The purpose of the link was to ease the traffic congestion on University Avenue by creating a new cross-town thoroughfare. A second purpose of the project was to give the North Park community greater access to San Diego High School and Roosevelt Junior High School. When the new link road was completed it was named Morley Field Drive for Balboa Park superintendent John Morley who retired in January 1939. Morley had been brought to San Diego to supervise the park development for the 1915 Exposition and had been instrumental in the 1930s development of the municipal swimming pool, tennis courts and recreation grounds on the southern border of North Park (Morley Field) (*San Diego Union*, March 1, 1939, page 4).

Loss of North Park Pioneers

Jack Hartley died November 5, 1937, at age 61. His obituary (*San Diego Union*, November 6, 1937) noted that he "helped organize the North Park Business club and the North Park Lions club and was elected as the first president of each. He also served on the board of freeholders in preparing the city charter." His father-in-law, John Mason Dodge, said, "This grand old boy was one of the best baseball players San Diego could boast of . . . Jack was called the 'Home Run King' of the bunch, and he certainly could handle the hickory." Emil Klicka said, "In the North Park district, where Jack's word was as good as a government bond, we did some teamwork in the upbuilding of North Park. I soon learned to know him as a man of high integrity. As a real estate man he did all he could to sell properties, but he always kept in mind a high sense of honor and ideals that made him a beloved citizen. When I organized the old San Diego State Bank, Jack became one of the directors. Later he became a member of the advisory board of the Bank of America and retained that place up to the time of his death. Residents in the North Park district have Jack Hartley to thank for many of the public blessings they enjoy now, because the growth of that section of the city came as the result of his leadership."

Jack Hartley's mother, Mary Jane Hartley, often referred to as the "Mother of North Park" and "Grandma Hartley," died December 9, 1940 at the age of 88. The funeral was held at Plymouth Congregational Church and she was buried at Mount Hope cemetery. Her obituary (*San Diego Union*, December 10, 1940) recalled a birthday interview given eight years prior, during the

Depression, in which Grandma Hartley said, "People may think they are having hard times now, but they should have been here back in [18]98. We really did have a desperate struggle trying to make a livelihood. But we got along all right, just kept smiling and did the best we could." Under the heading "City Grows Rapidly," the obituary for Grandma Hartley noted that, "Town lots were put on the market and homes began springing up as sage brush disappeared. San Diego pioneers have regarded the North Park growth as one of the most remarkable in the city."

Mrs. Hartley had been honored as the "Mother of the North Park district" the year before, on May 10, 1939, at a special Mother's Day meeting of the North Park Lion's Club. She had celebrated her 87th birthday on May 1st, and was given a large bouquet of roses. Her son, Paul Hartley, accompanied her to the affair. The meeting was held at the Trinity Methodist church on Thorn Street and the Rev. Moffett Rhodes gave the special address (*San Diego Union*, May 11, 1939, section A, page 5).

Maud Hartley wrote about her mother's later years in *Remembered Incidents in the Lives of the James Monroe Hartley Family 1882-1940*. Some excerpts follow.

Mary Jane Hartley
Photo courtesy of the Hartley Family

"She never got over marveling at San Diego, and its growth, and often said, 'Your father said it would be like this, some day', and I would answer, 'Yes, and you have both been a living part of it,' and she would smile, remembering the yesterdays.

And visitors were always coming, from far and near, as they always had, no matter where she had lived, for a week, or a day, or a dinner. It was all the same and they were always welcome. She liked to be busy, and she also liked to see everyone around her the same way.

Mother had a lot of happiness in her life, also heartaches and disappointments, but it seems that she made the most of the good that came her way, and the best of the other . . . She was interested in things in general, and therefore interesting, to all her friends."

– Maud Hartley MacDougall, 1950

Another pioneer in the North Park building industry died in November 1939. J. Herman Bjornstad was the founder of the North Park Lumber Company (later Dixie Lumber & Supply Company) in 1914. An early resident of North Park following his move to San Diego from St. Paul, Minnesota in 1911, Bjornstad had been a president of the North Park Business Men's Association prior to his retirement (*San Diego Union*, November 9, 1939, section B, page 9). The early years of the lumber company were recalled by Arthur Jensen, originally the secretary-treasurer and later president of the firm, in a December 8, 1949 *San Diego Tribune*

article. When he arrived in 1915, he said, "Ohio St. wasn't even graded, and the area across the street from the office was covered with sage brush. I kept a shotgun at the office so I could pop off a jack rabbit now and then." He related that none of the local streets, not even University Avenue was paved in those early years. "But I couldn't drive a horse down the street when it rained because the adobe mud would bog 'em down. The only thing that would get you through was a Model T Ford and I had a good 1912 model." Ohio Street was paved in 1925. Jensen said that lumber firms sold only lumber, plaster, cement, nails and shingles in those early days. "We never dreamed of handling paint, building hardware or any of the merchandise now carried by a building supply firm. Almost every house built in North Park in those days had redwood board and batten walls, which were given only one coat of brown stain. White or other paint was too expensive, and two or three coats were required," Jensen stated. But North Park started to come into its own in 1925, he noted, with tremendous growth in 1925-26 such that it was impossible to keep enough lumber on hand – "just as it was in 1947-48."

The Next Generation

The children of North Park's early entrepreneurs excelled in sports during the recovery years. In January 1938, a tennis players' ranking committee was formed of seven San Diego County tennis officials including Harper Ink of the Southern California Tennis Association; Roland Brock, Balboa Tennis Club; and Rodney McLeod Jr., North Park. The committee announced their 1937 ranked list of county players on January 16, 1938. Included in the ranking was Robert Klicka, son of George

Klicka, manager of the Klicka Lumber Company. Young Klicka was ranked #3 in the Boys' Singles division led by Robert Carrothers, the national champion of that division (*San Diego Union*, January 16, 1938, Sports Section, page 3). Another North Park boy who made good was Richard 'Dick' Essery, eldest son of the North Park Realtors Maurice and Eva Essery. Dick Essery had been building and flying sailplanes since his teen years in the 1920s. On June 8, 1939, he broke the distance record for "motorless distant flight with a passenger." Taking off from Wichita Falls he reached a height of 6,200 feet and glided down three hours and 20 minutes later in Oklahoma City, a distance of 109 air miles. Those who saw the skillful touchdown inside the Oklahoma capital city gave the report that there had been an air crash (*San Diego Union*, June 9, 1939, section A, page 1).

North Park Lion's Club

World events affected the local business groups as well as commercial development in the late 1930s. Frivolity coupled with a serious sense of charitable responsibility continued to be characteristic of the North Park Lion's Club. However, a new element entered into the fraternal meetings: discussions of world affairs and of the American way of life. In January 1939, one of the Downtown Lion's Club weekly meetings was disrupted and taken over by the surprise "invasion" of a group of North Park Lion's Club members. The North Park group, accompanied by C. E. Romero and his North Park Boys' Band, traveled from North Park to downtown San Diego on a new streetcar that they had decorated especially for the occasion (*San Diego Union* January 27, 1939, section A, page 11).

Arriving unexpectedly, the North Parkers entered the hall where the Downtown group was meeting, accompanied by the Band's rendition of "Hail, Hail, The Gang's All Here!" Officers of the North Park group displaced those of the Downtown club and Paul Hartley, North Park program chairman, took charge of the meeting. Although the incursion upon the meeting was accomplished in the high-spirited antics typical of the North Park members of both the Lion's Club and the Business Club, the main event of the afternoon was one of serious examination of principles. That event was a lecture by the Reverend George F. Williams entitled "The Meaning of Democracy." In the aggressive rise of world fascism, Reverend Williams contended that the typical citizen did not "appreciate the blessings in America that are his privilege" (*San Diego Union*, January 27, 1939, section A, page 11).

As a follow-up to the Downtown meeting, the North Park Lions Club held a forum on the topic of "Democracy" at its meeting of February 8, 1939. The discussion was led by William Hawks, the program chairman. The general opinion was that too many Americans fail to take a responsible part in the social and political life of their community. In his summary, James Robbins, a club member, stated that "there's too much of the feeling of 'let George do it', and the average good citizen stays at home on election day" (*San Diego Union*, February 9, 1939, section A, page 3).

At the February meeting, the Club went on record as being a supporter of the San Diego Union Shoe Fund, a drive to collect money and shoes for needy school children. Members present contributed to the Fund and the Union's representative indicated that he hoped "other clubs and organizations will follow that example" (*San Diego Union*, February 9, 1939, section A, page 2).

In May 1939, Lions Club president, Richard Siefert oversaw a remodeling project in the rear of the building at 2926 University Avenue. A restaurant had occupied the store space since the completion of the building in 1926. In the 1930s, a special dining room at the rear of the restaurant was used by the Lions Club for its lunch meetings. The last restaurant was succeeded by a stationery store in 1939. At that time, the Hays & Jackson project added a space to the rear dining room. Much of the work was done by members of the Club. The addition made "the place suitable for social affairs." The first affair in the new clubhouse was a "ladies night" dinner for the installation of new officers held June 19th. The new president was James Robbins. Paul Hartley, former Lions president, was the master of ceremonies. The North Park Lions Club was said to be the first service club in San Diego to build its own clubhouse for community use. Ten years later the members would build an even larger and more permanent clubhouse on Utah Street just off of University Avenue (*San Diego Union*, June 21, 1939, section A, page 4; and June 14, 1939, section A, page 10).

In October 1939, the North Park Lions held their second annual Halloween party for the boys and girls at the San Diego Children's Home. The party and dinner were held at the Home in Balboa Park and included games and gifts. Each member of the Lions Club "adopted" a child for the evening. James Robbins, president, was the master of ceremonies. Special musical entertainment was provided by members of the North Park Band (*San Diego Union*, June 22, 1939, section A, page 10).

North Park Festivities

The Silver Gate Masonic Temple on Utah Street was the site of several notable galas. On March 31, 1938, the North Park Business Club and its Women's Auxiliary held a special day-long celebration at the Silver Gate temple. Announced as a "spring fashion parade," the lengthy affair included tables of auction and contract bridge at 1:00 p.m. followed by a tea service. In the late afternoon, the fashion parade began during which "styles will be demonstrated by various North Park dress and clothing merchants, and beauty shops will display latest coiffures" (*San Diego Union*, March 31, 1938, section I, page 9). An evening of entertainment followed with dancing to the music of J. Ward Hutton. Co-chairs for the event were Mrs. Cora Whitaker and Carl Meeker. Master of Ceremonies for the evening entertainment was Dr. C. R. Miller. On Sunday, August 7, 1939, the Masonic Lodge celebrated the 50th anniversary of its founding with an anniversary dinner and meeting to which the 566 current members were invited. The Silver Gate, the third San Diego Masonic lodge, was instituted on July 31, 1889 during one of San Diego's most economically depressed periods (*San Diego Union*, July 30, 1939, section B, page 4).

The Vasa Order of America marked the 28th anniversary of that Swedish organization's Gustav V, 175 Club at 3094 El Cajon Boulevard, a 1927 building, on May 21, 1938. Following dinner, an evening of entertainment included two singers, a folk dancing group, a brief review of the history of the lodge and a reading in Swedish. Dancing to the accompaniment of an accordion orchestra culminated the evening. Hugo Erickson was chairman of the event (*San Diego Union*, May 17, 1938).

A special June event in 1938 was supported by every major organization in North Park and a large gathering of individual residents. This was the June 7 retirement party given to honor the long-term principal of Jefferson Elementary School, Miss Ida V. Meeks. Miss Meeks, a native of Illinois, became the principal of the school in 1917 shortly after the first eight-room segment of the facility was completed. During her tenure, the school more than doubled in the number of students. The building had also added three new wings to become a courtyard school. It was in that central courtyard, decorated with trees and flowers, that the 760 students of the school honored Miss Meeks with an afternoon ceremony. A large crowd of her current students was joined by scores of alumni who came to pay their respects for "all that she has stood for in North Park" (*San Diego Union*, June 8, 1938, section 1, page 2).

> "Jefferson school this afternoon was transformed into a fine summer garden for the reception in honor of Miss Ida V. Meeks, one of the leading educators of this city, who for the past 21 years has been principal of Jefferson School."
> – *San Diego Daily Transcript*,
> June 7, 1938, Locals, page 8)

The school courtyard was again the site of an evening party on June 7th, attended by "Hundreds of her old students; many of the teachers who have worked with her and scores of friends" (*San Diego Union*, June 7, 1938, section 1, page 2). Those attending also included members of the North Park Business Club and Auxiliary; the North Park Lions Club; the board of education; and the Jefferson P.T.A. Entertainment for the evening included speakers and a musical trio of piano, violin and cello. The planning committee for the event included Hal Royle, Mrs. Howard P. Foley, J. P. Reilly (North Park Lions Club), Hampton Stevenson (North Park Business Club), Mrs. Cora Whitaker (North Park Business Club Auxiliary), and Mrs. J. M. McColl (Jefferson P.T.A.) (*San Diego Union*, June 5, 1938, section 2, page 6).

In July 1938, the North Park Business Club sponsored an evening celebration for the opening of a new baseball diamond on the community's University Heights playground. The new lighting system was considered one of the best in southern California and the playground was said to be "perhaps the city's best spot for softball activities" (*San Diego Union*, July 3, 1938, section B, page 5) The opening night's event featured two games, the main one a Class AA league contest. Opening the event, two local North Park teams offered an amusing game between merchants west of 30th Street challenging those with businesses east of 30th. Jim Seall's Westside Wildcats opposed Dwight Willis' Eastside Easy Losers. The North Park Boys' Band was the musical entertainment of the evening. Hampton Stevenson, president of the North Park Business Club, was master of ceremonies for the event.

The following spring, on May 21, 1939, the North Park Business Club's annual carnival opened the municipal pool in Balboa Park for the summer season. The event included several award winning swimmers, including Florence Chadwick who set a new County record in the 100-meter backstroke competition. Miss Chadwick followed that by taking first place in the 100-meter free style and the 120-meter medley. Mickey Riley, 1932 Olympics diving champion, performed for the 2,500-plus attendees who crowded the grandstand and vicinity around the pool (*San Diego Union*, May 21, 1939, section E, page 1; and May 22, 1939, section B, page 5).

Following the swimming meet and diving exhibition, the North Park Business Club sponsored a bathing beauty contest. Winner of that competition among 19 contestants was Miss Phyllis Potter, 18-year-old daughter of a local Marine Corps captain (*San Diego Union*, May 22, 1939, section A, page 4).

The Christmas festivals were grand in this period of recovery. As an indication of the revival of prosperity in the commercial district of 30th and University in 1937, the North Park Business Club did not request funds from the city for the purpose of decorating University Avenue for the annual Christmas parade and festivities (*San Diego Union*, November 28, 1937, section 2, page 1). More than 25,000 people lined University Avenue from 32nd Street to Arizona Street to watch 150 entrants in the parade. First prizewinner was Miller's Service Station, with Dixie Lumber Company taking second place. The General Chairman of the festival was Paul Hartley. Observers were heard to say that it was the "most successful Christmas show in the history of the community" (*San Diego Union*, December 11, 1937, page 3).

In 1938, the Christmas parade had seven sections, each led by a prominent San Diego band, including floats and drill teams. The first section was led by the North Park Boys Band. The mile-long parade was followed by the turning on of the decorative lights along the Avenue (*San Diego Union*, December 9, 1938, section A, page 5).

In 1939, the annual Christmas Parade on University Avenue took place on Friday, December 8th. As in past celebrations, University Avenue was decked with garlands and thousands of colored lights which were illuminated block by block as the parade progressed down the Avenue between 32nd Street and Texas Street. North Park's decorations were called the "most pretentious in the city." Four bands paced the parade led by North Park's "prize-winning" band directed by C. E. Romero. New to street decorations in 1939 were 200 eight-foot candles and a large mock organ that towered over the buildings at the intersection of 30th and University. Christmas carols were played each day until Christmas.

Chapter 15
War & Post-war ~ 1942-1946

Long-time San Diego residents can attest to changes in the city during and after World War II. Nearly all the facilities in Balboa Park except for the zoo were temporarily turned over to the Navy as a giant hospital complex, where beds replaced museum collections. North Park residents who were youngsters during wartime remember military encampments in Morley Field, with tents filling the canyons among the eucalyptus trees. The Japanese community suffered through relocation by federal order in April 1942, but many returned from the relocation centers to reestablish in San Diego after the war ended. The city's population expanded from 200,000 in 1940 to more than 330,000 in 1950, and then doubled to nearly 700,000 by 1970.

A trio of buildings that were new in North Park as the urban village approached its 50th year in 1946 created their own "stardust memories." The grandest building and most entertaining stories revolve around 2223 El Cajon Boulevard. This is the location of the block-long, Neo Classical Imig Manor, more recently known as the Lafayette Hotel, a colonial beauty that seemingly has had as many owners and names as rooms. Only a fond memory now is the Palisade Gardens, a roller rink with a flashy neon sign that stopped traffic at University Avenue and Utah Street. Finally, the J. C. Penney store on University Avenue heralded North Park's emergence as *the* place to shop during the 1950s.

Imig Manor (Lafayette Hotel)

Lawrence Henry (Larry) Imig, a young entrepreneur who started in San Diego selling Chevrolets and then built homes, had a grand vision for his first large-scale commercial venture. Imig billed himself as "an Orson Welles of the construction world, cutting through red tape, shortages and other problems that bog down the less aggressive." He operated from a main office at 4320 30th Street, billing his company as the "Fastest Growing Builders in the West." Early architectural drawings for his two-story hotel along El Cajon Boulevard between Louisiana and Mississippi streets were not suitable competition for the U.S. Grant and El Cortez hotels downtown. So he added two floors to the north side of the hotel, and an elegant penthouse for himself. Started in 1943 and completed in 1946, the hotel was the only hostelry project to be constructed in the country during World War II. The 243-room resort was both a hotel and apartment complex billed as a "city within a city." The main building contained hotel rooms, twenty shops, four dining rooms, a 15,000-square-foot patio terrace for dining and dancing, and an Olympic sized pool designed by Johnny Weissmuller, who starred in the movie *Tarzan*. The promotion material touted "Southern Style on the Miracle Mile," calling El Cajon Avenue the finest boulevard in San Diego.

Larry Imig Promotional Material

THE FIRST IMIG OFFICE

Photos courtesy of the Lafayette Hotel Archives Photograph Collection

A four-column, full-height entry porch welcomed "The cream of San Diego" and Hollywood celebrities. According to the *Reader*:

"Bob Hope was the first person to sign the guest register in 1946, a move orchestrated by the hotel management. Imig Manor became a playground for such stars as Lana Turner, Betty Grable, Ava Gardner, and Harry James. Big-name bands filled the band shell in the hotel's ritzy Mississippi Room, one of its four dining rooms. Ted Fio Rito entertained there regularly, as did Jack McLaine, and the crowds sometimes exceeded the room's 599-person legal limit.

English Channel swimmer Florence Chadwick practiced in the hotel's pool. Poolside loungers could watch themselves and the backsides of divers in the huge mirror covering the wall behind the diving board. The hotel lobby brimmed with shops selling hats, clothes, and flowers, among other things, and the in-house dentist flashed movies on a wall to distract his nervous patients."

– *Reader*, April 7, 1988

Despite its early success, the hotel was not profitable for Imig. In September 1949, he sold the property to a partnership consisting of Conrad Hilton, president of the Hilton Hotel chain; Joseph Drown, former operator of the U.S. Grant Hotel; and Spearl Ellison, who spent 40 years with the Hilton organization, retiring as executive vice president. The hotel was then renamed the *Manor Hotel*, and renovations included 34 lanai units built around the pool. In October of 1955, the name was changed again, to the *Lafayette Hotel and Club* which paid homage to the health and fitness program instituted for adults and youngsters at the hotel. After five years, hotel operations ceased, and the Lafayette became an office building. During that time, two local radio stations, XEMO and KCBQ, called the Lafayette home, along with the San Diego Chargers, who maintained their headquarters and ticket office at the Lafayette when they first came to town.

In February 1985, Sharon and Robert Wilson, real estate developers from Carlsbad, bought the property, wanting to return it to hotel grandeur (*San Diego Union*, July 6, 1986). In 1988, the hotel was purchased by Pioneer Mortgage under President Gary Naiman and became a Clarion Hotel. In 1993, under bankruptcy proceedings stemming from the Pioneer Mortgage scandal, the property was taken over by Travelodge, and then was nearly converted to homeless transitional and low-income housing. A group headed by Bud Fischer bought the property in 1995. The façade was blasted to expose the original brick, marble was buffed, and guest rooms renovated. The hotel operated as a Travelodge until 1998, when it was bought by InnSuites (*San Diego Union-Tribune*, February 21, 1999, page H-11).

Imig Manor (Lafayette Hotel), circa 1946
Photo courtesy of the Lafayette Hotel Archives Photograph Collection

Aerial View of Lafayette Hotel
Photo courtesy of the Lafayette Hotel Archives Photograph Collection

Imig Manor Lobby, 1946
Photo courtesy of the Lafayette Hotel Archives Photograph Collection

Continuing its tradition of restoration, the hotel is poised to undergo an extensive renovation along with the addition of 140 ultra modern residences at the outside rear portion of the block. Hampstead Partners, the developers of the residential project scheduled to begin construction in spring 2007, have appointed Ventana Hotel & Resorts to manage the historic property, while they continue to create a place where owners, hotel guests, and neighborhood residents alike can mix, mingle, and socialize in an eclectic and dynamic environment.

The Lafayette's new "L" lounge and grille continues to host live entertainment in the lobby, while the hotel's Red Fox Steak House, defined by its plush burgundy booths and piano bar, remains as one of San Diego's oldest night spots.

Independent of the hotel changes, the Red Fox Steak House, which was added on the northeastern corner of the Lafayette building in 1959, continues to flourish. The restaurant is decorated with 16th century artifacts with their own fascinating history. Promotional material for the steak house tells the story.

"The Red Fox was an old inn in Surrey, England, and dates from about 1560 . . . The bar, back-bar and the trim around the doors with the interesting, small carved figures, all come from Charles of London, and date 1560 . . . The fireplace panel, with its finely carved over mantel, bears the date 1642. The three arched panels tell the story of Rebecca and Isaac as found in Genesis, Chapters 24 and 27 . . . The room was dismantled in 1926 and shipped to the United States for the petite blond cinema

actress, Marion Davies . . . to be completely rebuilt at the 'Ocean House.' During the nineteen fifties this property was sold and Miss Davies' 'Ocean House' was converted into a hotel. Some time later, this property was dismantled and the Red Fox Room was placed in storage. It is from this source that the Red Fox has finally found its resting place . . ."

Imig Manor Sign
Photo courtesy of the Lafayette Hotel Archives
Photograph Collection

Palisade Gardens

The roller skating rink at 2838 University Avenue was a place to skate and a North Park landmark. It was built in 1945 just when the World War II building controls lifted. When it opened in 1946, it cost only 75 cents for an evening of skating. The price included clamp-on skates (shoe skates were an extra quarter). Day skating cost 35 cents. The weekend dollar special, good on Saturday and Sunday, included admission, skate rental, a soda and a bus ride from an outlying neighborhood to the rink and back.

Leonard Zlotoff was one of the original owners. He was born in New York and was the son of a Russian candy-maker who had come to the United States in 1903. Zlotoff's brothers Robert and Mortimer were co-owners. John Albert Wright operated the rink. A World War II veteran, he served in the elite 101st Airborne Division, the first unit parachuted behind the German lines during the Normandy Invasion. Later, his unit was the first to enter the Nazi concentration camp at Buchenwald. He came home from the war and operated the Palisade Gardens for the next 40 years. Wright was involved with community affairs in North Park, and helped revive the post-war Toyland Parade. He was also one of the original "rexers" who introduced the sport of smooth backwards skating that originated in San Diego. Rexing involved scissoring movements, hourglass patterns, speed and control to music with the right beat.

Palisade Gardens Decal

Palisade Gardens Roller Skating Rink, circa 1980
Photo courtesy of the San Diego Historical Society (#80:9144)

Generations skated at Palisade Gardens during the 40 years of operation, until the cost of insurance exceeded the income. Zlotoff recalled one of the highlights of the rink was when they had a party for the blind, setting up guide ropes around the rink for the skaters to follow, similar to a boxing ring. "They skated beautifully," he said. The rink was also used as a boxing venue and a concert hall as the popularity of roller skating declined.

In 1985, the *San Diego Union* noted that the Palisade Gardens Roller Skating rink was the oldest in San Diego. In April 1985, Wright told the newspaper that his marketing approach was focused on the older market, observing that current adolescents "may be less active than previous generations, and more interested in non-physical distractions such as television and video." He said, "If I could get 1 percent of my ex-skaters, I couldn't handle the business." Toward this end, he staged "Oldies but Goodies" public skating sessions on Monday nights, extravaganzas designed to get old-time skaters back on the floor. Wright noted, "It's a clean, healthy sport. It exercises more muscles than swimming. Just moderate skating burns 650 calories an hour. And it's a soother as far as hypertension. It does all the good things other sports do, and it's easier on the body" (*San Diego Union*, April 6, 1985). As late as June 1985, a Senior Olympics skating competition was held at Palisade Gardens. But by September 1985, the rink was closed. The *San Diego Union* reported:

> "Wright, the elder statesman of San Diego's roller rink entrepreneurs, reluctantly called it quits after 45 years of setting the mood for skaters, first at the Trocadero and then at the Palisade Gardens on University Avenue. 'Maybe I shouldn't have gotten out,' said Wright, who, at 66, lately has been living in self-imposed exile as a fisherman at Arizona's Lake Havasu. 'Well, I haven't missed that thing one time yet, though, and I sure don't mind having Saturday nights off.' The closing of Palisade Gardens is the latest in a recent shakedown within the roller-skating industry. Wright, who 'skated' more than two million people at Palisade Gardens until the wooden floor was worn too thin to sand, said he was 'making a buck up to the last day.'"
> – *San Diego Union*, September 16, 1985

In 1986, the City Directory shows Mary's Doll World at 2838 University Avenue, and in 1987, Rainbow Patio Deck is the business listed. Later, the building was torn down to be replaced by a mixed-use project with store fronts on the ground floor and apartments above. The whereabouts of the original roller skating girl neon sign remain a mystery, however.

J. C. Penney Store

On April 14, 1902, 26-year-old James Cash Penney started the J. C. Penney department stores when he opened The Golden Rule, a dry goods and clothing store, in Kemmerer, Wyoming, with two partners. The store was a one-room frame building located between a laundry and a boarding house off the main business district of the town. He and his family lived in the attic over the store.

In 1907, Penney started building his own chain of Golden Rule Stores. By 1911, he had developed 22 stores with sales topping $1 million. A new corporation, the J. C. Penney Company, was formed January 17, 1913, with the Company motto of "Honor, Confidence, Service, and Cooperation." In 1936, sales totaled over $250 million, and there were nearly 1,500 stores nationwide. In 1941, store number 1,600 opened. This averages out to one new store added to the Company every 10 days for 40 years. However, between 1941 and 1946, only two new stores were opened because of World War II. One of these was the North Park store at 3029 University Avenue.

War time was difficult for retail businesses. During World War II, many goods were rationed to assist in the war effort. Staple goods including work clothes, sheets, and blankets were purchased by the government from manufacturers, leaving smaller quantities available to retailers. Even shoes were on the list of rationed goods, and only limited amounts could be purchased. Despite rationing and merchandise shortages, the company flourished; annual sales for the J. C. Penney stores nationwide exceeded $500 million in 1944, and sales increased to $676 million in 1946.

The J. C. Penney Company bought the Hartley North Park Garage in the winter of 1941-42, demolished the building, and excavated a large pit for the building foundation and basement. An unfortunate construction accident resulted in the collapse of neighboring Fire Station #14, and that building had to be demolished as well. A new city Fire Station #14 was built at 32nd Street and Lincoln Avenue. It was dedicated July 8, 1943, and Paul Hartley was master of ceremonies. When the station moved, the J. C. Penney Company took over the old site, which had originally been donated to the city by Mary Jane Hartley.

Collapse of Fire Station #14, 1941
Photo courtesy of the Hartley Family

The J. C. Penney Department Store first appears at 3029 University Avenue in the 1942 City Directory. F. Carroll Tyler was the first store manager. He lived in Lewis P. Delano's semi-circular tract of "remarkable homesites" at 2869 Kalmia Place.

The department store anchored University Avenue for decades. After the war, other quality stores joined it. National Dollar Stores, Lerner Department Store, Bob Coffman's Men's Apparel, the North Park Gown Shop, Williams Corset Shop, Sach Shoe Store, Buford Shoe Shop, and Gordon's Men's Wear were some of the stores that came to University Avenue from 1946 to 1949, resulting in a second commercial boom in North Park.

J. C. Penney Store, 1966
Photo courtesy of the San Diego Historical Society (#92:18835-2065)

Epilogue

Here we end this book, with North Park poised to become a destination shopping area. That exciting time would last for more than a decade. In the 1960s, development of the regional malls in Mission Valley, Grossmont Center, and College Grove not only changed San Diego's shopping experience, but profoundly affected land use and growth patterns as well. Businesses moved from North Park, and there were several decades of decline.

But times change. The circle turns again, and North Park is experiencing a renaissance. The North Park Theatre, vacant for nearly 20 years, has been restored to its former glory. Once again, movies and live performances are delighting audiences. The new multi-level garage offers not only ample parking, but an amazing view of historic North Park from the top floor. New stores have found the commercial core. Living in this lively urban village is appealing. An appreciation for the charming Craftsman bungalow is growing, as is interest in the history of this unique corner of San Diego.

North Park flourished in its early days as a result of many people working together. James Cash Penney expressed that sentiment when he reflected on the large and successful company he started from a single store in a little Wyoming town in 1902. While he was the founder and guiding spirit of the company, Penney never took credit for its great success. That honor he reserved for his associates, saying:

"I am not inclined to think of the Penney Company as a creation of mine. It is bigger than anything one individual could ever create or be. It is the finest example I know of cooperative effort; people sharing in what they helped create have made it what it is."
— James Cash Penney,
J. C. Penney website

A company, a community, a city, all grew from the efforts of people with vision and determination. Through boom and bust, decline and recovery, perhaps "Grandma" Mary Jane Hartley, the "Mother of the North Park District," said it best in 1932, during the depths of the Depression, when she observed:

"People may think they are having hard times now, but they should have been here back in [18]98. We really did have a desperate struggle trying to make a livelihood. But we got along all right, just kept smiling and did the best we could."
— Mary Jane Hartley

Esteemed Reader, the North Park Community Association History Committee wants you to know that this book is not perfect. However, we did the best we could, and we are very happy to have it in your hands at last. We hope you enjoyed this journey through North Park's early years. Perhaps you will be inspired to research your house or investigate some other intriguing historical question. To our members and friends who left us too soon, especially Dennis Campbell, Dan Perkins, Brett Harris, and Don Covington, we say thank you for your contributions. Our community is your legacy. And whether our own contribution is as simple as a kindness to a neighbor, or as grand as the restoration of a historic building, we all share in that legacy whenever we work together to improve our neighborhood.

The Stevens & Hartley Building and Stevens Annex, 30th Street and University Avenue, 1953
Photo courtesy of the Hartley Family

Index